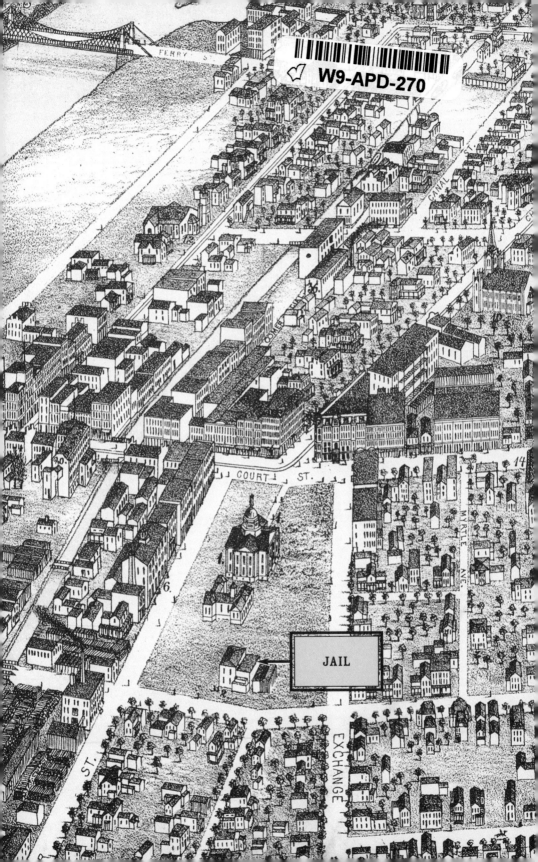

JAIL

ROGUE SCHOLAR

•••••••••

"Edward H. Rulloff, Scholar and Murderer." (From "The Life and Execution of E. H. Rulloff." *Frank Leslie's Illustrated Newspaper*, June 8, 1871, 189. Clements Library, University of Michigan.)

ROGUE SCHOLAR

•••••••

The Sinister Life and Celebrated Death of Edward H. Rulloff

RICHARD W. BAILEY

THE UNIVERSITY OF MICHIGAN PRESS

ANN ARBOR

2006   2005   2004   2003   4   3   2   1

A CIP catalog record for this book is available from the British Library.

Library of Congress Cataloging-in-Publication Data

Bailey, Richard W.
   Rogue scholar : the sinister life and celebrated death of
Edward H. Rulloff / Richard W. Bailey.
      p.   cm.
   Includes bibliographical references and index.
   ISBN 0-472-11337-2 (Cloth : alk. paper)
   1. Rulloff, Edward H. (Edward Howard), 1819–1871.   2. Murderers—
New York (State)—Binghamton—Biography.   3. Murderers—Psychology.
4. Murder—New York (State)—Binghamton.   I. Title.
HV6248.R8 B35   2003
364.15'23'092—dc21   2003001357

Endsheets: Bird's-eye view of Binghamton, Broome County, New York, 1873.
Courtesy of the Broome County Historical Society.

••••••••

**For the victims
and
those who loved them**

Preface

Since the beginning of national news, America has thrilled to a "trial of the century" nearly every decade. In the first three months of 1871, that trial was ordinary enough: a proceeding about the incidental murder of a clerk during the botched robbery of a store.[1] On its face, it hardly mattered beyond the limits of Broome County, New York. In the small city of Binghamton, the county seat, it had not even been the sole crime of the night of August 19–20, 1870, for that same evening a young man's nearly empty purse was stolen by a thief who knocked him to the ground and ran away. In another incident, toward morning, a despairing young prostitute poisoned herself under mysterious circumstances.

Crimes fit the times. But for them to do so, raw events need to be shaped into a story, and, to capture the imagination of the public, interpreters must gather powerful ideas and weave them into a compelling tale. In our own era, trials of the century have been elaborated out of our collective fears. In a different time, the deeds that enthrall us would have mostly passed unnoticed or, if noticed, attached to some other narrative entirely. We cannot imagine Timothy McVeigh as a murderer of the 1930s nor Bruno Richard Hauptmann as a killer in the 1990s.

Crimes in themselves hold almost no intrinsic interest: a young man shot in the back of the head dies, and there's an end on it. But in our case, the man gripping the handle of the gun took hold of both his victim and the imagination of the public. His narrators were many, but the principal reporters were two, both of whom wrote book-length biographies from the substance of their daily journalism.

One was from New York City—a "dapper Bohemian" who wore yellow gloves on his visits to the Binghamton jail. His paper was the *New York Times*, just another city paper given to lurid reporting in the days before Adolph Ochs. Edward Crapsey thought of the people of Broome County as rubes, and he did not conceal his contempt in writing for his big-city newspaper. His reporting on the Binghamton trial was reductive: the killer of the clerk was a brute, a fraud, and a sinner. The sooner he was done to death the better. Crapsey's book was supposed to appear just after the criminal was hanged, but the villain pursued yet one more of many niggling and legalistic appeals past the publication date, so the book lacked its last chapter, the story of the gurgling sound as the hangman's trap dropped him into space and the attending physicians pronounced him dead. People in Binghamton didn't like Crapsey much, even those who agreed with him.[2]

The other reporter was a local boy just starting in the newspaper business. He could not have known of Dostoyevsky's *Crime and Punishment*—it had appeared in Russian only five years earlier and was only much later translated into English—but he caught the idea of that novel in presenting the case as one involving a criminal intellectually sensitive and morally numb. The murder was, he thought, a sudden impulse involving madness and perhaps reduced blame. This reporter's name was Edward Hamilton Freeman, known to his friends as Ham. On his visits to the jail, Ham wore ordinary clothes and spoke in the accents of Binghamton. Just before the execution, he kissed the killer on the mouth and was thrust from his embrace when there was no capsule of poison or sharp blade delivered with his tongue.[3] Ham fully acknowledged their intimacy. His book appeared just after the hanging was done and the body buried. Ham was smart enough to sell the republication rights to someone who thought that the trial of the century would continue its fascination and sales. (It did not.) People in Binghamton liked him. As "one of the editors and proprietors of the 'LEADER,'" Ham was one of their own.

The murderer was Edward Howard Rulloff. He was a man waiting (and wanting) to be known, to have yarns spun about him, to become memorable.

There were reporters other than just Ed and Ham to tell the tale, of course, and all of them arranged circumstances into different narratives. Ed Crapsey had everything figured out: the man was a mountebank. Ham Freeman was not so certain, but, if some later theories of psychology had been available, he would have seized them. As it was, he made do with popular ideas about insanity. Another journalist, Oliver Dyer of the *New York Sun*, made Rulloff's quest for the origin of language the leitmotif of the murder. Dyer was willing to entertain the idea that Rulloff had unlocked the secret of an ancient mystery. He believed that marvelous benefits might follow from this discovery, and his coverage of the case almost single-handedly brought Rulloff's intellectual side to national attention. The proprietor of the local paper in Ithaca, New York, gave another angle to his newspaper stories. For a quarter century, Rulloff the murderer had been the scourge of the district, and the accounts written under the editorship John Selkreg in the *Journal* gave a historical perspective on the story.

Other writers had biological determinism on their minds: believing that nature had created a criminal, they set by science, to prove that Rulloff was a "natural" killer.[4]

Still others had literary analogies to offer: Milton's Satan was one—the brilliant rebel against high obligation; Byron's Manfred was another—defiant against inexorable fate. In mid-nineteenth-century America, literature was the coin of conversation. Americans were readers—and rememberers. The apt quotation and the telling allusion were scattered through every discourse.

The visual artists drew lurid images of the killing and marketed them in the sensational papers: that clerk at the moment of death; the drowned accomplices splayed on planks against a barn in the broiling August sun. Lurid instant books, with illustrations, found a ready if ephemeral market.[5]

Every newspaper across the country could tell the story and could tell it in what was almost real time. In San Francisco, the news that there was "no hope" reached Rulloff's brother in his morning paper at about the time of the execution. Technology and the telegraph enabled reporters to create a national narrative out of murder.[6]

Every American knew about the death of that clerk in Binghamton, New York, and everyone knew what to think about it—even if they did not think the same thing. The newspapers told them what to think. Editors considered whether a very intelligent murderer should be put to death as rapidly as a doltish one. Most agreed he should. In fact, intelligent murderers should be dealt with more swiftly, if anything, since they did not have privation or stupidity to mitigate their crimes. For such editors, it was galling to find that some English papers jeered at Americans for wanting to delay executions in the hope that arcane theories would be properly written up by condemned scholars like Rulloff. "We are as ready to execute our intelligent criminals as any country on earth," American editors and reporters patriotically claimed. We are like other civilized and moral nations.

More than that: America was a democracy and thus as ready to hang a genius as a fool.

But long after the execution there remained a mystery.

Who, exactly, was this particular criminal—the man with the gun in the dry goods store? Which was he: genius or fraud? Calculating murderer or pitiable lunatic?

Contents

Prologue: Guilty Secrets

Toward the end of his second year in office, in December 1869, President Ulysses S. Grant delivered a message to the Congress summing up the state of the nation and laying out the issues to be addressed next. It had been a year, he said, "of peace and general prosperity"; "We have, through a kind providence, been blessed with abundent [*sic*] crops, and have been spared from complications, and war, with foreign nations."[1]

But all was not well. The state governments that had declared themselves in rebellion nearly a decade earlier were not yet all restored to the Union; radicals in the Congress were intent on grinding the former Confederacy into bankruptcy, Southerners had just established the Ku Klux Klan to carry out vigilante justice and, through terror, to "restore" order. Conflicts with native peoples in the West were intensifying, and internationally the United States was mired in disputes with the European powers and prepared to launch its dominion into the Caribbean. These were not, as Grant had so confidently stated, peaceful times.

By the midsummer of 1870, things were no better, but across the country citizens readied themselves to celebrate the national day, the anniversary of the Declaration that had led to independence from Great Britain. If the damage done by the Civil War had not yet been repaired, nor the dead quite forgotten, there was nonetheless a sense that the time of national trauma had passed and the future presented limitless opportunities. Industries had provided materiel for the war and now were ready to produce even more for national consumption and international export. Railroads could be planned and built. A decade earlier, "rock oil" had been extracted in northwestern Pennsylvania, and, now that the war was over, venture capitalists were ready to turn petroleum into the fuel that would power the nation's energy. Agriculture, the country's largest industry, was becoming the great beneficiary of the railroads; products grown at a great distance from markets could arrive in prime condition. Barrels of oysters reached the midland; freshly slaughtered meats flowed from Chicago across the land.

The Fourth of July 1870 was a time for celebration. For the story that follows, it is a turning point in which to introduce three brothers at rest. Nothing in particular happened to them on that July Monday, but looking backward from it prepares us to look forward to the most eventful year in their lives.

Then as now the village that it takes to nurture a child also fosters the killer. The present-day criminologist Lonnie Athens invites those hoping to explain violence to consider that murderers see themselves as part of a "phantom community" where values are fostered that eventually make killing a rational act and even an obligatory moral choice. Self-respect and honor demand murder when the "phantom community" declares certain humiliations to be intolerable and therefore requiring a response. The person so unfortunate as to stand between the killer and his desire is done to death to clear the way. The phantom community seeks its satisfaction.

Athens sketches several types of violent actors; for our story, we need consider only one: the "frustrative" murderer who sees himself as a good person forced by circumstances into a violent situation. Frustrated persons may be coercive, Athens writes, but they may also be "resistive," doing evil to prevent a greater evil.[2] The killer can see himself, as ours did, as a victim of circumstances, forced to do violence to a person who might thwart him.

People learn violence in the same way that they learn the social graces: through their upbringing. Athens's phantom community creates killers by providing "significant" social experiences, though not all who experience the same events necessarily internalize the same lessons from them. In Athens's view, nearly all killers are calculating, and the calculus measures present frustration against past obstructions. Many times, victims are merely an obstacle. Murderers who have killed once are likely to kill again if they encounter circumstances they regard as like the ones in which they killed before. Society cannot tolerate the threat of repetition. Athens states this dour conclusion: "The ultraviolent criminals in our communities are outside the reach of any presently devisable long-term rehabilitation programs, much less short-term ones."[3]

The preliminaries to violence, whether rational or emotional, are shaped by the phantom community and thus offer insight into community values in the past. Our story is thus social history with murders in the middle.

It begins with Rulof Rulofson (1754–1840), a second-generation North American who lived in a German-speaking settlement in New Jersey where his father was prosperous and prominent. With the Declaration, only two months after Rulof had been elected to the vestry of Zion Lutheran Church in Hunterdon County,[4] the family saw every reason to uphold their loyalty to the Crown, and so Rulof promptly enlisted in the Loyalist New Jersey volunteers. During the war against rebellion, he rose to the rank of captain, and at the surrender he asked the king for a grant of land in Nova Scotia.[5] In due course, he received nineteen hundred acres along the St. John River, settled in Hampton, New Brunswick, and was appointed the first school superintendent of the province. In 1784, he married Mehitable Phinney. In 1809 he would become justice of the peace, and, at his death in 1846, would be celebrated for an honorable career as both a public and a private man.[6]

Rulof's son William Herman Rulofson (1792–1827) seems not to have been the equal of his father, except perhaps in producing children. William's wife Priscilla Amelia Howard (1798–1843) gave birth in 1818, 1819, 1821, 1822, 1824, and 1826. In those days of women exhausted by childbirth, it was not Priscilla but William who died in 1827. William remains mysterious, partly because his three surviving sons distorted the truth about their parents. In one obituary of the youngest in 1899, it was reported, "His father was a farmer, horse breeder, and at times imported blooded horses from Europe."[7] The same notice said that his mother "soon followed" in death, and another obituary said that "he was left an orphan when but a child."[8] These statements were not true.

In 1827, Priscilla Howard Rulofson found herself a widow with three surviving sons: John Edward Howard (1821–71), Rulof Isaac Allen (1822–99), and William Herman (1826–78).

However successful Priscilla's husband may have been in dealing with "blooded horses," he seems to have left little in the way of an estate, nor is there evidence that his prominent and still vigorous father was moved to support his grandsons. Priscilla returned to her childhood home and there, with the help of her mother, struggled to raise her children to measure up to their family record of talent, loyalty, ambition, and daring. Soon she married again and gave birth to yet another son,

James Henniger, who acts as a sidekick in the drama that follows.[9] Priscilla lived long enough to see all her sons grown or on the brink of adulthood. She was remembered as "a Christian woman of remarkable force of character and considerable education."[10] No records survive to illuminate the personalities of either of her husbands; all of the sons were romantics, were strivers, were violent men.

On July 4, 1870, the youngest of the Rulofson boys celebrated the nation's birthday in San Francisco. Though California had only been admitted as a state twenty years earlier, all the ceremonies of the eastern states had been imported intact and then elaborated. At ten o'clock, an open coach moved off down Market Street carrying three aged veterans of the War of 1812, and a long parade of military bands and troops in their ranks followed. Perhaps distinctive of freewheeling San Francisco were floats: the Chariot of Liberty, with goddess and Amazons, representing the American Republics, for instance. Perhaps not every municipality could boast of a Mounted Corps of Wholesale Butchers, with cleavers. San Francisco took pride in them. The excellent reader of the Declaration of Independence was "a native of California," and an anthem composed specially for the day, "Our Glorious Land," was performed to great satisfaction by the band and singers. The oration addressed the reconciliation of the states, and the orator was regularly interrupted by laughter and cheers. When he had finished, the band struck up "The Star Spangled Banner," and after that the Episcopal bishop of California pronounced a benediction. Out in the Bay, promptly at one o'clock, a regatta of schooners, sloops, and scows celebrated the Master Mariner Benevolent Association, and the steamers *Contra Costa* and *Goliath* carried spectators for a closer look, at fifty cents a head. At the Pacific Race Track, stakes races could be viewed (and wagers made) for a dollar admission. At the ballpark, the Eagles beat the Atlantics, 23–19. Woodward's Gardens was the venue for "Chang, the Chinese Giant" and the "First Appearance of the Two-Tailed Horse from Japan." In the evening fifty thousand people gathered to watch a display of fireworks. Among the spectacular terrestrial showers of sparks was the motto: "Westward the Star of Empire Takes Its Way."[11] Later in the evening were the predictable riots, drunkenness, arson, and shootings.[12] It was an altogether satisfactory occasion.

In the midst of it all was William Herman Rulofson, the junior partner of Bradley and Rulofson's Photographic Gallery at the corner of Montgomery and Sacramento Streets, an excellent viewing point for the parade as it passed along Montgomery. In the census of 1870, the value of the gallery was reported as thirty thousand dollars for the real estate and forty thousand dollars for the contents. It would shortly be improved by the installation of an elevator—driven by a hydraulic engine attached to the city water system—to raise sitters comfortably to the studios on the upper floors where natural light could be admitted and regulated through "the largest sky-light in North America." William was a booster for photography, and he predicted that it would go beyond art to foster "the progress of civilization" in myriad ways including aiding "justice by detecting the criminal."[13] So it would shortly do.

William was a wealthy and honored man, who, having been in California since 1849, had qualified himself for membership in the Society of California Pioneers. A brief episode of gold mining instructed him that the way to wealth lay in photography, a skill he had mastered before leaving Canada. With a huge wagon set up as a "daguerreotype saloon," he plied his trade in the goldfields before settling in Sonora, where once he managed to save his studio from a fire by having a team of oxen draw it out of harm's way. In 1863, he had moved to San Francisco, where he remained until the end of his life, as he grew increasingly prominent in photography. (In 1873, he was to win a gold medal at a competition in Vienna, and in 1874 he would be elected president of the National Photographic Association.) Innovation and creativity lay at the heart of his success. In a wonderful combination of the two modes of representation then competing with each other, he turned a room into a camera and produced life-size photographs. He then engaged a painter to add colors to make the image even more lifelike. He was a founding member of the Bohemian Club and its official photographer.

Beneath this surface of respectability and success lay small deceptions and dissimulations. One of his death notices declared that he was a native of Pennsylvania, another that he had been born in Maine.[14] Rulofson liked to relate that he had been shipwrecked in 1846 and landed, after "prolonged suffering," destitute, at Liverpool. Only his skill as a photographer, he said, had enabled him to earn his return passage. He wanted people to believe that he had overcome obstacles through self-reliance, ability, and determination. Only much later did close inquiry reveal that the ship in question was outbound from Liverpool when it went aground, and that its passengers were given free passage on the next available ship. Many episodes mentioned in reports of his election as president of the Photographic Association were similarly fictitious: he had not, for instance, been as a teenager "a wanderer over many lands, including Europe, America, and the islands of the sea."

William's biographies did not mention that in 1847, in Canada, he had made pregnant a fourteen-year-old girl: Amelia Violet Currie (1833–67). Their son was born there in 1848, and one of his biographers presumes that the precocious marriage may have hastened his departure, alone, for California. He returned for his family in 1850, and Amelia would bear five more children. She died at the end of January in 1867, and four months later William was married a second time, now to twenty-two-year-old Mary Jane Morgan, then employed as a receptionist at his studio. This union produced another five children. His second son, between the time of his mother's death and his father's remarriage, went to sea "to escape the severity of his father's punishment"; on his return, father and son agreed that the captain of the vessel should adopt the nineteen-year-old boy.[15] In 1874, William would stand up for one of his employees, Eadweard Muybridge, who had killed his wife's lover. Muybridge would be acquitted, in part on William's testimony that a "crime of passion" was only a manly act. In 1875, the youngest daughter of his first wife would die under suspicious circumstances; the inquest finding "welts . . . presumed to have been inflicted by her half-brother, Charles," then nine years old.[16] The old man seems to have spawned a young killer.

These acts of violence do not find their way into William's photography, but they are vividly on display in a book published in 1877 that he claimed to be his own, *The Dance of Death*. It is a violent attack on the "intolerable nastiness" of the waltz, and a morbid anatomy of sexual desire.[17] A man leading his partner in the dance is vividly described: "his eyes, gleaming with a fierce intolerable lust, gloat satyr like over her."[18] When it was published, some reviewers thought it must be a hoax, and Ambrose Bierce, who knew about its composition, later alleged that it was. Years later, Bierce said: "W. H. Rulofson (the 'William Herman' of the title-page) . . . suggested the scheme and supplied the sinews of sin,"[19] and the precise sharing of the authorship is unimportant for an understanding of Rulofson. William claimed the book, and no one denied his ownership of its message. A few months before his death, he told a visitor to the studio: "I have shown society what a loathsome ulcer festers in its midst."[20] For William, the book was no hoax, and the waltz was a matter of secret, hidden horror. That it was seen as hyperbole is a measure of how far it departed from even the most extreme expressions of moral outrage of the day, a time when fervor against sin ran high.

In northern central Pennsylvania, the celebration of Independence Day in 1870 was a far more sedate affair. The newspapers in Clarion County were in the habit of granting their writers and printers two week's vacation around the holiday, and they simply suspended publication. Consequently there is no definite record of what took place, but Rulof Isaac Allen Rulofson certainly did not have the rich menu of amusements open to his younger brother then in San Francisco. The village of Strattanville, where he lived, had only Central Avenue with two parallel streets to the north and to the south. A fast walker could travel from Rulof's house on the west side of the platted village to the east side in two or three minutes. Clarion, the county seat, was just three miles west, and any ceremony for the occasion would be held in the square opposite the magnificent courthouse. A speech or two and a band concert were likely to have constituted the ceremonials, and the love of small boys for blowing themselves up with fireworks was doubtless freely indulged.

Like his brother in California, Rulof was a prominent man. The 1870 census declared his real estate in Strattanville worth seven thousand dollars, and his personal property at one thousand dollars, but this was far less than his net worth since he was the manager and junior partner of Marvin, Rulofson and Company, a lumbering enterprise with ownership of eight thousand acres of prime timber forest. He had the family enthusiasm for children; he and his wife Amanda Jane Emerson (1828–98) had eight, five of whom survived to adulthood. Rulof was a fraternal, too, in both the Odd Fellows and the Masons, and he took pride in having written "a masterpiece": "A Mason for Sixty Years." An innovator, like his brothers, Rulof designed the floor plan of his residence in the shape of the Masonic square and compass. He was remembered as temperate, sedate, and a keeper of secrets.

When he arrived in Pennsylvania from the lumber mills of Maine, Rulof had been very much a man of the woods. He bought a gang saw in Maine, and it was transported at the last stages of its journey up the Clarion River on pole boats. Eventually replaced by a circular saw in the production of lumber, the newly designed mill allowed a skilled operator to extract the most valuable boards from the raw timber and increased profit for the mill owners. Every scrap could be made valuable, and the Rulof's mill produced lath and shingles in addition to finished boards.[21] A person with a long memory wrote in 1898 about the operation of Cobb and Rulofson in Elk County. Cobb was "the most eloquently profane man that ever stepped on pine timber"; Rulofson was "an educated man, polished in his manner, his early habits and training showing refinement in every act."[22] Rulof sold out his interest to Cobb in 1858, just before a massive flood swept the mill away. He then purchased the eight thousand acres near Strattanville with the proceeds and additional capital from Robert Marvin of Jamestown, New York. There he continued to be active in the forest, and another memoir writer recalled him as "the little man with the whiskers and the big boots."[23] The success of Marvin, Rulofson and Co., however, came from technical innovation, and in this respect Rulof's fascination with technique resembled his younger brother's combination of patents and promotion in the development of photography. Everywhere Rulof went, his half brother, James Henniger, another man handy in the woods and an utterly trustworthy companion, accompanied him.

Fabulous origins were part of Rulof's official biography, just as they had been for his brother William. He claimed to be a veteran of the Aroostock War, a bloodless conflict between Maine and New Brunswick that had erupted in 1836 when he was fifteen. In his maturity, he celebrated his own courage and strength. When he was nineteen, "he was nursed in the arms of a bear, and at another time was buried in the snow in consequence of a deer getting fast in one of his snow shoes." He said that in Pennsylvania he had seized a buck by the horns and wrestled with him in midstream until someone could bring a knife to finish the animal off.[24] All these episodes testify to a high standard of violence under circumstances where he might have behaved more prudently. Rulof thus promoted himself as more than what he seemed: a sedate businessman, Methodist, and Republican. As his past demonstrated, he was capable of subduing brute nature by brute force.

The most dramatic of these stories came from his older brother, who recalled that as a schoolboy Rulof had been beaten insensible by one of his teachers. Several days elapsed before it became clear that he would survive, and weeks before he had recovered. "The teacher afterwards begged his forgiveness, and was forgiven, but the incident has never been effaced from the memory of these boys."[25] Young Rulof was a survivor, and the beating taught him and his older brother deep lessons about the power of rage—and its uses.

8

In New York City, the July 4 celebration came early. Across the water in Brooklyn, there was a cannonade at dawn, and daybreak in Manhattan brought with it "a perfect pandemonium of jubilant sounds": fish horns, fireworks, and drums. As the *New York Times* reported the next day, these noises signaled that "the great birthday of the nation had come."[26] At seven o'clock the military units mustered for the huge parade on Broadway. At 7:30, the belfry at Trinity Church began with a peal of changes, followed by such selections as "Red, White and Blue," "Columbia, the Gem of the Ocean," and "Yankee Doodle"—the latter rung twice. The Atlantic Yacht Club had organized a race from Nyack to Stony Point, and all sorts of cruises and special rail excursions were available for those seeking a pleasant day away from the city. Ordinary citizens packed picnics; on the steamer *Vanderbilt* "a select class of our citizens" ate more elegant fare while being serenaded by the band of the Seventh Regiment. At Tammany Hall, the Grand Sachem, William Marcy Tweed, presided over the speeches railing against those who would impose tariffs and limit immigration. These edifying remarks were followed by a reading of the Declaration enacted by a descendant of Thomas Jefferson. At the Military Hall in the Bowery, thirty veterans of the War of 1812 were given "a plain but substantial repast." Between five and seven in the evening, the Central Park Band offered a concert and concluded with "The Union." More band music and fireworks were offered in the parks across the city, the program of each display having been meticulously listed in the morning paper. A popular choice was the "United States Coat of Arms," with wheels of Chinese, Egyptian, and radiant fires. Of course the day concluded with a predictable set of catastrophes attendant on drunkenness and celebration: stabbings, shootings, fistfights, and fires.

At 170 Third Avenue, in a pair of rooms over a dry goods store, the oldest of the Rulofson brothers awoke early in the morning. Beside him in the double bed lay his protégé and pal, Al Jarvis. The Jacob family, parents and two teenage children, were their landlords; they occupied the back rooms of the dwelling, and they were happy to have living with them two temperate men of regular habits. John Edward Howard Rulofson was known to them as Edouard Leurio, and out of respect for his studious habits and serious demeanor—not to mention his long, full beard—they called him "Professor." No one was very certain about his age (he was forty-nine), but people saw him as "elderly" or even "old." The word *harmless* seemed just right, especially as he played with two

9

abandoned youngsters in whom he took a grandfatherly interest. His companion, Al Jarvis, a handsome and dapper dresser, was about to celebrate his thirtieth birthday; the Jacob family thought his name was Charles G. Curtis.[27]

Neither Edward—the name John Edward Howard usually used— nor his friend Al enjoyed the prosperity of William and Rulof; they had no substantial property, nor any obvious means of maintaining themselves. Edward would occasionally take the ferry to Brooklyn to collect rent payments, as he had done a few days earlier, in time to pay the Jacobs the thirty-nine dollars in rent for July. In the early morning, he and Al were likely to have discussed a venture out of town that would help them improve their fortunes. Perhaps they took the holiday as an opportunity for relaxation, watching the parade or the boats racing in the harbor, admiring the fireworks. It is hard to imagine that they could resist a short walk to City Hall Park, where the most spectacular of the public displays brightened the darkness. The finale was "composed of red, white and blue, filling the air with streamers and colored stars, forming one of the grandest and most extensive pieces ever attempted in pyrotechny, exhibiting at one view over 50,000 square feet of fire of the most brilliant and beautiful colors known in art." For them, as for the diarist George Templeton Strong, it may have been "an uncommonly pleasant Fourth."[28]

More likely, however, is that "Professor Leurio"—that is, Edward— remained at home. When later asked how her senior tenant had occupied himself, Mrs. Jacob said definitely: "Studying, sir, studying; he was always studying."[29] The landlady did not know just what occupied him in these many hours of study, but her daughter Pauline could guess: "He was changing Greek, Latin, and German into English and French or else English and French into Greek, I hardly know which."[30] Pauline's brother Edward had little more to add to the mystery of these researches, but he recalled the intensity of Leurio's scholarly work. "Sometimes he would be playing with the children, when an idea would strike him, and he would go right to his desk, and begin to write."[31] The fruits of these efforts produced a huge and growing manuscript detailing that there was "method" in the apparent chaos of the world's languages.

This was not the "professor's" first attempt to distinguish himself in intellectual pursuits. Thirty years before, he had trained himself as a physician; later he had lectured on phrenology; he had invented an improved drill bit, a three-barreled pistol, a novel system of shorthand.

None of these had raised him to wealth or position. At last, late in life, he was on the track of an important discovery.

Grammar schools in nineteenth-century North America taught grammar in the expectation that more advanced study of languages would follow, especially of Latin and Greek. All educated young men of leisure were expected to be proficient in at least Latin, or to have been so at one time. Latin tags were freely used: the *New York Times* concluded its extravagant praise of the City's Independence Day celebration with *Valete et plaudite,* a shortened form of *Vos valete, et plaudite, civis* from Roman drama; as translated in the nineteenth century, "Farewell, citizens; we hope you are pleased." Few preachers, statesmen, or lawyers could complete an address without the use of such brief quotations.

A "key" to the mystery of language would allow persons with less Latin and no Greek to discover through English the meanings of classical expressions. This was only one of the many benefits "Professor Leurio" hoped would flow from his discovery. He was a contributor to the newly conceived discipline of *philology,* an inquiry devoted to unraveling the tangled web of words. The year before, in 1869, Leurio had attended meetings of the American Ethnological Society in New York, where a mixed group, mostly of enthusiastic amateurs, gathered to discuss voyages, discoveries, and exotic customs. (Craniometry, the measurement of skulls, was the subject of special inquiry by the society in those days.) In July, he announced his "key" in a flyer addressed to America's philologists, and he had made persistent calls on scholars in and around New York in an attempt to persuade them of the great value of it. He was far from the only scholar attempting to unravel the mystery, and magazines of general circulation summarized titanic battles between competing theories and theorists. Philology was more than just words; it was a field of study that combined history, literature, archaeology, and anthropology.

Above all, it was about race.

For most scholars, the races were settled scientific categories: some were "civilized," some "barbaric"; some "advanced," others "primitive." And scholars assumed that all aspects of human behavior are summed up and expressed in language. If philology could discover the sources of the diversity of tongues, scholars would be able to formulate a unified theory of human behavior. Laboring night and day, Leurio produced etymology after etymology, weaving together a network of relationships among words that revealed that languages contained encoded messages

11

from the past. He had discovered the secret to the code; he was still faced with the hard task of making the meanings of the messages known. He was sure that almost any day he would find the solution. All he needed was time.

John Edward Howard Rulofson was a man of many names; the one he had selected for himself as a young man was "Edward H. Rulloff," and it was by this name that he had become infamous. In 1870, there were reasons for him to disguise his identity, and he had used one alias after another for many years. By one of these names he was sure to beat his brothers in their intense competition for success. William was rich and famous in California; his contributions to "art" through photography were increasingly recognized nationally and internationally. Rulof Isaac was rich and famous in Pennsylvania; his contributions to the "mechanics" of forest products made him known far beyond his immediate vicinity. Edward was poor and ignored in New York; his discovery of *Method in the Formation of Language* would make him immortal.

Rulloff the philologist thought himself to be the victim of "misfortunes" that had dogged his career. Sometimes absorbed in self-pity, he was now ready at last for success. His abstemious life and humble circumstances would soon give way to considerable wealth if only he could find a buyer for his huge manuscript with its many speculations about words. In 1869, he had offered it for sale for half a million dollars, and, though he had not found a purchaser, he was certain that it was immensely valuable. The key would transform teaching and make schooling "efficient" in ways particularly admired by nineteenth-century America. Education could take less time producing the same level of skill; it could get to the sturdy heartwood of all the subjects with less distraction about the branches of learning. Al Jarvis, who had himself learned German as a student of Rulloff's, heartily endorsed the program. He was willing to put everything at risk to help Rulloff bring the project to a successful conclusion, and he fully expected to share in the wealth that would be realized from it.

Keeping close-mouthed about their secrets, on the Fourth of July 1870, the three Rulofson brothers were on the upward trajectory of success. All of them believed that the benefits of postwar progress would carry them along to yet more achievements. All three thought they were out of the ordinary. What was past was prologue.

And now our story begins.

1
········

Another Line of Work

In the fall of 1857, a stranger dressed as a farmer knocked on the door of Almon Benson Richmond—"A. B." his friends called him— lawyer, inventor, and occasional physician in Meadville, Pennsylvania. The man was of middle height with a thick neck and a broad, flat face. There was nothing very remarkable about his appearance. He said his name was James Nelson, and, after a few words of explanation, A. B. took a shine to him and invited him in.

A. B. took Nelson into his laboratory to inspect drawings for a machine he had invented while working as assistant director of machinery at the Crystal Palace fair in New York City. "I saw from the tone of his voice that he was evidently a gentleman of culture and education," Richmond later reported.[1] They entered A. B.'s museum and looked at the shells in his cabinet of curiosities, and Nelson noticed some confusion in the exhibit cases.

> He immediately stopped and called my attention to the fact, saying, "Mr. Richmond, that is certainly not correct. The shell is not correctly labeled. That shell is surely not Spondylus Spinosus, but is the Argonauto Argo."
>
> . . . Of course I was very much astonished to find that he should know anything about them, but I found, upon further conversation, that he was perfectly familiar with the science of Concology, and also equally well acquainted with the science of mineralogy. My astonishment increased when, a little further along, he picked up the skull of an Indian that had been found on a Western battlefield, and remarked, "Ah! that man received a terrible blow

upon the right *parietal* bone. See it has fractured the temporal bone and the *zygomatic* process": and remarked further, "he must have been a man of considerable age, as the *lambdoidal suture* is almost obliterated."

Every word they exchanged increased A. B.'s sense of wonder; Nelson seemed to know everything about the objects on display.

> He passed around the collection and repeated a quotation in Latin, with which, by mere chance, I happened to be familiar, and I continued the conversation as though he had spoken to me in English.
>
> Then he repeated a sentence in Greek. I discovered that he was evidently trying to exhibit his best phases intellectually, and remarked to him that it was something unusual to find a visitor so well acquainted with the sciences and languages.
>
> He then took from his pocket a certificate from the late Rev. Dr. Barker, President of Allegheny College. The certificate stated that he had examined Mr. James Nelson in Latin, Greek, Hebrew, French and German, and that he took pleasure in stating "that he found him one of the best linguists it was ever his pleasure to meet."
>
> Nelson said that he had obtained the certificate, as he desired to obtain the situation of principal in some school or academy.
>
> We then passed into the laboratory, where we found on a shelf some apparatus that I had used in the stomach of Daniel Brewster, who had been poisoned by arsenic. I found him perfectly familiar with all the tests for detecting poisons, and apparently as much so with my galvanic, electrical, magnetic and chemical apparatus as I was myself, or even more so.

A. B. Richmond thought he was in the company of an unusually learned man, as measured against the scale of his own erudition. A. B. was, of course, celebrating himself as one "well acquainted with the sciences and languages," and, further, as the sole proprietor of a law practice, a laboratory, and a museum. By the time he wrote up this account in the winter of 1870, A. B. had become even more successful, and in the twentieth century a local historian in Meadville would declare that A. B.

had been as famous as Clarence Darrow for his clever defense of hopeless cases.[2]

To secure a patent on his machine, A. B. needed to submit a model
to the Patent Office, and he invited Nelson to build it. Several weeks
passed as Nelson worked on the model, mostly at night for, he said, his
eyesight was bad and the sunlight hurt him. A. B. was delighted with
Nelson's progress.

> In going into the laboratory one day, he asked me if I had an
> emery wheel, for polishing. I showed him one, which he said was
> not rightly constructed, and described to me a method of con-
> structing one which I had heard was used in the Auburn Peniten-
> tiary, in the State of New York.
>
> I remarked to him jocularly, "Mr. Nelson, this is the way they
> polish cutlery in the Penitentiary. Were you ever there?"
>
> He turned suddenly upon me, and his eyes fairly blazed with
> fire, with a look like a tiger ready to spring upon its victim, as he
> said, "What do you mean?" and a more fiendish expression on a
> human countenance, I think I never saw.[3] But he perceived from
> my look, that it was only in joke. He said that he had seen that one
> in use in polishing cutlery when there on a visit.

But Nelson had not been there on a visit. He had spent a decade there
as a prisoner. He was, then, Edward Howard Rulloff, who had escaped
very recently from the Ithaca jail and had fled westward to Meadville.
He worked at night not because his eyes hurt him but because daylight
might reveal his identity to those who could earn a generous reward by
capturing him.

A. B. Richmond, like so many others, found his encounter with
Rulloff memorable. He did not forget him. Like nearly everyone else,
A. B. wondered how this learned monster grew up to be a murderer.

In creating their lives of Rulloff, journalists Ham Freeman and Ed
Crapsey had very different ideas, but they quoted A. B. Richmond's
narrative in full. Ed Crapsey saw Rulloff as a prodigy of egotism.

> The immeasurable vanity of the man had been displayed before
> his accomplishments were paraded to the astonishment of Mr. Rich-
> mond, and to as little practical purpose, except its own gratification.[4]

In Crapsey's view, Rulloff had played a trick on the "estimable" president of Allegheny College, the Reverend Dr. John Barker, and he had imposed himself on the most intelligent part of Meadville's population. He was "a mountebank murderer."[5] Meadville, in his view, had had a narrow escape: Rulloff might have been taken at face value without his evil becoming apparent until too late. Crapsey saw Rulloff as an impostor and titled his book *The Man of Two Lives*—one life virtuous and the other vile. Rulloff was a dissembler, a demon in disguise.

For Ham, the story spoke for itself: Rulloff was something approaching a genius with practical skills (for instance, model making) and theoretical knowledge (for example, of the geography of the human skull). Ham concluded by noting the barest of facts: "Mr. Richmond learned shortly after that his James Nelson was no other than the notorious Rulloff, who it was supposed had murdered his wife and child at Ithaca, N.Y."[6] Ham put journalistic distance between his report and the facts; Ed Crapsey would have no such evasions. Rulloff was not *supposed* to have murdered his wife; he had unquestionably done so in a spasm of violence.

Ham Freeman called his book *The Only True and Authentic History of Edward H. Rulloff*. At the last minute, having seen what Crapsey had written, he added a surtitle: *The Veil of Secrecy Removed*. Ham's Rulloff was far more complex than the figure held up to scorn by his competitor. Searching beyond what he saw as Ed's simplistic judgments, Ham hoped to come at his truth of the real Rulloff. In the end, he was convinced that he had not entirely solved the mystery. He declared that

> though he was undoubtedly a great scholar, possessed of various literary attainments, still there was a species of insanity or monomania which affected all his intellectual faculties, prevaded [*sic*] his whole soul and irresistably [*sic*] controlled all his actions, and that such being the truth, he was not morally or legally accountable for his deeds.[7]

(*Monomania,* in the psychology of the day, was lunacy brought on by a fixation with one thing. In 1851, Melville had given monomania an enduring fictional life in Ahab's quest for the white whale; in 1859, Dickens displayed monomania in *A Tale of Two Cities* in Dr. Manette's constant treadling at his spinning wheel. It was a form of madness especially congenial to the nineteenth-century imagination.)

Ed Crapsey had no truck with such nonsense. Rulloff was not a great scholar, and his knowledge of languages, he asserted, was both superficial and acquired in prison when he was an adult. He had had no more than a fleeting common school education in his youth.[8] He had not been a child prodigy and was a grown-up fraud.

With his school certificate in hand, in Ham's version, Rulloff was thrown upon the world. An uncle might have supported him for further study, Ham said, but he was adamant that any education that he paid for be commercial (and hence worthy) rather than liberal (with little likelihood of economic value). They quarreled and Rulloff's conventional education ended. Perhaps the argument with his uncle was early evidence for his lifelong warfare against commerce.

Ham reported that Rulloff had read law with Duncan Robertson and acquired not only a taste for it but also an expertise in its practice. Crapsey thought that he had been merely a copyist of legal papers. Whatever the truth, in later life Rulloff had no compunction about representing himself as a lawyer, and his performances had as much plausibility as his display of genius in A. B. Richmond's museum. As a lawyer, he produced results: he could get crooks acquitted.

Ham wanted his readers to know that he had affecting stories to tell, though tact required him to keep silent in order to protect delicate feelings.

> While in the office of Mr. [Duncan] Robertson, Edward got himself into trouble by trying to assist another, a friend of his, who was in distress, out of trouble. What the precise nature of that trouble was we do not know, as the matter was kept private, but we are assured by those who ought to and do know that it was no misdemeanor, that it was nothing disgraceful to Edward, but on the contrary it was highly creditable to him, inasmuch as he sacrificed himself and his own interests and happiness to honorably save another.[9]

This is unreliable nonsense. Ham had no independent corroboration of any honorable self-sacrifice. He had only Rulloff's word to go on, and he trusted it even though (he would later admit in the preface to his book) Rulloff never trusted him.[10]

Ed Crapsey, poking into Rulloff's youth, came up with a different story. Rulloff had been a clerk for Keater and Thorne dry goods.

Although the studious and conscientious clerk had impressed his employers with his diligence, things began to go wrong. Twice fires broke out in the store, and circumstances led them to suspect an arsonist. The virtuous Rulloff—an active, willing, and obliging young man in the view of his employers—had been above suspicion.

Borrowing against their good name, Keater and Thorne managed to resume business after the two fires, latterly in the same building occupied by lawyer Duncan Robertson on Prince William Street. But then there were thefts, most memorably of some suiting goods. The merchants hired a detective to help, and he soon traced the stolen goods to a less than scrupulous merchant on Water Street.

Shortly after that theft, Rulloff appeared in an elegant suit made of the very material that had been stolen. Thorne saw at once what the source of that suit had been, and he tried to reason with his clerk. But Rulloff declared himself outraged at being accused. Other members of his family rose to his defense and circulated unpleasant rumors about Mr. Thorne. Since Rulloff would not come clean, Thorne notified the authorities.

The source of the suit having been ascertained at trial, Rulloff was sentenced to two years in the St. John Penitentiary. In the fall of 1841, he was released. He was twenty, and, with the remarkable talent for renaming himself when occasion arose, he styled himself Edward Howard Rulloff. He had also learned how to serve time.

In 1841, St. John was a thriving city of some thirteen thousand inhabitants, twelve churches, two public libraries, and a chamber of commerce. Rulloff had not been forgotten during the two years he had been imprisoned, and, despite his very respectable family, the likelihood of his future employment there was slim. So he walked out of the penitentiary and down to the docks, where he found a boat to the nearest American town—Calais, Maine, at the mouth of the St. Croix River. In the forest just above Calais his younger brother Rulof had settled and was learning the lumber business. The two brothers must have affirmed their kinship, and much later, Rulof would provide Edward with invaluable assistance. Calais was not far enough from St. John and the penitentiary so, after a short visit, Rulloff went on to New York City.

There in 1842, Rulloff said, he enrolled in a commercial school conducted by a Mr. Gourand, where he learned bookkeeping and other useful skills. In Ham Freeman's sentimental account of Rulloff's life, he "went out into a strange world, poor, inexperienced, without powerful influence, with nothing to recommend him but his learning, and the great ability with which he was by many supposed to be endowed."[11]

Seldom grateful to anyone and always wanting people to believe that he had gained skills by unaided study, Rulloff said later that Gourand had promised to set him up in some business but only took his money. He called him "a humbug and a fraud." But why had he enrolled in Gourand's school in the first place? Perhaps two years in the penitentiary had made a commercial education seem less repellent than it had before. Whatever his state of mind, Rulloff became skilled as a penman in the many hands that were expected in the commercial world of the day—and his distinctive handwriting would be recognized by others until the end of his life.

Though Rulloff hardly ever left any town without having drawn the attention of the police, he left New York City unnoticed, taking a boat to Albany and then traveling by canal westward. Arriving at Syracuse in May 1842, he met the proprietor of a passenger boat, William H. Schutt, then twenty-four years old. Rulloff told Schutt that he was out of money and hoped to find a place where he could set up a school. Schutt agreed to let him earn his passage and then made a fatal mistake: he invited Rulloff home.

There was nothing in their early friendship to arouse Will Schutt's suspicions. Rulloff was an eager worker, helping out along the towpaths, assisting in operating locks, and even jumping into the canal to remove snags impeding the boat's progress.

At the end of the journey, Will took him home to the town of Dryden, between Ithaca and Cortland in the Finger Lakes region. The more he came to know him, the more he marveled at Rulloff's accomplishments.

In 1842, this part of New York State was still emerging from the wilderness. Named in 1815, Dryden was originally built on the lumber business (it had fifty-one sawmills in 1835). By the time Rulloff settled there, there were still good farms and a community of industrious people. There were Germans, not only the Schutt family but Snyders, Krums, and others whose handsome tombstones still ornament the beautiful cemetery on a knoll west of Dryden village. Education was valued, and the octagonal schoolhouse built in 1827 was a landmark.[12]

As a guest of the Schutt family, Rulloff began his career as a schoolmaster, not at the "common school," which any child might attend, but at a "select school," where fee-paying parents thought they were getting something better. Among the pupils were Landon D. Krum, a cousin of the Schutts, and two of Will's bright and attractive sisters, Jane and Harriet Schutt. Rulloff taught them in the fall of 1842 and the winter of 1843.

Harriet Schutt was much attached to her family, but before long the schoolmaster was paying court to her, and she responded enthusiastically to his attentions.[13] Later Ephraim Schutt, Will's older brother known as "Eph," said that they were suspicious of the outsider, but the family "was not much opposed to the marriage." In the summer of 1843, Rulloff abandoned schoolteaching to go to Ithaca, six or seven miles away from the Schutt farm, in order to become a physician, but continued his attentions to Harriet.

On December 31, 1843, Rulloff and Harriet were married. The next day, Will Schutt married too, and a crowd of family members celebrated: Harriet's brothers Eph, James, Henry, Aaron, Francis, and John; her younger sisters Mary, Hanna, and Ellen; and her oldest sister Jane.[14] Rulloff had no relations or friends to stand beside him.

There were omens, even as the Rulloffs were married. At the end of the ceremonies, the minister had kissed both brides. Rulloff was enraged. If he were a woman, he said, he "would murder a minister before he would permit him to kiss her."[15] A few days later, some of the family and the Rulloffs went to a shilling party where card games and merriment would have been expected. Again the minister kissed Harriet and again Rulloff was very angry. He said he would never take Harriet anywhere again. She refused to eat for two days, punishing herself for her new husband's violence.[16]

The marriage was not off to a good start.

Rulloff was restless. He resumed his schoolteaching for a while and continued to learn more and more about medicine from Dr. William Stone, who called himself a "botanical physician," though others thought of him as a root doctor. In his practice, Dr. Stone continued the age-old methods of treating disease with herbs and other organic medicines. Soon Rulloff bought a copy of Hooper's *Lexicon-Medicum* and found listed in it the "materia medica" of healing as practiced by his teacher.[17] There were two lists of medications. One described medications such as ipecacuanha, squill, and mustard; these had been used by physicians since the Middle Ages. The other named medications such as Anthemis nobilis, Sulphas zinci, and Hydro-sulphuretum ammoniæ, which look forward to modern chemistry. Dr. Stone represented the good old ways (the first list); a cousin of Harriet Rulloff's, Dr. Henry W. Bull, represented the latter.

And Dr. Bull was a problem.[18] Bull then lived just three miles from the Schutt farm, where Rulloff and Harriett continued to live after their marriage, and was a regular visitor there. Whenever opportunity presented, he kissed the young Schutt women, and Rulloff took great offense at this custom, once shouting his jealousy at Harriet and leaving her in tears.

Bull came regularly to see the Schutts, and the kissing continued. Rulloff pleaded with the Schutts to decline any further visits, but they refused. He was their relation; they had known him for years; he intended no harm.

In February, only weeks after the wedding, there occurred the first act of violence any of the Schutt family could remember. Harriet was crushing peppercorns in a mortar, and Rulloff said that she had not ground them fine enough. Although she said she would pound them more, Rulloff snatched away the pestle and struck her with it on her forehead, leaving a bruise that lasted for some days. He told Jane Schutt that he was only being playful, but she saw no playfulness in her sister's face.

The following summer Rulloff sometimes thought his wife and Dr. Bull were lovers, and that she liked Bull better as a sexual performer. He told a neighbor, Gerrit Van Pelt, that he had been present when Dr. Bull encountered his wife at the sawmill close to the Schutt farm. Rulloff had been so angry that his words stuck in Van Pelt's mind, and he would later testify to what Rulloff had told him.

> Had con[versation] with Dft [defendant] in June or July '44. Dft s[ai]d he saw Bull & his wife talking together in saw mill. Bull sd (Dft sd) Harriet, you have been screwed & he believed she might be again. That Harriet turned it off with a laugh & didn't warrant it.[19]

(As the last chapter of this book will disclose, the young lawyer keeping these notes, Francis Finch, will eventually tell the tale of Rulloff in poetry. Like so many others, he found Rulloff unforgettable.)

The Schutts still thought that Bull was engaging only in harmless social pleasantries, but Rulloff believed otherwise.

Against Harriet's wishes, Rulloff demanded that they move to Ithaca, and in the summer of 1844 they did. There they boarded with Jane O'Brien in rooms over a tailor shop kept by Harriet Ackerman. Rulloff clerked some of the time in Hale's hardware store nearby. The young couple was hard up now that they had to pay rent and buy food in stores. And Rulloff was still obsessed with Dr. Bull.

One day Will Schutt passed through Ithaca on the way to an errand in a distant town, leaving his younger sister Mary with the Rulloffs. Evening came, and Rulloff demanded that Mary walk home. Harriet feared for her sister's safety: she was only eleven years old, and the distance in the dark was too great—eight or nine miles.

Rulloff pushed Mary toward the stairs leading down to the tailor shop. From below, Harriet Ackerman heard a noise and went upstairs. Through the door she could see Harriet Rulloff standing at the foot of the bed with a pillow in front of her mouth. Rulloff had a vial in his hand. Rulloff claimed that his wife was going to poison herself and that he was trying to stop her. Harriet Rulloff asked Harriet Ackerman to go back to her shop, and, with some hesitation, she did. Other people, including Jane O'Brien, came to see what the commotion was. They heard what sounded like a blow. They saw Harriet Rulloff.

> As I went up [Jane remembered] I saw her, and she said, "Oh, Jane, come up quick!"
> Mrs. Rulloff said, "Edward is going to make me take poison and take it himself."
> They were clinched together; he had the bottle in his hand, and I and she tried to take it away; I took hold of her.
> He said, "By the living God, this poison will kill both of us in five minutes," and that would put an end to their troubles.

Some of the rescuers tried to pull them apart, and then Rulloff threw the vial out of the window.

> [H]e began to twit her about Bull.
> She dropped on her knees and said, "Oh, Edward, I am innocent as an unborn child."
> He struck her in the face, and said, "Get Away, God damn you!"[20]
> "You know better than to come near me when I am angry as I am now." . . .

He then told her she could go and live with Dr. Bull, and seek all the pleasure she wished to, for he didn't want to live with her any more. He charged her with sexual improprieties.

His language was pretty broad.

That was about all that was said; I advised him to go away and leave her.

Rulloff said that before he would leave her to another he would serve her as Clark did his wife; Clark murdered his wife; said Clark was a gentleman, and he would chop her as fine as mince meat.[21]

That night, Rulloff took Harriet and Mary to the Schutt farm and left them there.

Two or three days later he went back to the Schutts to collect his wife's clothes, telling Jane that "no other man should have them." But the family would have none of such nonsense, and Rulloff returned empty-handed to Ithaca at midnight. Harriet's father told him not to come back.

Rulloff told Jane that "he sometimes felt like destroying the whole family, and then being hung like an honest man, as Clark was." These were remarkably prescient words and demonstrate how much Rulloff had taken to heart the violent "phantom community" in which he was even then a devoted communicant. At his trial Clark had declared, "I swore I would kill the d——d bitch, and I have killed her." At the gallows, he said that "he had done his duty."[22] Though more than a decade had passed since the hanging of Clark, his memory remained vividly alive.

Later Rulloff would tell Ham Freeman about these terrible events as "circumstances" accumulated that would make him a murderer.[23]

A fellow by the name of Bull, an ass, who pretended to be a regular physician, and perhaps he was, was very often hanging about the house. I saw him kiss my wife the same afternoon we were married, in the pantry. I smothered my rage. He was always lolling around the girls, and I thought for no good purpose. I was not used to anything of the kind. In all the society which I have ever been in, which was not much, such things were not allowed or tolerated. I imagined that my wife liked him better than she did me. I was disconsolate—I was wild. All sorts of ideas and plans passed through my head. After a few days matters grew worse. I resolved to put an end to her existence and mine.

I did procure a vial of poison, and I did attempt to make Harriet take it first, and then I intended to dose myself, and we would die together, but she screamed so as to attract attention, and I pretended it was only in fun.

Harriet Ackerman and Jane O'Brien saw no fun in it and were worried. Still, as long as the Rulloffs remained apart, things might be all right.

Then Harriet Rulloff discovered she was pregnant.

And it did not make it any easier that on October 23, 1844, the world was going to come to an end.

2

•••••••

Oh, That Dreadful Hour

In 1831, a New England preacher, William Miller, had calculated on the basis of biblical prophecy that the familiar world would be consumed in fire and a new world would arise from the ashes. He thought that the latter day, as this end time was known, would occur sometime before the end of 1844. At first Miller did little to publicize his prediction, but as the years passed other preachers converted to "Millerism" and took up the cry. Omens were detected: spectacular displays of the northern lights, vivid meteor showers, earthquakes. Millerites sharpened their pencils and refined the calculation.

As best as anyone could tell, the end would come in late October. One Philadelphia storekeeper was so convinced of the predictions that he put a sign in his store: "This Shop is closed in honor of the King of Kings, who will appear about the 23rd of October. Get ready, friends, to crown him Lord of all."[1]

Speaking of the last days in the Gospel of Matthew, Jesus had sketched the calamities that would occur. It would be particularly agonizing, he had said, for women who were pregnant. Harriet, especially, must have been troubled by the prophecies.

For Rulloff the idea of the Advent was liberating. A baby, on the other hand, would chain him even tighter to the Schutt family, making it even harder for him to move west, where opportunities might be more abundant. As Harriet heaped up obstacles to his dreams, he was increasingly tormented.

> Harriet said that she would never go to Ohio, or so far away from her family, that if I went away she would not remain and

keep house, and that she would take her child and things and go home, that she was tired of living with me any how, and that her mother was anxious for her to return home. Of course this made me very angry; it rather upset my plans, and I did not know what to do. I could not make a decent living there; my practice amounted to nothing, and I had no taste for it; besides, I was poor, and too proud to have the neighbors and people generally know how poor I was. Angry words ensued between us.[2]

Here Rulloff begins to accumulate the reasons to justify his violent acts. His talents were yet unformed and certainly unappreciated. Harriet was settled and ready for motherhood; Rulloff was unsettled and ready for anything.

October 23 came and went. For some, the Great Advent became the Great Disappointment, and angry crowds burned Millerite meeting houses roundabout Ithaca.[3] But the months in Lansing, where Rulloff and Harriet now lived, seemed to Harriet's family and the neighbors happy ones. Rulloff was "getting forehanded with the world," somebody remembered, and he had acquired a library. He was reading Latin and Greek with DeWitt Clinton Vosbury, an older scholar in Ithaca,[4] and he could afford to pay for lessons. For a fee, he lectured on the new science of phrenology.[5] Whether from his lecturing, medical practice, clerking in the hardware store, or thievery, Rulloff had some ready money and bought small presents for Harriet, including an orange, an exotic and expensive gift in those days.

On the night of April 12, 1845, their daughter was born. She was named Priscilla after Rulloff's mother, according to family legend.

Harriet's mother Hannah persuaded her husband to relax his prohibition made the previous summer against Rulloff, and in early May the couple and their baby paid an extended visit to the Schutt farm.

Toward the end of the month, the Rulloffs returned to their "humble house" in Lansing, a ninety-minute walk from the center of Ithaca. Harriet liked to visit her brother Will and his wife, Amelia. Having married just a day apart, the two women had had babies just two months apart, and they enjoyed being together. Since Will and his family lived above Hale's store, where Rulloff sometimes worked, both parents and the baby were frequent visitors.

Then, at the very end of May, Amelia Schutt fell ill. Will Schutt asked his doctor brother-in-law to minister to her. He might have asked Dr. Oliver W. Bonney, who had attended her in childbirth three months before; he might even have asked Dr. Bull. In picking Rulloff, he made a mistake he would regret for the rest of his life.

In 1857, Hannah Schutt recalled these terrible days.

> Rulloff was called to William's wife, who was sick first; she went into a decline and had a cough; she was sick about two weeks; she had been unusually smart but took cold; she never recovered her health after her child was born; was imprudent in going out too soon.[6]

Before the germ theory of disease was accepted late in the century, sickness and death were fearfully mysterious. It was not clear why so many women died in childbirth; imprudent behavior—"going out too soon"—was about as good an explanation as anyone could provide. *Childbed fever* was a dreaded and often fatal affliction of new mothers.

Suddenly the Schutt baby—bearing a name echoic of her mother's, Amille—was wracked with convulsions, and Rulloff made her his patient too. The sickness got worse and mother and daughter declined.

Rulloff asked Hannah Schutt to come to Ithaca and help him. On the way there, he continued to talk darkly about Dr. Bull. He said that Will Schutt had misused him in allowing Dr. Bull to hang around Harriet. Ominously, he said that "that thing would yet mount up to the shedding of blood."

Later Hannah remembered that Rulloff had said it was strange that she had raised all her children to adulthood without losing any. But life was not finished with her yet. "My gray hairs would go down in sorrow to the grave," he predicted, and Hannah worried that he might be right. She little reckoned that Rulloff would be the cause.[7]

In 1871, Ham Freeman asked Rulloff if Hannah's account were true.

> I do not remember of telling the old lady that I would bring her gray hairs in sorrow to the grave, and that I had poisoned William's wife and child, and that others of the family would go next. Still I may have said something of the kind to her when in a passion. She was a very good old woman, but ignorant and suspicious, and easily influenced.[8]

On June 3, Amille died. On June 5, her mother Amelia died too.

In later years, most people would believe that Rulloff had murdered them both. Clearly he had been angry with Will Schutt for not taking his side in his obsessive effort to banish Dr. Bull. Still, at the double funeral, he did not behave in a way that aroused suspicion, nor for many months did Will Schutt and others in his family begin to doubt him. After all, in those days mothers and infants died in great numbers. There seemed to be no mystery about it.

Rulloff may have been treating his two patients according to the established scientific practice, though Ed Crapsey would never believe it, and he suspected that he had deliberately murdered them.[9] Rulloff had an unusual capacity for feigning innocence when confronted with his crimes, and his failure to show "outward manifestations of any consciousness of agency" during the funerals and the grieving does not allow any inferences about his sense of guilt or innocence at the death of his sister-in-law and her child. The deaths were a sad but ambiguous episode, and, like so much else in Rulloff's story, the truth was elusive.

What followed that funeral in June 1845 was even more ambiguous and the truth even more elusive: the disappearance and apparent deaths of Harriet Rulloff and baby Priscilla.

On June 16, 1844, the Rulloff family returned home to Lansing. On June 23, in the morning, Harriet went across the road to visit her neighbor Elizabeth Robertson. Wearing a dark calico dress with the sleeves torn off at the elbow, she was getting ready for housework, and she borrowed some soap from Elizabeth. She said she might do her washing that day or maybe the next; Edward was away, she told Mrs. Robertson, and she would wait until he came back so he could carry the water from the well to the washtub. About midday Rulloff came home, and in the afternoon Harriet again walked across to the Robertsons, this time dressed up and wearing her ring; "it was a valuable ring with a set in it," Elizabeth noticed. She commented on it when she and Harriet were drying the dishes after the tea and cakes Elizabeth served for the Rulloffs and for her own family.[10]

Later in the day, two Indian women wearing blankets and headdresses appeared in Lansing. Rulloff thought that Harriet might be frightened of them and asked Olive Robertson, age fifteen, to sit with Harriet and Priscilla, though a young girl would hardly seem the best choice to reassure a frightened adult. As a result of this strange invitation, Olive was the last to see Harriet and Priscilla alive.

Sometime between eight and nine in the evening, Dr. John F. Burdick drove up in his horse and buggy to visit a patient at another neighbor's, just fifty feet or so from the east end of the Rulloffs' house. The doctor stayed until about eleven o'clock and then went out and turned his horse toward home. As he passed between the Rulloffs' and the Robertsons' houses, he heard both doors close. Mrs. Robertson remembered a heavier vehicle, a double lumber wagon, arriving at about the same time that Dr. Burdick first came by. It stayed at Rulloff's only about fifteen or twenty minutes, and she had opened her front door to look at it too. But the night was dark and she couldn't see much.

Rulloff's memory of that evening he reported to Ham Freeman in 1871. He said he had been talking to Harriet, once again, about moving westward where his prospects might improve.

> This was the subject of our conversation on various occasions, and on the night of the 23rd of June, 1845, after Miss Olive Robertson was there and went away, I told her that I had got hold of a little money; that I was going west to find something profitable to do, and that I wished that she would remain there and keep house until my return, or until I sent for her; that I had been corresponding with persons in Ohio, and I expected to get to be a Principal of an Academy out there; that I intended to drop practicing medicine, and to become, in time, either a Professor in a College, or a lawyer.[11]

Harriet had no wish to live alone in Lansing during Rulloff's absence and said she would return home. Once again Rulloff accused her of wanting to be with Dr. Bull.

> At this I told her that she might go where she pleased. I think I said she might go to hell if she chose to, but that she should not take the child, that I would take care of that. At this I attempted to take the child away from her, and she clung to it. In my passion I reached for the pestle of the mortar in which I pounded medicines, and which stood near by, and struck her with it over the left temple. I must have struck very hard—I was a young man and

very strong, and the blow broke her skull. She fell senseless with the child still in her arms, which was crying. Oh! that dreadful hour! that horrible moment which I would have given worlds to blot out![12]

For the first time, late in his life, Rulloff confessed to murdering Harriet.

Even in his last weeks, Rulloff remained the owner of his narrative and wanted to craft its telling. He kept a copy of Amasa J. Parker's *Reports of Decisions in Criminal Cases* in his cell, and the "confession" that he related to Ham Freeman in 1871 was built on the minute circumstances of the testimony of his 1856 trial for Harriet's murder. There are no inconsistencies between the two, and very little information of consequence that had not already been put on public display. He wanted to say that he had killed Harriet but was not to blame for murdering her. He described a crime of passion, the brutal act brought on by his jealousy of Dr. Bull. But it was not murder in the first degree, at least as far as Harriet's death is concerned. He declined to address the fate of his daughter. (Rulloff's self-absorption is grammatically expressed in the abundance of first-person pronouns in his account of the murder.)

"I took the child and lay it upon the bed—I gave it a narcotic to stop its crying." These, I can testify [wrote Ham], were his exact words. He said then, with a significant smile: "I had raised Harriet up and placed her in a position so that I could examine the wound. Oh! God, I tried to bring her to life. She never spoke a word after she was struck. I administered every restorative I had at hand; dressed the wound carefully, and did all I could to restore her. Once I went out of the house, and intended to call the Robertson family, but when half way to their house I returned. She died about one o'clock, I think. Oh! think of me bending over her in her last moments gasping for breath, and I attempting to breathe life into her. She died easy—I do not think she ever realized any pain. The pestle broke the skull, and sunk into her brain. It was all the work of a moment. She bled some, but not much. From that hour I knew that I was a ruined man. Everything that had before been bright or hopeful turned black and forbidding in my mind. I realized at once my awful situation; there was no premeditation;

no preparation about it whatever; whoever says or intimates that there was, lies; all the facts go to show that there was none. In my despair I did not know what to do. I finally concluded that I would kill myself too, and let that be the end of it, and with that intention I prepared some poison which I had."[13]

"I wrote a letter to be left on the table to be found by whoever should enter the house, detailing all the circumstances of what had happened, and giving directions as to the disposition of the remains, and my effects, then I closed all the shutters of the house, but something seemed to stay me from committing suicide, even when the cup was to my lips. Thus I passed the time alternately adopting and rejecting different plans. It would take a week to relate all my thoughts in these few dreadful hours. Each minute seemed a day, and each hour a week. Morning came at last. I had been out, in and around and about the house dozens of times. When daylight appeared I awoke, as it were, from my reverie of despair. I realized that something must be done before the neighborhood was astir. I pulled out the largest chest I had, emptied it of its contents. I wrapped *her* in some strong bed-ticking, and then in two sheets. I had previously bandaged the head, and I then crowded *her* into the chest, which I had much difficulty in doing. I also placed some flat-irons and the mortar in the chest. I had about made up my mind what I should do with the *body*. About eleven o'clock I went over to Robertson's and asked them for the loan of their horse."[14]

Evaluating the truth of Rulloff's description of these events is difficult. Certainly they match the facts as they had been revealed. But Samuel Halliday, the only twentieth-century observer to describe the crime in detail, thought Rulloff was telling more lies, and he said as much in a lecture he gave at the Ithaca High School in 1901.

Halliday was sure that there would have been blood everywhere if Rulloff had killed Harriet in the way he had described to Ham, but he offered no other reason to question the account. He further quoted the deathbed story attributed to one of his lawyers, Stephen B. Cushing. Cushing said that "Rulloff told him that he strangled his wife and then took up a board in the floor, and opened an artery, bled her to death. The child was smothered." When this tale emerged during Rulloff's last imprisonment, he vehemently denied it.

Halliday did not make clear whether he doubted Rulloff's story or Ham Freeman's report. Both had reasons to make yarns differing from the truth, and Ham scooped the other writers in reporting Rulloff's confession. Rulloff, too, would benefit if people thought that he was driven to kill his wife through his well-documented jealousy of Dr. Bull. They would not be so sympathetic, of course, if he confessed to killing his infant daughter, and Rulloff carefully avoided talking about her fate. He even convinced the half-skeptical Ham that Priscilla had survived and, in 1871, was living happily with her uncle in Pennsylvania.[15]

On June 24, the day after Harriet's fatal injury, between ten and eleven o'clock in the morning, Rulloff went across to Tom Robertson's house to see if he could borrow that horse and wagon. During the night, he said, Uncle Henry Snyder—or maybe Emory Boyce, the Robertsons disagreed about just which—had visited and taken Harriet and her child to Mottville, a village some eight or ten miles away. To make room for them, Rulloff said, they had unloaded a box, and now he wanted to deliver it and bring his wife home again. Robertson, reluctant at first because the day was hot and a twenty-mile round trip would be hard on his horse, finally agreed to help. With his son, Newton, Robertson helped Rulloff load the chest onto the wagon.

In the early afternoon, then, Rulloff set out in the direction of Mottville. Those who embellished the story later described him as giving a ride to a group of children who sat beside him and on top of the chest; they were singing and whistling, it was said. Some thought that a couple of corpses matching the descriptions of Harriet and her baby had been sold for anatomizing to the Geneva Medical College at about that time. All the tales were vivid and presumed that the chest in the wagon contained the bodies. Lurid details like these helped fuel the idea that Rulloff was a monster.[16]

Truthful neighbors testified to only the facts without embellishment. Elijah Labar, a kinsman of the sheriff, told what he had seen.

> I . . . remember the time of his wife's disappearance; saw him pass my house, with Robertson's horse and wagon, about two o'clock P.M.; was a chest in the wagon; he was alone; he was going south; the road led to Mottville and Varna.[17]

Everything in Labar's account was unemotional and seemed entirely factual. Rulloff pretended that nothing unusual had happened, but later he said he was wracked by torment. In his "confession" to Ham, Rulloff presented himself as a sufferer submerged in anguish by the horror of his deed. At midnight before his execution in 1871, he was visited by the reporter for the *New York Tribune* who had with him the proof sheets of Bayard Taylor's translation of Goethe's *Faust,* a work that powerfully influenced Rulloff's presentation of himself. Like Faust, he was accidentally damned by an "unfortunate" act of bad judgment.

> Rulloff took great interest in [the proofs], took them in his hands, read extracts in the English, and then from memory reproduced the German, which he pronounced beautifully. When he had finished and had handed them back, Rulloff said, "I want to get a copy of that work when it is published." But when he was reminded that he probably would not be alive at that time, a fact which seemed to have passed out of his mind, he laughed, and, as far as any could observe, his laugh was not pretended or forced, but perfectly natural.[18]

Faust instructed him in feeling. It showed him how a genius in torment should behave, and he hoped to triumph over suffering as Faust had. It is not too hard to imagine the lines that he quoted that last morning of his life—Faust's death speech. In Taylor's translation, these are Faust's words.

> The Night seems deeper now to press around me,
> But in my inmost spirit all is light
> I rest not till the finished work hath crowned me:
> The master's Word alone bestows the might.
> Up from your couches, vassals, man by man!
> Make grandly visible my daring plan!
> Seize now your tools, with spade and shovel press!
> The work traced out must be a swift success.[19]

Like Prometheus, another of the great heroes of nineteenth-century romanticism, Rulloff would benefit human kind through revelation. In place of Faust's vassals, Rulloff had Ham Freeman at his command.

A high romantic in the most sentimental of centuries, Rulloff knew how to express anguish through melodrama. His account of the day after Harriet's death is suffused with righteous suffering. And in re-creating for Ham the events of June 24, 1845, he made images of heroism fully apparent. He was capable of broad gestures, and it would not have been out of character for him to fall to his knees, press the back of his right hand to his brow, and wail.

> After I had left with the horse and wagon with the chest, I again became undecided. I fancied that everyone I met knew of my crime, and what I had in the chest. I tried to assume a composed manner. I drove on slowly and listlessly, taking cross-roads to the lake, little knowing where I was going. I was so completely confused and overcome by the horror with which I was filled, that had any one charged me at the time with the crime, or arrested me, I would instantly have confessed all. Such has always been the case with me, believe me or not, as you please. I never committed a crime of any kind but what its commission overcame and perplexed me. I could never been expert in crime. I had no adaptation to it. It was repugnant to my nature. I despise a thief as much as you do. I am a victim of circumstances. It is a fatality with some. I am almost, yes, I am quite a *fatalist* sometimes.[20]

These musings are Rulloff's re-creation of his younger self from the vantage of a quarter century later. His continuing literary and linguistic education had refined and shaped his feelings. In 1845, with a corpse in the chest at the back of the wagon, his thoughts were likely to have been more practical than philosophical.

Heading toward Mottville, Rulloff skirted the edges of Ithaca and passed around the southern end of Lake Cayuga and into the town of Ulysses.

> It was, at one time, partly my intention to drive boldly into Ithaca and procure some potash, and to bury my charge some where, covered with the potash. The potash I thought would, in time, absorb or eat up the remains and thus destroy all trace of them, but I was not good enough chemist then to know whether it would, so I abandoned that idea.[21]

In all his statements to Ham, Rulloff used euphemisms like "my charge" or "the remains," all of them both abstract and unnumbered. He did not reveal whether he was carrying one corpse or two.

I drove into the woods near the lake, about six or seven miles from Ithaca, and while planning what to do, I think, being very tired, I fell partly asleep, and was awakened by hearing two persons pass conversing; I listened; fortunately they went on without discovering me.

I dismounted from the wagon, and went to the lake. I looked about cautiously for a boat. I found one suitable to my purpose, after a long search. I returned to the wagon, opened the chest, and took out the contents. I made two trips from the wagon to the boat.[22]

Ham refrained from asking him why two trips were necessary. Were there two corpses? Or was the second trip only necessary to carry to the boat the weights Rulloff had brought with him from Lansing?

I used weights of iron and stone tied to what I sunk into the lake. The stones were tied up in the clothing, and the clothing tied to the body. I placed all when ready into the boat, and rowed out into the lake. I rowed a long way, until I found a spot where I thought the water was the deepest. I then carefully placed what I had with me in the water, and letting go of it the same sunk rapidly to rise no more, as I intended it never should.[23]

In years to follow, repeated efforts were made to drag the lake for the bundle Rulloff had dropped into it. It was said that in the 1850s more than ten thousand dollars had been spent on dragging the lower end of Lake Cayuga—an impossibly large sum for the times but indicative of the insatiable craving for the evidence of Rulloff's crime. Toward the end of the century, a workman was laying sewer pipes far out in Lake Cayuga, and, with the water a "glassy smoothness," saw what he thought was the lid of a box in some ten feet of water. "That box contains the bodies of Mrs. Rulloff and her child," he thought. Returning with a long pole, he attempted to pry the box loose but failed, and was later unable to locate the spot again. In 1901, Samuel Halliday told the Historical Society that he had wanted to try to find the spot, though there should be no box. After all, Rulloff had returned with that chest, now empty, to Lansing. Still, if two corpses, or even one, could be discovered, that would settle at least part of the mystery of Rulloff.[24]

In articulating his story to Ham, Rulloff inflated his emotions to the bursting point: "I fancied that everyone I met knew of my crime, and what I had in the chest."[25] Rulloff yearned to be caught and did everything he could to arouse the curiosity of those who so credulously believed him. He wanted to turn the Schutt family into his pursuers. This goal he accomplished but not nearly as rapidly as he seems to have wished.

Returning from the west shore of the lake with Tom Robertson's horse and wagon, Rulloff felt hungry. "Arriving at Ithaca I tied the horse under a shed, and got something for it to eat. I then went over to William Schutt's and Jane gave me something to eat."[26]

Jane's recollection was that he behaved far more erratically.

> About the time of my sister's disappearance, defendant was at Ithaca, the day after the Indians were there, twenty-fourth of June; it was before noon; don't know how he came; he said he and Harriet were going away out between the lakes; that a family visiting in Lansing had advised him to go; that he thought he should go and stay five or six weeks, and might return; he said he was hungry; would not wait for me to get him something to eat, but went down to the cellar and eat ravenously, taking his food into his hands; I understood his wife was at home then; I gave him some of William's babe clothing; he first objected to taking it, but finally did so; he stayed half an hour; said he was going back home.[27]

Tom Robertson was glad to see Rulloff and glad to have his rig back.

> He brought the horse and wagon back about twelve the next day; the horse didn't seem to have been driven, wasn't sweaty; was as hot a day as the one previous; he took his dinner with us that day; at three or four P.M. I saw Mr. Rulloff going towards Mottville or Ithaca with a bundle in his hand; bundle was tied up in a reddish shawl or handkerchief.[28]

When Rulloff came back, the chest was in the wagon. Newton Robertson, the boy, watched the proceedings with interest.

> Rulloff returned next day with a chest; I didn't help lift chest out or lift it after it was out; I think it was the same chest that went

away; he got back some time in the forenoon; I believe Rulloff took it out himself without difficulty; it did not seem heavy.[29]

At the 1856 trial, as in other cases in which he was a defendant, Rulloff took an active role in the proceedings. His tendency to scrutinize irrelevant details appears in the cross-examination of Newton Robertson. Was he sure it was the same chest?

Newton Robertson: "I looked at the chest and thought it was the same one; I did not examine it to see if it was the same or another chest; I saw Rulloff take it out of wagon in front of his house, before the horse was taken from the wagon."[30]

There was no theory of the case in this questioning, no leading up to a dramatic conclusion in which one chest or two might make for an alternative explanation to the disappearance of Harriet and Priscilla. Rulloff only muddled the details.

Soon Tom Robertson saw Rulloff about to set out on foot, and he and his family were troubled. Yet Rulloff had seemed so cool and relaxed as he departed that Tom could not believe anything serious was amiss. "Good-bye, Mr. Robertson; don't be alarmed if we don't come back in two or three weeks. I and my wife talk of going on a visit between the lakes!"

"He added jocularly, 'Please don't let any man carry away our house while we are gone.'"[31]

Elizabeth Robertson had been particularly attentive to Harriet's pitifully few clothes, and even ten years later she remembered them in detail. When she went away from home, Harriet wore a large woolen shawl. To Elizabeth, Rulloff gave yet another of his brutal answers: "I asked him when he was agoing to bring his wife back; he said in three or four weeks, maybe never."[32]

From Lansing, Rulloff walked back to Ithaca to Will Schutt's rooms; tormented, he did all he could to arouse suspicion.

I remember Rulloff at my house the day after the disappearance; I saw him at tea; he spoke of his face burning; asked if it didn't look red; said he had walked some ways; after tea he took the ring out of the vest pocket; he asked if I recognized the ring; I said it was one that I gave his wife several years ago; he said, "Don't you want to take it back?" I said, "No, give it back to your wife"; he put the ring back; said he had carried it since his last visit to my father's; my sister usually wore the ring; he said he was going between the lakes next morning; should take his wife along; that he had some prospects of getting in business; he stayed till after tea and went down to the store with me, and after a little he went out; returned shortly after and got a rocking chair that belonged to him; saw him about nine o'clock that night, at Dr. Stone's office, bringing a chest out or pulling it towards the door; he had studied at Dr. Stone's; I don't know what he was going to do with it.[33]

Jane Schutt remembered as vividly as did her brother the conversation that evening, and her testimony in 1856 corroborated Will's and added additional detail.

Mrs. Rulloff had a ring with a set in it; she had had it several years; after tea he said don't my face look red; I said it did; he said he had walked five miles very fast, and it made his face red; he then read the Mysteries of Paris, and commenced weeping; said he could never read that part of the book without crying; after that he took out the ring from his pocket and asked William if he remembered it; William said he did; he gave it to his sister years ago; defendant said, Don't you want it? William said, No, give it back to your wife; defendant said his wife gave it to him while at her father's, a number of weeks before, and he had carried it since.[34]

Jane Schutt must have thought it odd that Rulloff abruptly turned his attention to Eugène Sue's sensational novel, just published in English translation. Even more bizarre was the emotion on his face, and he soon commenced weeping over the book. Many passages might have brought Rulloff to tears, but perhaps one, in which the evil notary Jacques Ferrand confronts his crimes, would have suited his mood. Certainly Sue had created a character Rulloff wished to resemble:

He remained there a long time, dumb, immovable, petrified. With wan eyes, his teeth compressed, his mouth foaming, tearing mechanically with his nails at his breast he felt his reason totter, and was lost in an abyss of darkness. When he awoke from his stupor, he walked heavily, and with an ill-assured step; objects trembled in his sight; he felt as if recovering from a fit of intoxication.[35]

Sue's description portrayed exactly the "reverie of despair" that Rulloff would convey to Ham Freeman in 1871.

Later on the evening of June 25, Rulloff went to Eber Babcock's livery stable and hired a horse and lumber-box wagon. He told Milton Ostrander, who was on duty at the time, that he wanted to take some goods a distance of three or four miles.[36] At 3:00 A.M. on June 26, he returned it. The date and time were written in Babcock's ledger.

About 7:00 on that same morning, Rulloff appeared at the stage office in the Clinton House with two chests. Edward H. Watkins was the agent, and Rulloff approached him to buy a ticket on the stage leaving for Geneva at four o'clock the following morning. He told Watkins to book the seat in the name "John Doe." Watkins thought that a strange request. "I was a little surprised at the name; by information I knew him; I did not know him personally."[37]

Next day, as the stage passed through Jacksonville, just up the western shore of Lake Cayuga, one of the Schutt relatives saw Rulloff and was surprised that he was traveling without his wife and child. At Ovid, he took the boat across Seneca Lake and then overland to Keuka Lake, where he took another boat to Hammondsport at its southern end; taking yet another stage, he reached the Genesee Valley Canal, where he seemed to disappear. It was a route west where he would likely escape detection.

Some weeks passed. The Robertsons grew increasingly anxious about Harriet and her baby, and so did Will and Jane Schutt.

In early August, Rulloff was in Chicago and penniless. His ingratiating manner, and the dubious security of one of the chests, helped him obtain money on a three-month note.

By the time of Rulloff's trial a dozen years later, the prosecutors had tracked him to Chicago and brought back a witness, Richard K. Swift.

I . . . think in 1845 my brother [Elijah Swift] was applied to for a loan by a man; my brother refused; heard the man say he had lost his wife and child, and was out of money; I said to brother if he didn't let him have the money I would; I let him have $25 or $30, for which he gave me his note, signed, I believed, James H.

Revillee; he left as security for the payment of his note, a brown chest, snuff brown; I think about eighteen or twenty inches across ends, three feet or more long; as near as I can now remember, he said his wife and child died south of Chicago, on the Illinois river, in Illinois; I think he said they died about six weeks before.

He told me if he didn't return in a certain time I was to write to a certain place near, I think, the Mohawk river, and he would remit the money; I wrote and received no answer; I then, with Dr. Dyn and others, opened the chest;[38] found a good many books; the box now in court, a sheet and some other things; he [Rulloff] was there with me and got the money August 4, 1845; that was the date of the note; I have a statement made out February 18, 1847, of contents of the box; I remember a large bundle of papers, lectures on phrenology; Hooper's Dictionary, E. H. Rulloff written on inside cover; some of the names were erased; names of places rubbed out; so of names of persons; small box contained women's fixings; papers in bottom of box; letters; cards marked Edward H. Rulloff; a paper on which were the words, 'Oh, that dreadful hour!' one lock of light brown hair in paper, labeled a lock of Harriet's or Mary's hair; I thought Harriet; think the chest was heavy with books; saw a pocket-book in box; can't identify it; style of card is the same; pair of hose like these; remember a piece of silk and a bead bag like this; remember a collar like this; the small box was in our house for many years; the lock of hair was lost, and so of the loose pieces of paper on which the words were written; I remember a figured lace cap for an infant; the silk was light colored, ash colored; there were a lot of small sea-shells.[39]

These pitiful fragments provide an archaeology of Rulloff's life: the shells, his fragments of a museum that might rise in time to rival A. B. Richmond's; the medical dictionary, his failed efforts as a physician; the women's fixings and the lace cap, his dead family.

"That dreadful hour" was a phrase used by several of the poets known to Rulloff. Most likely, he applied it from James Beattie's fable "The Bees." Beattie invited readers to imagine a "system-building sage" who is blessed with a "foundation dream," "a goodly scheme," upon which he hopes to explain "all nature by his rules." Then, suddenly, a catastrophe: "that dreadful hour" when everything is reduced to ruins.[40]

3
•••••••

Doctor! Where Is Your Wife?

A few days after Rulloff left Ithaca, one of the younger Schutt brothers, Henry, went to the house in Lansing with a present of clothing and furniture sent over by Harriet's parents. When he arrived, he found the shutters closed and the house locked. The Robertsons told him that the Rulloffs were "between the lakes." Henry returned home and reported the news to the rest of the family without exciting much curiosity. The Schutts, by this time, had grown used to their son-in-law coming and going in unannounced and unpredictable ways.

Several weeks passed without anyone's paying much attention to where the Rulloffs might have gone, but, when Dr. Burdick once again visited his patient at the house next to the Rulloffs, they got to talking about what had become of them. Together they discussed the strange circumstances of Rulloff's departure and determined to enter the house. Elizabeth Robertson, who—it must be said—was a busybody, went with them. Eleven years later she testified to what she had seen.

> Went in the house with the family of Schutts three or four weeks afterwards; went with others; I saw that wash-dress lying at the foot of the bed on the floor; it lay on the floor in a heap; saw some shoes and stockings; knew they were Mrs. Rulloff's, that she had worn the day before [she disappeared]; they were before the bed on the floor; saw a skirt in another room hung up; part of the bed was on a chair; bed was not made; saw her traveling basket there, which she carried when she traveled; she had but one; saw a small pair of child's socks in the basket; saw the dirty clothes in the wash-room; the soap had been emptied out of the tin pail into a wooden pail; some of the table dishes were on the table.[1]

Harriet, with her new baby, might not have been much of a house-keeper, but she would not have taken a trip without her basket and shawl or have left the house in such disarray. The baby's socks in the basket were somehow poignant. Elizabeth was worried.

Dr. Burdick also remembered what he had seen in the Rulloffs' untidy house.

Harriet's skirt, in a circle just as she had stepped out of it, seemed a sign of a hasty departure. Surely she would normally have draped it over a chair or hung it from a hook in the wall. Still there was no sense of urgency about her disappearance.

After three or four more weeks, the sheriff of Tompkins County took charge. The saloons of Ithaca were soon filled with rumors of foul play, and forty or fifty men came with him to the house, Eph and Will Schutt among them. Dr. Burdick said it was just as he had seen it before. Imagination filled the cluttered house with dire deeds.

On the afternoon of that same day, Will and Eph Schutt were sitting in Hale's store when an amazing thing happened: Rulloff appeared. Will cordially shook Rulloff by the hand as soon as he entered the store. When asked where Harriet was, he said that she was "between the lakes,"[2] some place near Geneva, but he didn't name it.

During the trial, Eph told the court that when he looked over the house in Lansing he had noticed that the huge pestle Rulloff had for his medicines—it must have weighed twenty-five or thirty pounds, he thought—was missing. So were the flat irons. Probably these missing pieces of heavy metal only came to his mind after he and his friends had developed the theory that Rulloff had used them to sink Harriet's body in the lake, but he said he had noticed that they were gone and suspected Rulloff of having done something sinister with them.

Will Schutt was not suspicious at all, just mightily relieved.

> I asked him up to my lodging room, and asked him if he had heard of a report there was about his murdering his wife and child; he said he had not; he seemed to be somewhat surprised that they should think any such thing. . . .
>
> He stayed in the room with me that night; his eyes were sore; I wrapped them up in cloths; he appeared restless during the night; I asked him what troubled him; he said it troubled him to think the people had that opinion of him, that he would murder his wife

and child; I told him to be easy and I would explain it; the next day, in the afternoon, he left the store to go to my father's.[3]

How could anyone suspect that a murderer would go to stay with the parents of his victim? In Dryden, John and Hannah Schutt greeted him warmly and of course asked about Harriet and the baby. This time he said that she and their daughter were in Madison in Lake County, Ohio.

The Schutt brothers wanted evidence that Harriet was alive. They were not the only interested parties by that time. A lynch mob was forming. Eph Schutt was present in Hale's when a delegation arrived. "I was there when several gentlemen came in to ask him about her; he would give no definite satisfaction; they left him and told him that he would probably be detained."[4] *Detained* was a high-sounding word for some quicker form of retribution.

Eph hit on an idea. If Rulloff would write a letter to Harriet and wait for her to reply, that would solve everything. Rulloff immediately agreed.

He drafted one letter and destroyed it, then began another, which he finished. He addressed it to Harriet Rulloff in care of N. Dupuy in Madison, Ohio. Eph showed the letter to the "gentlemen" who had taken such an intense interest in Harriet Rulloff's fate, and he took it to the post office to be mailed.

When Eph got back, he discovered that Rulloff was gone.

Eph might have asked for help in his search; instead, he set out alone. He traveled to Geneva but found no evidence of Rulloff. He continued on by train to Rochester, on his way to Madison, Ohio.

At the train station in Rochester Eph caught sight of Rulloff on the platform; Rulloff saw Eph and vanished into the crowd. Eph jumped aboard the train. He found Rulloff with his bundle of clothes hiding in the back among the "emigrants" who were going west.

Rulloff said he would take Eph to Harriet. Soon they arrived in Buffalo, where they spent the night. When Eph went out, he locked Rulloff in the hotel room to keep him from escaping. On his return, Rulloff was quaking in fear at the sound of the key in the lock; he thought that some of the "gentlemen" from Ithaca had come after him.

The next morning they went down to the docks and—an odd detail— Rulloff paid for the tickets. They arrived in Fairport, Ohio, the nearest stopping place to Madison, and Rulloff disappeared once again. As the steamer left the dock, Eph searched everywhere but Rulloff was not on board.

At the Erie wharf, Eph went to visit his brother Uriah, who had heard nothing of Rulloff or Harriet. Eph took the next boat to Fairport and went to the small village of Madison. There was no Dupuy family there, and no one had heard of Harriet Rulloff either. Leaving word where he might be reached, Eph took the boat to Cleveland, where he obtained a warrant for Rulloff's arrest.

Rulloff might have gone anywhere, but Eph still believed he could find him. Sure enough, two large steamers crowded with emigrants were just then arriving from the east and from the second one Rulloff emerged. He didn't notice Eph in the waiting crowd.

This time Eph knew he needed help, and he took his warrant and engaged a famous detective, "Old" Hayes.[5] In a "low eating saloon," behind a dry goods box, they found Rulloff. He denied his identity, and, taking Hayes aside, Rulloff nearly persuaded him that Eph was persecuting him and that there was no truth to his accusations.

Eph locked Rulloff in the strong room of the Buffalo boat until they were well clear of the shore. Then he took Rulloff up to the pilothouse and begged him to tell what had become of Harriet. Rulloff sullenly refused and said he would put an end to Eph's questions by jumping overboard. Eph allowed as how that would be all right with him, but Rulloff changed his mind.

Eph told the heartbreaking story of Harriet and the baby to the captain and the passengers. Some of them wanted to kill Rulloff then and there. But Eph still hoped to discover Harriet alive and so returned Rulloff to the strong room.

Once in Buffalo, Eph had himself appointed a "special constable" for the purpose of taking Rulloff back to Ithaca, and he clapped him in handcuffs to discourage further escapes. When they arrived in Ithaca, the Schutt family and the hangers-on at Hale's store were delighted at Eph's success. This time the lynch mob assembled in earnest, but the sheriff locked Rulloff in the jail and kept the mob at bay.

In September 1845, Rulloff was indicted on the charge of abducting or murdering his wife. Spencers' Bookstore, seeing a good thing for business, published a pamphlet containing an account of Harriet's disappearance.[6]

Elected officials in Ithaca were determined to plumb the depths of the mystery. On November 17, the Board of Supervisors of Tompkins County voted to provide a reward of four hundred dollars.

> $300 for the discovery of the bodies of the wife and child of Edward H. Ruloff, or of the body of the wife alone—and a further reward of $100 for the discovery of the luggage of said Edward H. Ruloff, consisting of two chests which he took with him when he left Ithaca in June last past, and which have been traced as far as Rochester.

The chests, the supervisors thought, contained Harriet's clothing and other material evidence. Relying on the most recent of Rulloff's tales, they declared: "For six weeks between 25th June and 24th August Ruloff was absent, supposed to have been at work on a farm in Ohio or Michigan." The sheriff of Tompkins County was authorized to publicize the reward. Rulloff, the notice said, "was very quick in his movements, and quick tempered."[7]

In late November, Rulloff was brought to court and bound over for trial. In January 1846, he was tried before Judge Hiram Gray of Elmira. By this time, people were sure that Harriet and Priscilla were dead, and so a substantial, though unsuccessful, effort was made to drag Lake Cayuga in search of the bodies. The district attorney instructed the grand jury to indict Rulloff for the lesser crime of abduction.

Stephen B. Cushing led as Rulloff's defense counsel, but then, as later, Rulloff took charge of the strategy, trying to escape prison by a series of legal quibbles. He did not testify, hoping that the lack of evidence would keep the jury in reasonable doubt, but he often asked pointless questions of the witnesses.

In his instructions, Judge Gray told the jury that if they believed that Rulloff was responsible for Harriet's death, they should acquit him of abduction so he could be charged with murder.

Most of the jurors were convinced that Rulloff had murdered Harriet. After the trial, one of them told the judge that he was sure of it.

> "How, then" inquired the Judge, "could you find him conscientiously guilty of abduction?"
>
> "Well," replied the Juror, "we did not know as we should ever get a chance at him again, and we were bound to convict him of something."[8]

Rulloff was found guilty and sentenced to ten years in Auburn Prison. Sheriff Porter delivered him to the imposing prison, a building designed to resemble a medieval English castle, whose grim exterior would inspire fear in those who passed by it and terror in those who were confined in it.

In the "Auburn system" inmates were given ill-fitting and deliberately ugly striped coats and trousers, often ones already having been worn by freed convicts and infested with whatever lice, ticks, or skin diseases had thrived on the body of the previous owner. Routines were rigid and regular. All cells had the same equipment; the prisoners ate the same food; and they walked to and from their cells in the same order in an unvarying routine. In this system, individuality was thoroughly crushed, and in the early days inmates were not allowed to speak to each other or even to raise their eyes from the floor.[9]

Prison workshops were encouraged, however, since any money that could be earned reduced the burden on the taxpayer. Under the best of circumstances—seldom or never achieved—prisons could be self-sustaining through profits from inmate's labor. To keep costs down, food was poor and scarce, and even blankets could be rationed to keep prisoners in a constant state of deprivation. Reforms in 1847 mandated by the legislature did allow inmates to have visitors, correspondence with the outside world, and books. Taking advantage of this new opportunity was a seminarian from Auburn who had graduated with high honors in the class of 1849 at Amherst College: Julius Hawley Seelye. They began a correspondence that would end only with Rulloff's life.

One of Rulloff's favorite poems was Byron's "On the Castle of Chillon."[10] The theme of the sonnet is "Liberty," but its opening lines had a more particular meaning for Rulloff: "Eternal Spirit of the chainless Mind! / Brightest in dungeons, Liberty! thou art, / For there thy habitation is the heart." However highly colored Rulloff's literary taste, it is no surprise that on entering the brutal regime of Auburn Prison he suffered in his first few weeks from what the prison doctors called "acclimating fever."

Labor in the shops was a central part of prison life, and daily work details gave at least some variety to the monotony of incarceration. Sundays were, in fact, dreaded because there was no work done in the shops, and, except for the briefest church services, prisoners were shut in their cells from midmorning to the following day.

At Auburn the shops were arranged against the perimeter of the prison with an observation corridor between the wall and the shop to allow guards to oversee goings-on. Work by prisoners was rewarded with token payments, and outside contractors operated the shops in the expectation of making substantial profits.

Rulloff first worked in the cutlery shop, where he became proficient in the use of an emery wheel to sharpen and polish metal. That shop was closed 1848, and he was employed in a carpet-making enterprise organized by a contractor named Josiah Barber. To keep his products at the height of fashion, Barber employed a French designer outside the prison and, as designer on the spot, Rulloff became his assistant. According to his biographers, he soon surpassed the designer in imagination and excellence[11] and

> made . . . carpets with a wonderful prodigality of invention and more beautiful than had ever before been produced in the United States. Twenty years after[,] this accomplishment was to be a solace in moments of unutterable agony; but in Auburn Prison it was no less a delight to him than it was a source of profit to the State.[12]

(This effusion was penned, very atypically, by Ed Crapsey.)

With extra work, prisoners could accumulate cash. As a designer, Rulloff profited from extra payments, since he could do his design work during the evenings and on Sunday while locked in his cell. He also drew money from his brother, Rulof Rulofson, who had now moved to Pennsylvania, and with these funds he was able to buy books, some of which, it was later said, were even imported from abroad for his use.[13]

Having found something to praise in Rulloff's life, Ed Crapsey soon showed that the darker side of Rulloff's character was never far distant during his decade of imprisonment.

> His demeanor during his ten years of service was in keeping with his contradictory character. Generally he was docilely submissive to rules of prison discipline, and gained the favor of the keepers by his readiness to assume any task and his zeal in performing. . . . But, notwithstanding all his advantages, the malevolence of his nature would sometimes flame up almost to the point of a flagrant violation of prison rules. Generally these displays were provoked by some trivial act or deed of a fellow convict, for it has always

been the fate of this monstrosity to set loose his consuming passion without sufficient cause. But while he was at Auburn he
seems to have kept better control of himself than ever before or
since, and he was there known only as a man subject to sudden
bursts of passion, but placable, if not equable, in his disposition.
. . . His powers of fascination had been exerted to good purpose,
and there were among the officials some who believed him to be a
man outraged by the vindictiveness of the Schutts.[14]

Rulloff's own account of his time in prison was made to the commissioners asked to investigate his sanity the week before his execution in
1871. One of the interviewers on that occasion, Dr. John Perdue Gray,
had a firmly held conviction about the sources of insanity: "The exciting
causes of insanity, as far as we are able to determine, are physical; that
is, no moral or intellectual operations of the mind induce insanity apart
from a physical lesion."[15] Such a "lesion" might arise under various circumstances, Dr. Gray claimed, among them "irregular or excessive use"
of the brain. There was much in Rulloff's behavior to support the idea
that he had been using his brain "excessively," and there was also the
chance that at some earlier period in his life he had acquired a "lesion"
that would account for his behavior.[16]

While Rulloff awaited the end of his sentence in 1856—there was no
such thing as time off for good behavior in that era—he had not been
forgotten in Tompkins County. The Schutts' enmity had hardened into
hatred and a desire to see Rulloff hanged by legal means or otherwise.

Just two years after Rulloff had been imprisoned, District Attorney
Marcus Lyon obtained an indictment in Tompkins County accusing
Rulloff of having murdered Harriet, and it was filed away until his sen-
tence expired.

On January 25, 1856, a cold, cheerless winter day, Rulloff was called
to the warden's office at Auburn. He expected to be released from the
prison: his sentence had been completed; he had paid his "debt." To his
astonishment, a stranger entered the office and declared himself to be
Smith Robertson, sheriff of Tompkins County. He had with him a warrant, based on the 1848 indictment, for Rulloff's arrest on the charge of
having murdered his wife. To the amazement of those present, Rulloff
expressed no feelings but merely extended his arms so he could be put
in handcuffs for the journey to Ithaca.[17]

The first question to be settled was whether or not Rulloff could be charged with his wife's murder after having been convicted of abducting her. In April 1856 this issue was argued before Judge Ransom Balcom, sitting as a judge of the Court of Appeals. Rulloff himself had composed a writ of habeas corpus declaring that he should be released from custody on the grounds that he could not be tried a second time. The district attorney, John A. Williams, opposed the motion; Rulloff appeared on his own behalf. Judge Balcom ruled that the matter should be settled at a trial on the indictment. Having heard Rulloff's arguments, however, Williams dropped the charges.

Public outrage and a desire for revenge could not be satisfied by letting Rulloff go free, and so district attorney drew up another indictment and presented it to a panel of three justices of the peace. This time the crime alleged was the murder of Rulloff's daughter.

This lengthy document described in detail multiple methods by which the murder could have been committed: it was alleged that Priscilla had been kicked to death, throttled with a silk handkerchief, poisoned with arsenic dissolved in milk, or bludgeoned with a weapon "to the jurors aforesaid unknown." Sad to say, the drafters of the indictment did not know the baby's name.

A motive was imputed: Edward H. Rulloff, laborer and late of the town of Lansing, did not have "the fear of God before his eyes" but was "moved and seduced by the institution of the Devil." "Laborer" must have been a particularly galling description of the learned Rulloff's occupation.[18]

Rulloff entered a plea of not guilty. On August 21, 1856, his counsel, Boardman and Finch of Ithaca, applied for a change of venue on the ground that an impartial jury could not be impaneled in Tompkins County. When jurors drawn from Tompkins County were asked their opinion of Rulloff's guilt, it became apparent that this was so. The request for a change of venue was granted.[19]

On October 28, Rulloff's trial began in Owego, the county seat of Tioga County just to the south of Tompkins. No one seems to have considered that anger at Rulloff's crime might be almost as intense in this adjacent county. With Judge Charles Mason presiding, again the question was raised as to whether a murder trial could be held when the accused had already been convicted of abduction. Like Judge Balcom, Judge Mason decided to put off his ruling on that motion until after the jury had considered the evidence.

The evidence was presented in great detail with lengthy testimony by the Schutts, the Robertsons, and all the neighbors with any knowledge of the events of June 23, 1845, and afterward. Somehow Richard Kellogg Swift and his wife were discovered in Chicago and brought to testify at Owego, bringing with them what items from Rulloff's chest still remained in their household eleven years after "James H. Revillee" had left them there in pawn for twenty-five or thirty dollars. All of Rulloff's conflicting stories about where Harriet and the baby had gone were placed in evidence, and so too were the tales of his erratic behavior and his unsuccessful attempt to evade Eph Schutt's pursuit.

In his instructions to the jury, Judge Mason addressed in particular the "sudden disappearance" of Harriet and baby Priscilla and the fact that they had not been seen or heard from in eleven years.

> [A]lthough this unaccountable disappearance and failure to ascertain any trace of them may lead to a strong suspicion that those parties have come to an untimely end, yet they are not alone sufficient proof of the death of this child and mother to justify a conviction because the fact may be accounted for on the hypothesis (however improbable) that they may have absconded and eluded all inquiry, or may be kidnapped and concealed and be still alive.[20]

Prosecuting in the case was Daniel S. Dickinson. Joshua A. Spencer, from Utica, acted on Rulloff's behalf. As Ham Freeman would later recall, "These eminent gentlemen were both then in their prime, and very giants of the law."[21] At the end of the prosecution's evidence, Spencer declined to put up a defense, alleging, as he had at the beginning of the trial, that there was no proof that a murder had taken place. The jury found Rulloff guilty.

In January 1857, a three-judge panel took up the question of whether or not the trial at Owego had been properly conducted, focusing particularly on the proof needed when no dead body could be found. Joshua Spencer spoke eloquently on Rulloff's behalf, citing the celebrated dictum of a British judge that "no person should be convicted of murder or manslaughter unless the fact were proved to be done, or at least the body be found dead." Spencer cited many American cases in which that principle had been applied, concluding that "modern writers have in no respect called in question the safe old rule of Lord Hale." The verdict should, therefore, be set aside.[22]

Dickinson argued that circumstantial evidence made it plain that Rulloff had murdered his daughter and said that Lord Hale's dictum was "merely advisory." Many other cases, he explained, showed that "direct evidence is more unsatisfactory than a chain of strong consistent circumstances."[23]

The judges deferred their decision until the coming May term, though Joshua Spencer must have been convinced that the outcome would not favor the position he had argued as Rulloff's advocate. Rulloff was returned to jail in Ithaca.

When the opinion was finally delivered, Judges Mason and Gray sided with Dickinson and declared that the verdict would be allowed to stand. Judge Balcom, however, agreed with Spencer's analysis:

> Persons accused of murder must be proved to be guilty, by certain and reliable evidence, before they can be lawfully convicted. The case does not do this when there is the least uncertainty as to whether the person alleged to be murdered is dead. It is infinitely better for society that guilty persons should sometimes escape deserved punishment than for courts to establish a precedent that may be used to deprive innocent persons of life.[24]

During the long wait for this decision, Rulloff was constrained in the Ithaca jail not only by the locks and iron bars but also by a shackle around his ankle attached by a chain to a ring in the floor. Yet he was not idle. Some local citizens saw no objection to having their sons, and even a few of their daughters, attend school with Rulloff as the teacher. Among those who saw an opportunity for education at no cost was the undersheriff in charge of the jail, Jacob S. Jarvis, a cabinetmaker who had turned to law enforcement. In 1857, he was forty-six years old, and he and his wife Jane Curtis Jarvis, age forty-two, lived with their family in the house that formed part of the jail. Their children were Francis (age six), Helen (age eight), and Albert (age sixteen).[25] Albert became Rulloff's pupil, and the whole family came to occupy a prominent place in his story.

Rulloff recalled the details for Ham Freeman.

> My acquaintance with Albert Jarvis began in 1856, when I was confined in the jail at Ithaca, charged with the murder. His father was the Under-Sheriff of the County, and kept the jail. [Albert]

was a bright, active boy, about sixteen years of age. He was as generous a fellow as ever lived, but was impulsive and rash. My attention was attracted to him first by a present of some fruit he made me. We soon came to be on very good terms, and I used frequently to employ him to do little errands for me in the village, such as to procure paper, pens, books, candles, etc. The attachment which he began to have for me attracted the attention of his parents, who did not object to our intimacy.

I began soon to give him instruction in the languages—German and Latin. I found him an apt pupil. He made fair progress in his studies. At the time of his death he was a fair linguist.

The mother of Jarvis encouraged him, and sometimes came with him to my cell. Mrs. Jarvis was a very amiable woman, and I became indebted to her for many considerate acts of kindness. Jarvis' father and mother did not live happy. The father was a brute. I could hear him curse her in the night, and threaten to shoot her. He would often, I was told, go to bed with pistols under his pillow, and would brandish them about her head to frighten her. She had no love for him—how could she have? He became jealous of me, and would sometimes come in front of my cell door and abuse me by the hour, calling me everything he could think of. This was not very pleasant for a poor devil locked up as I was. If I could have got to him on one of these times I would have fixed him, he was so abusive. He was naturally of a very jealous disposition, and he treated his wife cruelly. He sometimes beat her and threatened her life.[26]

Eph Schutt warned Jacob Jarvis that Rulloff was not to be trusted, but Jarvis seems to have been dazzled by the accomplishments his son was acquiring under Rulloff's teaching—not only German and Latin but French and stenography as well.[27] The son of a physician, Jacob Jarvis admired book learning, and his mother Margaret had been a Schermerhorn, a family prominent in the state since the days of New Amsterdam. Though Jacob had not done so well in life, Al might restore the family's fortunes.

Al Jarvis did not, however, use his education to gain a respectable career in commerce, and his father was himself ruined as a consequence of Rulloff's treachery. Ed Crapsey felt genuinely sorry for the family; Jacob Jarvis, he would later write, "was a man of excellent repute and blessed with the most happy domestic ties."[28]

While Rulloff was in the Ithaca jail, Jacob Jarvis found himself in financial trouble. Leander Millspaugh had sued him for an unpaid debt, and the matter was in court. Philip Stephens was seeking a judgment against him too. It was humiliating for the undersheriff to appear as a litigant, even in a civil suit. But that was not all. Jacob Jarvis's "happy domestic ties" would soon end in bitterness and rancor. He was about to be disgraced and ruined at the same time.[29]

As Rulloff waited in the Ithaca jail, he once again took the law into his hands.

On May 5, 1857, he escaped.

4
• • • • • • •

That Cursed Word *Moral*

STOP THE MURDERER!!
$500 REWARD!
Escaped from the Jail in this village on the night of the 5th inst.
EDWARD H. RULLOFF

He has been convicted of Murder, and was awaiting his sentence. Said Rulloff had on when he left a pair of brown pantaloons, no coat or vest as known. He was about 5 feet 10 inches high, heavy shouldered, large head, thick neck, blue eyes, light hair, weighs about 180 pounds, when walking stoops a little forward. He will undoubtedly be disguised. He has served 10 years in Auburn State Prison.

Whoever will return said Prisoner to jail in this village will receive the above reward.

    R. J. Ives
    Sheriff of Tompkins Co.
    Ithaca, May 6, 1857[1]

Official news of Rulloff's escape came in this handbill from Sheriff Ives. Then the *Tompkins County Democrat* published a story May 8, followed on May 13 by a longer one in the *Ithaca Journal*. The details were breathtaking.

One reason that Rulloff had escaped, it was said, was his fear that a lynch mob might remove him from the jail and summarize justice. The editor of the *Journal,* John H. Selkreg, dismissed that possibility;

Rulloff's anxiety, he declared, was "entirely unfounded of course, because however indignant our citizens might be, they have too much regard for 'law and order' to be participant in such an affair."

Seven locks had separated Rulloff from freedom, and it seemed increasingly likely that he had had the help of insiders. The daunting locks were not quite what they had appeared to be.

> To show how often appearance passes for that which it is not, we may mention that three of the jail locks, each nearly the size of a dining plate, were unlocked by a machinist of our village, in the space of less than a minute, on Monday last, without the aid of anything except a crooked wire![2]

Ithaca's third newspaper, the *American Citizen* (the organ of the American, or Know-Nothing, Party), published a report that an "unknown person" had some weeks earlier appeared at the Ithaca jail and supplied Rulloff with a very substantial sum of money—seven hundred dollars. The paper also reported that James Quigley of Auburn had been arrested "on suspicion of having something to do with Rulloff's escape."[3]

Quigley had formerly lived in Ithaca and had worked for some years as a guard at Auburn Prison. Jacob Jarvis had needed a reliable assistant, and, the week before the escape, he invited Quigley to look over the jail. During the visit Quigley spoke a few words with Rulloff. With no better clues to follow, Sheriff Ives took the boat to Auburn, arrested Quigley, and brought him back to the Ithaca jail. On May 12 and 13, just a week after the escape, Quigley was brought before Judge Samuel P. Wisner and Police Justice C. B. Drake. The district attorney, Marcus Lyon, assisted by George D. Beers, led the examination. (All of these legal worthies would later be involved with Rulloff's career.)

While the proceeding brought many fascinating details to light, it seems to have been conducted in an atmosphere of hysteria. Witnesses arriving on Tuesday were immediately locked in the courthouse basement until called to testify; those held over to Wednesday were allowed to go home in the evening but locked up the next morning. One by one they were brought before the judges.[4]

Milton Ostrander—from whom Rulloff a dozen years earlier had rented a horse and wagon to transport the box in which he hid his wife's corpse; Ostrander was now a police officer—gave a straightforward account. Albert Jarvis had come to him in the early evening to say that his father had gone off to Ovid and needed Ostrander to lock up (as he was in the habit of doing when Jarvis was away). About nine o'clock, he and Al Jarvis had moved Rulloff from the day cell and locked the padlock holding the leg shackle to the ring in the floor. A little later Ostrander walked to the station house, where he found George Burritt, who wanted to see the "cooler."

George Burritt was certainly a suspicious character. Just a few weeks earlier he had been a prisoner himself, sharing a cell with Alfred Warner. Pardoned the week before Rulloff's escape, Burritt remained at the jail to assist Jacob Jarvis and slept in the family quarters. Having a former prisoner given free run of the jail was not, in the opinion of most people, an excellent idea, but Jarvis needed help. He was also attempting to farm about three miles south of town and went regularly back and forth between the farm and the jail.

It was not quite clear why, on the night of the escape, Burritt wanted to visit the jail. But Ostrander let him have a look, and then he began to patrol Main Street and the center of town. He saw nothing out of the ordinary, only a "top" carriage driven at moderate speed down Cayuga Street just before midnight. About six the following morning, Burritt came to Ostrander saying that Jarvis wanted him at the jail at once: "Rulloff was out." When Ostrander arrived, he saw all the doors open, the lock to the shackles broken, and the leg band cast aside.

None of the testimony implicated James Quigley, though it emerged that Quigley had regularly corresponded with Rulloff and was attempting to collect sums of money owed to Rulloff by various prisoners at Auburn.

Caroline Jarvis, Jacob's niece, described the routines of the jail. Usually she slept in a large downstairs bedroom, but, the night of the escape, only Al shared that room with her little sister Flora. She got Flora settled, and, when she went upstairs, Helen, Al's eight-year-old sister, was already asleep. Not long thereafter Burritt came to bed, and Al came upstairs to get something from his usual bedroom. Before midnight Caroline awoke from a sound sleep and heard "a light pounding" from the jail. She testified that the "pounding sounded as if on iron," and she thought it came from Rulloff's cell. Between midnight and one o'clock, she heard her Uncle Jacob come home and go to bed.

When I got up in the morning Albert came and bro't Flora to my room, left her in hall, I got up, put her in bed and dressed and went down stairs. Albert said nothing up stairs about Rulloff's escape, found Jacob and Albert in sitting room, Jacob in rocking chair, Albert standing by shelf. Jacob said that Ruloff had got out and went and showed me how said locks were unlocked; Albert said nothing.

Then Caroline made public the astonishing information that Albert had spent quite a lot of time with Rulloff studying French and getting help with the hard words. Rulloff had also undertaken to write a life of Jacob Jarvis. The biography seemed, in fact, to be a project designed merely to inflate Deputy Jarvis's already inflated sense of self-importance.

Two men who were prisoners in the jail were called to testify. Though Caroline Jarvis had heard only a light pounding, Lewis Hammond, occupying the cell above Rulloff's, heard a great deal more.

Didn't hear any one speak night of Rulloff's escape, heard considerable noise in Rulloff's part of jail, in his cell; heard something go off like a pistol, kind of a crack, after Jarvis came home; heard a noise of a cane on a door; heard Rulloff cough in cell after Jarvis came home, heard nothing after this; noise sounded below; I was over Rulloff. Heard on Tuesday Rulloff's door open several times, and some one went there and whispered, at different times during day; took the voice to be Albert Jarvis'; Burritt went there but he talked out loud. Warner said he was to be locked up for listening to Al Jarvis.

Locking the prisoners in their night cells seems to have been a matter of judgment by the keepers, even by the teenage Al Jarvis.

Jacob Jarvis testified about the errand that had taken him away from Ithaca on the evening of the escape. Just before three o'clock, a man had come to the jail with an urgent letter reporting that a notorious counterfeiter was in the county. Al had taken the letter out to the farm at about four. There was six dollars enclosed, he said, and it promised an additional reward if the counterfeiter were captured. Jacob walked to town, picked up a horse and wagon from Babcock's livery stable, and headed south. Then he remembered that he had left his handcuffs at the jail and went back to collect them. As dusk began to gather, he found himself in Halseyville, and snow on the road made it almost impassable. Estimating that he could not reach Ovid before midnight, Jacob returned to Ithaca and went to the hotel for something to eat. He didn't get his dinner but spent an hour there. (He didn't say so, but he almost certainly had a drink to ward off the cold.) After midnight, he got to the jail. Al got up and let him in. Jacob did not check on his prisoners.

None of these reports filled citizens with a sense that Jarvis was a capable deputy.

The testimony of Catherine Maloney, a former jail employee, made things at the jail seem even worse than had already been revealed. She admitted that just the night before, Jane Jarvis had asked her to come to the jail to talk over what she would say. Though there was no love lost between the two women, Jane Jarvis hoped for testimony that would conceal some of the goings-on.

> Jarvis and son had care of Rulloff when I was at jail, sometimes I took meals to him; Rulloff was treated better than all the other prisoners; he had good victuals. Albert was with Rulloff most every day alone; . . . always heard Albert and Mrs. Jarvis say Rulloff was a nice man. Rulloff had same provisions family had; other prisoners had different food; little girl [Helen] used some-times to be left alone with Rulloff in cell; sometimes Albert and sometimes Mrs. Jarvis let her in; Mrs. Jarvis unlocked door; some-times Albert in cell with Rulloff till 10 or 11 o'clock at night; he was studying something with Rulloff, and A. locked him up when he got through with his studies; Mrs. J. locked up cell one night with Burritt when Albert and Jarvis were gone.

When Jane Jarvis's turn came to testify, she had plenty to answer for. She had been at the farm for some weeks, she said, and thus had an alibi for the night of the escape. The hired man said he had been to town with a load of wood that day, but when he got back in the early evening Jane Jarvis was there and, after tea, went to bed as usual at ten o'clock.

> Heard results of Rulloff's trial in Mass.; have seen no strangers around where I live; have no particular opinion as to Rulloff's guilt or innocence; I said I did not think he murdered his family, can't tell why I thought so; did not derive that opinion from what Rulloff said; R. gave Albert his books. I gave Rulloff a ring; neither directly or indirectly did Rulloff give me anything. Mr. Warner's

girls danced in Rulloff's cell; I did not dance, stood on the floor; don't know that Rulloff understood dancing; he did not stand on the floor to help form a figure; think they were there but twice; Jarvis not there; think bar in door, but cannot say door was locked; can't lock door from inside. Rulloff was not chained or shackled, can't say when girls left; don't know whether boys went home with them in evening; dance did not commence till after dark; can't tell how long it lasted; Alf. Warner musician; can't say who closed door when company went away.

I was in hall after they went away; Sarah Babcock was there; we were reading a bird book. George Burritt locked up that night under my superintendence; he was not locked up that night. I have received no communications from Rulloff since I left or sent any. Saw man who brought Rulloff money; never asked Rulloff who he was; heard Rulloff say who he was; heard Rulloff say he had a brother.

Dancing at the jail? Private moments between Jane Jarvis and Rulloff when her son and husband were away? Carelessness about locking cell doors?

Only Rulloff's recollections in 1871 survive to suggest that the Jarvis's marriage was something short of blissful, and the notion that Jacob threatened his wife with pistols has no corroboration beyond his claims. Rulloff had great magnetism, as Ed Crapsey was fond of pointing out, and he had endeared himself to Jacob by promising to write his life. His affection for Jane may have had a more selfish foundation, but it is undeniable that they found each other "amiable" (to use Rulloff's word). Ham Freeman would find something mitigating in almost all of Rulloff's crimes, but in the case of Jane Jarvis he could do little more than lament: "the wife of the jailor was corrupted by him, and forgot those vows and promises that should be as sacred to the humble and lonely as to the refined and better taught classes."[5]

Jane herself could not (or would not) tell why she believed that Rulloff had not murdered Harriet, but she seems to have believed that so nice a man could not possibly have committed so horrible a deed. She was flattered by his attentions, and for a vigorous man, starved for the company of a woman, to find her attractive was very pleasant. Powerless against her husband's violent temper, she was supremely powerful in her relationship with Rulloff. He could not come near her unless she released him from his cell; when locked in at night, he could not reach beyond the radius of the chain shackling him to the floor. She could be teasing and playful; she could arouse him to a pitch of high excitement; she could grant her favors or withhold them. Just as Rulloff liked to think of himself as very powerful—like Faust or Manfred, for instance—so too could Jane think of herself as a sylph entirely in control of the muscular and intellectual prisoner.[6]

Hardly could her testimony have been more shocking.

Al Jarvis's direct testimony had explained that the letter calling his father out of town had been given to him by

a stranger, a tall well proportioned man, with black dress coat, black round top fur hat, 35 or 40 years old; sunburnt, light complexion, no overcoat; did not notice vest, don't think; black pants, no whiskers except little before ear, middling well dressed; hair dark brown.

Out for a stroll, he had met the man outside the jail. Marcus Lyon, the prosecutor, peppered him with questions. Yes, Rulloff had been writing his father's life—he had commenced two or three months earlier and stopped about four to six weeks before the escape. Yes, Rulloff had "considerable money." No, he did not know that the locks could be opened with a wire. Yes, he had gone directly to fetch Sheriff Ives, as instructed by his father, when Rulloff's escape was discovered.

Now, after his mother had testified, Al Jarvis was brought back so the questioners might probe inconsistencies in his story. He confessed that he had walked with the stranger up to the burying ground and had talked to him for half or three-quarters of an hour. This he was forced to admit because someone had seen the two talking and kept track of the time. What had they talked about? "He inquired about Rulloff, how long R. had been in, and how he was confined, if he was in chains, asked how the chains were put on; I told him." He now added that the man had asked to see Rulloff but that the prisoner had declined.

Rulloff had also sent letters, Al Jarvis testified, though he didn't know to whom they were addressed. All letters were supposed to go through the sheriff, but Alfred Warner sometimes carried letters to the post office for Rulloff. Even Timothy Maloney, editor of the *Democrat*, got into the witness box. He had received letters from Rulloff, some through the post office and some through a little girl nine or ten years old—not Helen Jarvis but a girl he didn't know. He looked over the letter the mysterious man had given to Al Jarvis for delivery to his father; "the formation of capital letters," Maloney said, made him think that it was in Rulloff's hand.

At the end of the testimony on Wednesday, there was no evidence to keep James Quigley in jail. Both the prosecutors and the public were convinced that he had had nothing to do with Rulloff's escape. But Ithaca was alive with speculation about far more interesting matters.

Sheriff Ives now acted. Regretting that he had not done so earlier, he fired Undersheriff Jacob S. Jarvis and put a more reliable deputy in charge of the jail, Edward Tilton. The following week, the *Ithaca Journal* reported that Jarvis was indignant at the accusations against him and his family. "Mr. J. S. Jarvis, lately under-sheriff, has, we learn, commenced suits for libel against the editors of the Owego Gazette, Elmira Gazette, Elmira Advertiser, Albany Statesman and New York Daily News."[7] He was disturbed by stories such as this one in the *New York Evening Post*.

> The circumstances attending the escape of Dr. Edward H. Ruloff from the Ithaca jail inevitably establish the fact that he was aided in his escape by outsider friends, who effected their object through the bribery of the jailer. There were nine locks between the outside door and the cell where Ruloff was confined. The prisoner was securely ironed and chained to the floor. These locks were unlocked—the irons upon the person of the convict cut, and he was evidently carried off by his friends. These circumstances alone would sufficiently indicate the complicity of the jailor in the escape.[8]

Rumors from afar gave speculative news about Rulloff. At Owego, a man and a woman had spent Monday night at the Ah-wa-ga House. On Tuesday they went out but returned to the hotel to take their meals in their room. On Wednesday, the day after Rulloff's escape, they departed by train.

> It is moreover believed that the woman who returned to the Ah-wa-ga, after the temporary absence in the morning, was not the woman who slept there the night previous, but the murderer RULLOFF in disguise.[9]

The *Tompkins County Democrat* would have none of that story.

> We consider all this nonsense, as we are certain all the women's clothing in the world could not disguise Rulloff so as to make him pass as a woman, to any man outside of the Utica Insane Asylum.[10]

With little real news to enrich conversations, rancor and vituperation increased in Ithaca to a high pitch. The *Journal*, the Republican paper in Ithaca, reminded readers that Sheriff Ives and his cronies were members of the American Party.[11] *The American Citizen* responded that prosecutors Lyon and Beers were both Republicans and had discharged James Quigley on their own motion; the Republicans were most likely outraged, stated the *Citizen*, because they wanted to run Rulloff for "some *high office*" (the double entendre encompassing both electoral politics and lynch law).[12] The Copperhead *Democrat* sneered at the Republican *Journal* as "the negro organ of this place" and hinted that John Selkreg, its editor, was a traitor obscurely in cahoots with Rulloff.[13] With equal indifference to the facts, the *Journal* suspected the editor of the *Citizen* of having felt "joy" at Rulloff's escape.[14] The *Journal* commenced a four-part series on Rulloff's trial in Owego and then offered the series in a pamphlet edition "on superfine letter paper" for fifty cents a copy.

A promising rumor reached Ithaca from Corning. Deputy Sheriff John S. Knapp heard that a suspicious team had been left at the livery stable of Pier's Hotel on the morning of May 6 by a man calling himself Isaac Allen. Later a James Henry arrived with a bill of sale from Allen and attempted to collect his property. Knapp arrested Henry and informed Sheriff Ives.

Richard Ives had been humiliated by Rulloff's escape and by the mismanagement at the jail. An anonymous critic, in a letter to the *Democrat*, had questioned "the fitness of the men [holding] the important offices of Sheriff and Under Sheriff of the county of Tompkins" and wondered why the taxpayers should allow incompetents to "draw their 'weasel-skins' so often."[15] Other armchair officers complained that none of the obvious methods of pursuit had been employed.

Sheriff Ives could only increase the size of the reward and hope for good news. By the middle of June, $1,250 had been promised, including $500 added through a proclamation by Governor John A. King.[16]

A poster gave details of Rulloff's appearance, the team and buggy, and details about the man who attempted to collect them. But by the time this poster was issued, the trail was cold. Sheriff Ives had an excellent matched team, costly harness, and a fine buggy in hand—but no Rulloff.

Once a description of Rulloff and the team of horses and buggy seen near the jail began to circulate, clues fell into place.[17] The top buggy Milton Ostrander had seen driving at a moderate pace through Ithaca on the night of the escape was declared to be the means of escape; he now recalled the muddy rubber coat mentioned in the inventory of confiscated equipage. Henry Halsey and George Blood had seen the team. At Corner-of-the-Lake, a settlement just to the south, the rig had been stabled at the "public house" during Tuesday and driven away toward Ithaca in the early evening. Someone remembered having seen the horses tied to a railing opposite the park from nine to ten o'clock on the night of the escape. But on the crucial evening, no one had thought any of these details important.

James Henry was haled before Police Justice C. B. Drake on May 27. He said that sixteen or eighteen days before the team fetched up in Corning, he had met Isaac Allen at Cuba, New York. He had examined the horses then, and on May 11 he met Allen again, bought them, and received a bill of sale. When he tried to collect his property from Pier's Hotel, the landlord refused to release the horses and declared that they were stolen. Not long after, Deputy Knapp arrived in Corning and, accompanied by Sheriff Ives, arrested Henry, searched his person, took his money, breast pin, and pocketbook, and brought him (and the team) back to Ithaca. Henry's defense counsel, John S. Williams, drew attention to the fact that Henry had persisted in claiming ownership and had not taken the ample opportunity to escape. After the summation, Justice Drake discharged Henry on the charge of helping Rulloff escape, but he did not settle the question of who owned the team.

The *Democrat* suggested that, lacking a person to indict, the sheriff might well charge the horses with the crime of "carrying Rulloff off." Should that happen, it would be a shame to let "two such fine horses run the risk of being sent to State Prison for want of a little of the 'needful.'" Perhaps citizens would like to contribute to a defense fund for the team.[18] The *Journal* demeaned "the withering sneer and overpowering witticism of the *Democrat* about indicting the horses." Sheriff Ives and District Attorney Lyon, the *Journal* confidently predicted, would have Rulloff's accomplices in prison "before the summer is out."[19]

Since there was not much else he could do, Sheriff Ives let the public know that new locks were being considered for the jail, and details were provided to testify to their excellence should Rulloff or someone else attempt to repeat the escape: "the best kind of Swiss wrought iron," "heavy cast iron," screws "worked down even with the surface of the plate," and other marvels. There was muttering about stable doors and stolen horses, and the new locks were considered by the Tompkins County supervisors in June. In July, the taxpayers recovered the value of the escape vehicle. Frederick Goodwin of Lansing bought the team for $221.00; John Wilcox bought the buggy for $35.00; and Atwater's bought the harness and other gear for $18.50. James Henry got nothing.[20]

The first week in June, the grand jury in Tompkins County indicted Albert Jarvis for aiding in Rulloff's escape. He was granted bail on a bond of one thousand dollars.[21]

Back in Ithaca, the energetic Schutt brothers must have considered various ways of pursing Rulloff, but there was no trace of him to be found beyond the cold trail to Corning and the abandoned buggy, team, and that muddy rubber coat.

This time Rulloff put more distance between himself and his pursuers. Before he decided to provide Ham Freeman with more circumstantial details, he characterized his time as a fugitive as if he were an Ishmael wandering in the wilderness.

> I lived by foraging upon the farmers, and upon beech nuts. I lived like a beast, and I fear that I became almost one. I was cornered once in a cow shed—eight men surrounded me. Some fired upon me. I escaped and left that part of the country. Winter came on and I was at one time for forty-eight hours without a mouthful of food to eat. A large reward had been set upon my capture. I was in constant danger of re-arrest or death by starvation and exposure. I kept to the woods. My feet were so badly frozen that I lost two of my toes, but even in that condition I was obliged to make excursions in the night, for food, to the farm houses. Finally I made the acquaintance of some good friends. I wandered to a village not a great ways from Towanda. I got some money and some good clothing.[22]

Like most of the agony he described, Rulloff's account of his escape was highly exaggerated. With more than seven hundred dollars to fund his escape, he would have had no difficulty in locating persons willing to assist him. (Jacob Jarvis had told the tribunal in Ithaca that he had heard that James Quigley was offered "a considerable sum" to help him escape as early as the time in January 1856 when Jarvis and Sheriff Ives were bringing him from Auburn Prison to Ithaca.) But Rulloff could count on more than mere hired help, and the elusive Isaac Allen was the key to his escape. Sheriff Ives would have been delighted to know the full name of the brother who consistently used the name R. Rulofson: Rulof *Isaac Allen* Rulofson. And he would have been happy to know the name of their half brother too: *James Henry* Henniger.

Sheriff Ives would have been glad to know of a minor little proceeding in the county seat of Clarion County, Pennsylvania, just a few weeks earlier. Having been in the United States for sixteen years without seeking citizenship, Rulof Isaac Allen Rulofson had decided that it was a good time to renounce his "allegiance to Victoria, Queen of Great Britain," becoming a citizen on March 4, 1857.[23]

Driven through snow and mud by his beloved brother, Rulloff fetched up in Ridgeway in Elk County, but it was not safe there. After a few days, they went to Rulofson's mill at Beech Bottom in Spring Creek Township, where Rulloff worked as a mill hand. But that too was unsafe. Penetrating the deep forest, they built a hideout at Blue Rock on Little Toby Creek, a narrows where steep hills rise nearly seven hundred feet on both sides of the water. Rulloff, however, would not stay put. Before long a wanted poster was on display in the general store in Beech Bottom. According to a later recollection, Rulloff's "personality and intelligence were such that everyone was wondering why he was laboring in a sawmill."[24] A doctor, in particular, asked R. Rulofson if it did not seem to him that the intellectual mill worker seemed to match the description in the poster. It was time for Rulloff to leave Blue Rock and go elsewhere.[25]

So Rulloff went west to Meadville and introduced himself to A. B. Richmond.

Having worked hard to build the model of Richmond's invention, Rulloff said it might be easy to raise the cash to become the co-owner of the patent. A. B. later recalled,

> A few days after this, he informed me that it would be difficult for him to get money, and wished to know if I would take four or five gold watches as payment in the place of money, stating that he

could get them easily. By that time I had become so much attached to the man that I would have let him have the invention upon any terms. I said I would. He stated that he would go and see his brother.

Rulloff postponed his departure so he might attend a murder trial in which A. B. was defense counsel. He was particularly interested in A. B.'s opinion as to whether a murder conviction could be obtained in a case where the dead body could not be located.

A few days after he went away, as he said, to see his brother, taking with him some handbills, which he had got printed, advertising my invention and that of Mr. Stewart [another Meadville inventor]. He borrowed five dollars of his landlord, and on the night he left a boot and shoe store near his hotel was broken open and some boots and leather taken therefrom. In a day or two his landlord received five dollars from him by mail, from a little town in the country a few miles distant, and where we ascertained that a man answering to his description had sold some boots and leather.

A trail of robberies followed in Rulloff's wake, as he "raised" money.

A few days after, our postmaster received a letter from Warren County, Pa. [just east of Meadville], stating that a jewelry store had been broken open, and some watches taken, which were afterwards found concealed in a pile of lumber, with one of those handbills wrapped around them. This led to an inquiry of our postmaster as to whether two men resided in Meadville named, respectively, A. B. Richmond and George Stewart, and inquiring as to their character, etc.

Mr. Stewart, when informed by the postmaster of the circumstances, was very much annoyed, as he was a most exemplary member of one of our most prominent churches, and I annoyed him still more by informing him that there was pretty strong evidence against us that we had committed the burglary. Mr. Stewart recollected that Nelson had had his photograph taken in this place, and immediately had one printed and sent down to Warren county, whence we shortly after received information that James

Nelson was the celebrated Edward H. Rulloff, who, it was suspected, had murdered his wife and child in Ithaca, N.Y.[26]

A. B. Richmond was a humorist and had a good laugh at the very respectable George Stewart's expense. But something important had just taken place: a photograph provided a clue to Rulloff's crimes.

Not nearly so amused by the robbery, P. R. Bennett, the proprietor of the jewelry store, was happy to have the valuables back, and the Schutts and their friends in Ithaca were glad to know that Rulloff had been sighted at last.

A further consequence of the burglary was described by Ed Crapsey.

[Rulloff traveled] direct to Jamestown, N.Y., where he went into the drug store of Dr. G. W. Hazeltine, and wrote a prescription for a frozen foot which he had compounded. The remedy was for his own use, and the Warren burglary was far reaching in its retributive effects, as the destruction of the great toe on his left foot by the frost during its perpetration was the chief means of convicting him of the murder of Frederick A. Mirrick at Binghamton, N.Y., ten years and seven months later.[27]

Jamestown, in far western New York, was a poor choice of destination, for it put Rulloff back into the neighborhood of people connected with Ithaca. A hostler at the Allen House hotel, a former convict at Auburn Prison who recognized Rulloff, realized that he had a good chance at that $1,250 reward still pending for his capture. But Rulloff threatened the man with "a three-barreled pistol of his own invention,"[28] and extracted from the hostler a promise to keep his presence a secret. Nonetheless, at the earliest opportunity the hostler went to the office of the sheriff of Chautauqua County, where he found Deputy James Dennin and told him that he had seen Rulloff.

Deputy Dennin set out in pursuit, but Rulloff fled westward, and in March Dennin went to Cleveland, where he asked advice of yet another of the detectives for which the city, at least among Rulloff's pursuers, had become famous. "Old" Hayes, who had helped Eph Schutt capture Rulloff in 1845, was no longer active, but Marshal Gallagher then bore the reputation of "one of the sharpest detectives in the country." On Gallagher's advice, Dennin scoured the whole northern portion of the state, from Cleveland to Sandusky, to Tiffin and Toledo.

Near Sandusky, a farmer, Charles Curtis, overheard Dennin describing Rulloff's appearance and mentioning the circumstances of his crimes and the generous reward. Dennin even told of the three-barreled pistol that Rulloff had brandished back in Jamestown. Curtis told his wife the extraordinary story, and she said that a man of that description, claiming his name was Wilcox, was teaching writing at a school in the inn in a nearby village and boarding with the Smiths, their neighbors. Curtis, Smith, and another neighbor, McCoy, decided to act quickly before Dennin could return with an Ohio warrant for Rulloff's arrest.

The farmer procured the services of a young but courageous constable, and three neighbors, and went to arrest Rulloff, who, with the utmost sang froid, told him he was not the person they were in quest of, and if they arrested him it would be at their peril. They put him into a wagon and started with him to a railroad station and magistrate's office, and while on their journey Rulloff got out of the wagon a short distance away, and told the constable he did not propose to go any further with him, as he had no warrant or authority to arrest him.

His captors surrounded him, and picked up stones and threw at him when Rulloff fired at one of them, shooting off a part of his whiskers. The constable, being more plucky than prudent, started to grapple with him, when Rulloff fired a second time, the ball penetrating through the overcoat, coat, vest, and under clothing of the constable, and marking but not entering his person. Rulloff then told them, as he was crippled with sore feet, and had but one more charge in his pistol, and there were five of them, he would surrender and go along quietly. After getting into the wagon, he ridiculed the constable for being so pale and scared, and apparently was the least excited one of the party.

On their arrival at the magistrate's, the constable made a complaint against Rulloff for shooting at him, but fearing that Dennin would return with the Governor's requisition and take the prisoner from him, the constable informed Rulloff of Dennin's purpose, and persuaded him to go with him without a requisition to Ithaca. Rulloff consented, with the understanding that he was to be quietly and secretly delivered into the Sheriff's hands, as he was afraid of the enraged populace, who had previously tried to lynch him.[29]

So Rulloff returned to the Ithaca jail. The three Ohioans had certainly fulfilled the terms of the reward by bringing him back. Rather ungraciously, the *Ithaca Journal* reported that letters useful for identifying his accomplices in the escape had been in Rulloff's pocket but they had mysteriously vanished. The *Journal* said they should receive the reward "when they agree among themselves. They are now quarreling about it, and the Sheriff is not bound by law to pay over the money, until they settle the matter with each other."[30] In the following week's paper, Curtis wrote in some distress to protest against the suggestion that they had been careless or were motivated by something less than concern for the public good. The *Journal* declared that Curtis "seems to be a fair, manly and open spoken gentleman," but there was still some skullduggery suspected in their innocent narrative.[31]

While the authorities in Ithaca were slowly sorting out the dispute over the reward, they also were engaged in intense conversations about Rulloff. He should not escape hanging this time, they thought, but the difficulty was to discover how he might be brought to the gallows. The corpses of Harriet and the baby were nowhere to be found, it seemed, but then they hit on the idea of accusing Rulloff of murdering two people whose corpses they could find: Will Schutt's wife and infant daughter.

A murder in New York City offered a possible strategy. In that case, James Stephens was accused of having poisoned his wife, Sophia. Although buried for a year, her body was exhumed, tested exhaustively for arsenic (along with her grave clothes, the casket, and the surrounding soil). Stephens was found guilty of poisoning his wife and was executed.[32]

Dr. R. Ogden Doremus, who had analyzed Mrs. Stephens's body, was asked by Rulloff's former counsel, Joshua Spencer, and prosecutor, Marcus Lyon, to examine Amelia Schutt's remains. In a deposition sent to Ithaca he reported his results.

A quantitative analysis of a small portion of the spots before referred to, and found in said tissue, demonstrated that they were composed of *Carbonate of Copper.*[33]

He then tested the other samples that had been sent to him from Ithaca, and "no cupreous deposit" was detected. The bones and the wood did not show copper either, though a small trace was detected in the earth taken from the neighborhood of the grave.

Those who despised Rulloff had no compunctions about declaring him the murderer of Will Schutt's wife and daughter, and Crapsey's sensational biography expressed no doubts about Rulloff's diabolical character and dreadful crimes. Yet the copper deposits found in the tissue might well have had a more benign origin. Hooper's *Lexicon-Medicum*—the reference book Rulloff had carried from Ithaca to Chicago in 1845—recommended medications containing copper for various conditions.[34] "Cupri sulphas," for instance, "is esteemed as a tonic, emetic, astringent, and escharotic, and is exhibited internally in the cure of dropsies, hæmorrhages, and as a speedy emetic." "Cuprum ammoniatum" was viewed as a medication that would produce "tonic and astringent effects on the human body" and, taken internally, was good for epilepsy and "other obstinate spasmodic diseases." Not until a subsequent edition of Hooper's *Lexicon-Medicum* were doctors warned that metallic copper was a poison or told the intriguing, but untrue, information that the remedy for copper poisoning was a spoonful of sugar. Copper in some soluble form was definitely in the materials of medicine during the years when Rulloff was practicing.

Rulloff thus may have been treating the two patients according to established scientific practice, though Crapsey and others were unwilling to entertain that hypothesis once they had persuaded themselves of Rulloff's irredeemable evil. It was a sad but ambiguous episode, and, like so much else in Rulloff's story, the truth was elusive.

Back in the Ithaca jail, Rulloff resumed his correspondence with Julius Seelye, the seminarian who had visited him in Auburn Prison. Seelye had returned from philological study in Germany to take up the professorship of "mental and moral philosophy" at his old college, Amherst.[35] Writing to him in October 1858, Rulloff apologized for the two-year hiatus in their exchange of letters, declaring, with conscious irony, that in the meanwhile he had been "otherwise engaged." Rulloff's letters to Seelye from October to December 1858 show him arguing a fatalist position against Seelye's orthodoxy of revealed truth. From "the invisible animalcule to the leviathan of the deep, one order of creatures is constantly preying upon another, and can subsist only by doing so,"

Rulloff declared.[36] The letters are full of learning with citations to both classical and New Testament Greek authors; Rulloff shows here an interest in eighteenth-century Scottish philosophers that will emerge later in his theorizing about language.[37]

Having turned against Rulloff, Joshua Spencer refused to represent him in any further proceedings; then Spencer unexpectedly died. Samuel Halliday thought that Spencer's death was Rulloff's salvation, since the line of defense that Spencer had taken in the trial at Owego had been unsuccessful, and there was little reason to think it would do any better at a still higher tribunal in Albany.[38] A recent graduate of Yale College and an unknown in legal circles, Francis Miles Finch, now had full charge of the case. In May 1859, Finch was successful in his application to bring "exceptions" to the Court of Appeals, but the court declined to hear the exceptions until Rulloff had been sentenced. All these tedious technicalities aroused considerable impatience in Ithaca.[39]

In July, Rulloff was taken to Delhi in Delaware County and sentenced to hang in Owego on Friday, August 27, between the hours of ten and two o'clock.[40]

> We are informed that during the whole period of the Judges' remarks, and during, and at the pronouncement of the sentence, the prisoner exhibited no outward emotion. When asked what he had to say why sentence should not be pronounced, he rose and spoke ½ to ¾ of an hour.[41]

Rulloff made a series of persnickety legal points, and these, with the supporting authorities, were duly noted in the *Journal*. First, the court lacked jurisdiction because the certiorari called for a proceeding in a special term and a court reform act of 1847 had designated special terms only in circumstances not present in this case. Consequently, Rulloff said, his case should be dismissed entirely. Second, Rulloff argued that since Judge Mason had presided at the Owego trial, he should not be part of the panel at the appellate level. Third, he had not been present for the proceeding at which his appeal had been granted, though the last constitution of New York and common practice allowed him to appear in his own behalf and with counsel.

The court agreed to consider these points. On Wednesday morning, the court announced that, because their decision on the bill of exceptions had not been announced in Rulloff's presence, they would direct the clerk to enter an order denying his motion for a new trial, and then proceeded to pronounce the sentence of the law. In a solemn tone, the court set the date for Rulloff to hang. In a routine expected by all, Finch moved that the exceptions be appealed, and the case moved on to the capital in Albany.

Now it was possible for Francis Finch to press forward with the appeal, and in September 1858 he did so. Finch undertook the case himself, in part to present an alternative view that Spencer had dismissed out of hand in Owego. In Albany, Finch would face Daniel S. Dickinson, who had been opposing counsel when Finch was Spencer's junior at Owego.

Dickinson, a Democrat, had been the first village president of Binghamton when it was organized in 1834, and in 1836 he became a state senator. In 1844, he was appointed to fill a vacancy to complete a term in the United States Senate, and the following year the legislature elected him to a full six-year term in that body.[42] With the expiration of his senate term, Dickinson remained prominent in New York and in national politics. In the Congress, he had debated the great questions of the day—the Mexican War and the extension of slavery to newly admitted states were among the most prominent—with Daniel Webster and Henry Clay, and he was highly regarded by them both. During his years of public service, Dickinson had not amassed a fortune, and, returning to New York from Washington in 1851, he resumed an active law practice to provide money for his personal and political ambitions. The attorney-general of New York assigned him to quash Rulloff's appeal.

Rulloff, it turned out, had not liked Finch's proposed approach any more than Spencer had, and it was with great difficulty that Finch persuaded him to rely on it. Only after many law books had been brought to Rulloff's cell in the Ithaca jail did Finch obtain his client's reluctant consent.

Finch arrived in Albany with his enormous brief, replete with cases from the English common-law tradition. The day before the case was to be heard, he met Dickinson at the hotel. Dickinson looked the part of an oratorical equal of Clay and Webster, wearing a cutaway coat and with his magnificent white hair falling almost to his shoulders and forming a halo around his face. His brother would describe, in phrases echoing phrenological doctrine, the senator as having "a head of massive proportions and a countenance indicating at once intellectual activity and strength, force of character and benevolence of disposition."[43] Dickinson was majestic and mature; Finch was neither.

Halliday told the DeWitt Historical Society about this meeting, and Finch, reading Halliday's lecture in 1906, approved of his account.[44]

Dickinson rather contemptuously asked Finch if he had used a freight car to bring his brief down in. The sarcastic remark cut Finch to the core. He felt it keenly. He thought his situation was trying enough, anyway, and that at least he should be treated with kindness if not respect.

Finch entered the imposing courtroom with considerable anxiety, and Nicholas Hill, one of the leading counsel then in practice, was curious enough about the case to appear there that day as a spectator.

"Young man," he said; "don't be afraid; you are right in this case." This encouragement must have done much to stiffen Finch's resolve since Hill was famous as an expert on evidence, and, as one of his colleagues would memorialize him at his death in 1859, "he was a walking library."

The line of argument that Finch pursued was exactly contrary to the one Spencer had argued in Owego. He admitted that it was not necessary to produce a corpse to show that a murder had been done and that circumstantial evidence could, in principle, establish that a crime had been committed. Even more audaciously, he said that if Rulloff's daughter was dead, there was sufficient proof to show that he had murdered her.

"But," said Finch, "I assert that the circumstance of *mere absence* in and of itself is not sufficient in a criminal case to establish death."

Dickinson was flabbergasted, suggesting that he had not spent much time reading Finch's long brief. In oral argument, he attempted to refute the position that Spencer had taken. Judge Hiram Denio soon brought him up short.

Mr. Dickinson, the counsel upon the other side admits those propositions and says that the only question is whether the mere absence is a circumstance strong enough in a criminal case to justify a verdict that the party was dead, and upon that point we would like to hear you.

Nicholas Hill was pleased to see the legal Goliath discomfited by the young David. Dickinson attempted to thwart Finch's argument by claiming that he was addressing a matter not listed in the "exceptions" to the lower-court trial but was improperly bringing in new material. The judges denying this claim, Dickinson made a few more remarks and sat down.[45]

Recalling the argument in 1906, Finch summarized once again the point he had made in Albany in 1858.

> I avoided all discussion resting upon the difference between direct and indirect proof, and argued that, whatever its character might be in that respect, it must at least be *certain* and *unequivocal* and such that, conceding its truth, the supposition of remaining life would not be a *rational possibility*.

In writing the opinion of the court (there was one dissent, by Judge James J. Roosevelt Jr., but no written record of his grounds), Chief Judge Alexander S. Johnson carefully reviewed the case law as presented by both sides.[46] Dickinson's collection of cases, he concluded, showed no departures from Lord Hale's rule.

> The rule is not founded in a denial of the force of circumstantial evidence, but in the danger of allowing any but unequivocal and certain proof that some one is dead to be the ground on which, by the interpretation of circumstances of suspicion, an accused person is to be convicted of murder.

This principle, as articulated by Finch, was subsequently adopted as part of the New York Penal Code. As a result, Finch wrote in 1906: "The distinction I drew, with much of study and care, has thus ceased to have any importance except that of an historical character; but it at least serves to illustrate one of the ways by which, through judicial interpretation, the law develops."[47]

The result of the decision was that a new trial was ordered, though, without any additional evidence that Priscilla was dead rather than merely absent, it would have little hope of success.

Judicial millstones did not grind rapidly over the small particles of the arguments urged by Dickinson and Finch, and, while awaiting the decision of the Court of Appeals, Rulloff bided his time in the Ithaca jail. Finally, in January 1859, he was granted a new trial.

In Ithaca there was a rising thirst for blood, and Smith Robertson, the sheriff of Tompkins County, was worried. (Smith Robertson's brother Tom had helped Rulloff load that suspicious chest into his wagon on June 24, 1845.)

Early in March appeared an inflammatory handbill apparently calling for the angry populace to take Rulloff's punishment into its own hands. It was written, in its final form, by B. G. Jayne, printed in Ithaca, and distributed throughout the region by, among others, Sewell Thompson and James Mix.[48] Halliday was well acquainted with these personalities, though he had been a young man when the sensational events had taken place. Some indication of the popular preoccupation with Rulloff is suggested by the youthful Halliday's visit to see Rulloff in jail; he went there, as part of a crowd of curiosity-seekers, in the company of his oldest brother.

> "I expected to see a monster in human form. In fact, I was a little timid about going at all. It was a long time before I could be convinced that the gentlemanly and mild-mannered man that I saw in the cell was Rulloff, the murderer. One thing impressed me; it was the way in which he carried his head, a little to one side in not a coy but a gentle, winning and winsome manner, while his voice was gentleness itself." Sewell Thompson and James Mix, Halliday said, "regarded the whole affair at that time as a huge joke."[49]

At the *Tompkins County Democrat*, Timothy Maloney interpreted the joke for readers in doubt that the region would erupt in mob rule.

> AN IMMENSE HOAX.—Some unmitigated wag or wags have made an awful attempt to pull the locomotive extremities of the citizens of Tompkins County. There has been hand-bills circulated by them extensively through the country, calling for a meeting of the citizens, at the Clinton House, on Saturday next, to take into consideration the propriety of breaking the jail and lynching Rulloff. The whole thing, from beginning to end, is one of the

most transparent *leg-pulling* operations we have ever heard of. Our friends of the Citizen and Journal, have bitten, like gudgeons, at the bait offered; and if they do not confess to the *core,* when they see the *"immense"* crowd on Saturday next, then are we no prophet. The authors of *the* hoax of the season deserve a leather medal at the hands of those duped by them. *Vive la Humbug!*[50]

Maloney was right in saying that John Selkreg of the *Journal* had "bit." The very idea of a lynch mob made his civic blood boil.

Have those instrumental in calling this meeting fully considered the consequences? Have they counted the cost of an attempt to storm the jail, when the law makes it imperative on the Sheriff to defend it with all the force which he is empowered to call to assist him? If they have not, it is time they looked the matter square in the face. We are not speaking of the guilt or innocence of Ruloff, and certainly are no friend of his, but declare it as our conviction that those who advise and participate in the movement, are more dangerous members of society than even Ruloff himself. It would be a disgrace to our village and county should such a meeting be held from which we could not for long years recover. If laws are wrong correct them by proper means; but to subvert and over turn them by a mob is more to be deprecated than ought else besides.[51]

B. G. Jayne and those who contributed to the language of the handbill did not find Rulloff "gentle, winning, and winsome," and they were not in a joking mood. They were ready to step in where the law seemed likely to stumble over an obscure quibble in Albany on a point barely discernible to the untrained legal mind. The handbill asked a simple question and offered a clear answer. The question was not even graced with a question mark (see p. 77). This notice evoked an energetic community response. A gallows was constructed, a rope was found and a noose tied in the end of it, and a battering ram was constructed to break down the jailhouse door. This ram was a particularly impressive apparatus. Sam Halliday remembered it vividly years later.

This was a large piece of timber about as large as the ordinary telephone pole, but not so long. At one end of it there was an iron ferrule, or ring, to prevent its splitting. Through the timber holes were bored and large sticks passed through for handles. It would take about twenty men to handle it.[52]

Shall The
Murderer Go Unpunished!

EDWARD H. RULLOFF will soon gain his freedom unless prompt and effective measures are taken by the people to prevent it. It is confidently believed that the new trial that has been ordered by the Court of Appeals will not be had, but on the contrary it is the intention to *Secretly Smuggle* this atrocious *Murderer* out of the country, where he will be set at liberty, to add fresh victims to the number he has already sent unannounced before their **GOD.** Since his confinement he has repeatedly threatened that if he is once more a free man, he will seek satisfaction in the *Blood* of the relatives of the *Murdered* wife. Shall these things be? Shall this *Monster* be turned loose to glut his tiger appetite for Revenge And Blood? Shall the ends of **JUSTICE** BE DEFEATED? We trust not! We hope not! We implore you, citizens of Tompkins County, let it not go out to the world, that there can be no **JUSTICE** had in your midst! In the name of **HUMANITY,** in the name of the relatives of the *murdered* wife, whose heart-strings have been lacerated by this *Fiend* in human shape, in the name of the Murdered wife and child, whose pale ghost calls to you from the silent tomb to do your duty, we ask you— **SHALL THE MURDERER GO UNPUNISHED?** Shall we let this convicted felon *escape*? Will you allow Edward H. Rulloff to breathe the same pure air of freedom we enjoy? Will you allow this man, who bears the mark of *Cain* upon his brow, to go forth in this community and add fresh victims to the grave? **NO,** you will not! You cannot.

We call on those who wish JUSTICE done to the *Murderer* to meet at the CLINTON HOUSE in Ithaca on Saturday, March 12th. 1859, at 12 o'clock noon. It will depend on the action you take that day whether Edward H. Rulloff *walks forth a free man, or whether he dies the death he so richly deserves.*

MANY CITIZENS

Sheriff Smith Robertson was, of course, aware of these preparations and anxious about them. His first plan was to call out the DeWitt Guards, the local militia, but he felt that its members would not be enthusiastic about defending Rulloff. Then he considered deputizing the less hotheaded citizens to defend the jail, but he found difficulty in locating persons willing to help.[53]

> I felt myself alone; there were *so few* who could breast the horrible tornado that was sweeping our people all in one direction. All believed him guilty, and all wanted him hung, nor did they care how it might be done. Very few would make the least effort to allay the excitement, and fewer still would volunteer their influence and manly effort to meet the threatened storm. At your distance you can have no conception of the feeling here. When I found myself powerless for any defense that promised success, I felt I might do by stratagem what I had no hope to accomplish by force, *to-wit, a horrid crime!* Hence on the night of the 10th I made my plans to be off in the morning by the boat with the object of the people's vengeance to Auburn. None except actual performers were let behind the scene.

Rulloff was reluctant to travel even the short distance to the steamer without an escort of guards. But the sheriff spoke to him sharply: "Rulloff, you will go to Auburn to-morrow or to the devil the next day." Rulloff agreed to go tomorrow.

Accordingly, on Friday morning a carriage drove up to the jail, and the sheriff entered it and drove away. The two men deputized by the mob to watch for a trick decided to go to breakfast.

As soon as the scouts had departed, the carriage returned and the sheriff's trusty helper emerged with Rulloff from the jail. As quickly as possible they drove to the dock and waited until the steamer had cast its lines. As it turned outward in a northwesterly direction, Rulloff was "jumped" aboard.

Word of Rulloff's departure soon spread through the town. Just before noon, George W. Schuyler entered the offices of Boardman and Finch and suggested that it might be well for the attorneys who had defended Rulloff to avoid the angry crowd that had gathered. In 1906, Halliday described their reaction.

Judge Finch has told me that, so far as he was concerned, he was perfectly willing to go down a back street, but Judge [Douglass] Boardman would have none of it. They had simply done their duty as attorneys and they should go to their homes by way of the Clinton House, as they always did. There was, in fact, no personal violence done to either of them, but when they saw that crowd they regretted that they had been so rash. When they returned after dinner they were both of the opinion that the longest way around was the safest, if not the shortest, way back to their office.[54]

When the lynch mob met on Saturday, the leaders announced that their quarry had fled, thus dampening the zeal of those who had worked so hard fabricating the battering ram and the gallows. But the intensity of feeling was still strong, as reported by the *Ithaca Journal* the following Tuesday.[55]

A resolution was passed by the meeting announcing the determination to summarily hang Rulloff, should he be caught, and from the tone and temper of the gathering, there would be no reasonable doubt of the strength and earnestness of their determination.

Feeling against the sheriff, who had prevented the lynching, ran high, but the *Journal* reporter was still on the side of institutionalized justice. Some condemned Robertson, but others were less passionate and "admitted that the Sheriff had but made a mistake of judgment."

In his letter to a friend, Sheriff Robertson was more dramatic.

At first, when the news of my movement with the prisoner spread among the people, one universal howl of indignation and rage went up, as from a lot of hungry wolves who have been cheated of their prey after having tasted blood.

Robertson wanted backing for his position, and he went straight from Auburn (where Rulloff was safely settled in the county jail) to Albany, where he conferred with the governor, the attorney general, and persons he described as "many other of the first men of the State." All of them congratulated him and warmly approved his decision.

A newspaper reporter in Auburn went to the jail to obtain a reaction to these events from the local sheriff but found him absent. He did, however, manage to interview Rulloff himself, who expatiated on the bloodthirstiness of the Ithacans, and the story gave the impression that Rulloff and Robertson were of one mind in condemning them.

The following week, the *Ithaca Journal* corrected this impression.

> The Auburn journals have contained statements of the matter but these statements were not obtained from the Sheriff as has been charged. In his absence from that place and also in the absence of the Sheriff of Cayuga co., access was obtained to Rulloff's cell, and expressions charged as emanating from Mr. Robertson in regard to our citizens and the circumstances of the case were colored by the prisoner to suit his own notions of the matter.[56]

Maloney's *Democrat* also commented on the sheriff's decision.

> The Sheriff of our County, impelled, no doubt, by a desire to avoid the consequences likely to result from such a scene of excitement, very prudently as we—with all deference to the adverse opinions of respected friends—cannot but think, removed Rulloff on Friday last to the jail in Auburn for safe keeping.
>
> Whether the Sheriff acted in precise conformity with *the letter* of the law, or not, we are not competent to say—that in obeying *the spirit* of the law, for the avoidance of apprehended riot and violence, we are very willing to believe. . . .
>
> With Rulloff we have no fellowship, and for him we have no sympathy. He was guilty of abduction, and he paid the penalty— but that don't wipe away his guilt—Perhaps he is a murderer— that being yet *sub lite,* our opinion is not obtruded. We wait for the law. It is fast enough for us—but too slow for many persons.
>
> One thing we are fully decided upon, viz: that we would rather that the greatest villain in the State shall—for want of legal evidence—escape his deserts, than that Lynch Law, Mob Law, or any other law than the law of the land, shall be resorted to for his punishment.[57]

On the Wednesday following the thwarted lynching, another "vast assemblage" gathered in the Ithaca Village Hall.[58] George Beers denounced the precipitate action of Sheriff Robertson in removing Rulloff to Auburn: "running him off was illegal and wrong." Marcus Lyon, the district attorney, expressed confidence in the people of the county. But, he said, that without evidence of the murder, it would be difficult to prosecute.

> Mr. Lyon was in favor of securing, if possible, the proof; and if found impossible by human agency, then the prosecuting officer would do all he could, legally, to hold him in custody, in the hope that Providence might, in the mean time, furnish such proof as would be necessary.

A committee to formulate resolutions was named, and, while they were drafting them, others addressed the body. On their return, it was declared that Sheriff Robertson's removal of Rulloff had been "without authority of law" and "unwarranted"; that by removing him, the sheriff had occasioned "the means of casting unmerited reproach on the good name of the citizens of Tompkins County as a law-abiding people"; that the way to create social change was through the ballot box and the justice system; that the removal also led people to believe that the militia could not be counted upon. Having satisfied themselves with expressions of patriotism and confidence in the citizens, the meeting now authorized George D. Beers, O. B. Curran, and G. W. Schuyler to receive contributions toward the cost of dragging Lake Cayuga for the bodies. At the end of the day, the meeting passed a resolution urging that Rulloff be returned from Auburn, and those present pledged themselves to protecting him.

While incarcerated in the Cayuga County Jail in Auburn, Rulloff wrote a steady stream of letters to Francis Miles Finch, many of them on lined paper from an exercise book or even, when the sheriff declined to supply him with more such paper, on the back of the printed transcript of his 1856 trial in Tioga County.[59]

In the jail Rulloff had resumed his carpet-designing work for Josiah Barber. That gave him money on account; he could also "command" money from his prosperous brother in Pennsylvania. In one undated note, he urged Finch to unabated efforts to free him.

On June 20, 1859, he wrote to Finch about the proposed plan to return him to the Tompkins County Jail: *"Tone* and *energy* must characterize our proceedings or I am a dead man."

Three days later he wrote again with a mixture of bravado and apprehension, viewing his plight as if he had some choice about whether or not to return to Ithaca.

> That this course is highly dangerous I know very well. I feel that I will not be safe in Ithaca jail, that my return there may be the signal for an immediate assault upon the jail—and that every moment I stay[,] surprise parties will to be apprehended. But we have got to choose between risks and by all odds this is the least.

Attempts to transfer Rulloff from the jail at Auburn to the one at Ithaca did not, however, succeed.

In July 1859, Rulloff was taken to Cooperstown in Otsego County, accompanied by Francis Finch and Sheriff Hoskins, the officer who had taken charge of Rulloff in the Auburn jail. The court in Cooperstown set the time and place for the new trial: September in Owego. In October, Francis Finch's delaying tactics continued to be effective. Now Rulloff's trial was further delayed, and proceedings were expected to begin in February or March 1860.

Suddenly, Rulloff's fortunes took a turn toward freedom. In the face of the appellate decision, the district attorney in Tompkins County decided that there was no likelihood of success in attempting to convict him of any of the murders, and, apparently, there was little interest in prosecuting him for breaking jail. Consequently, in March 1860, he was transferred to Erie, Pennsylvania, to await trial on the charge of robbing P. R. Bennett's jewelry store in Warren.

Apparently Bennett did not urge the local prosecutor to bring Rulloff to trial; after all, he had recovered his valuables, considerable time had passed, and perhaps the evidence of those handbills for A. B. Richmond's invention had been misplaced. Further, Rulloff was supplied with a pair of powerful lawyers, paid for no doubt by his brother, and they were ready to argue strenuously on his behalf. Judicious payments might also have soothed the discontent of Mr. Bennett and others victimized by his thefts. For whatever reason, in the early summer of 1860, Rulloff was released from jail a free man.

Soon he had a nasty letter from Al Jarvis, who threatened violence if he did not at once secure money to support himself and his mother. Rulloff told Ham Freeman that he sent them all the money he could get his hands on.[60]

Almost everyone in western New York and Pennsylvania, Rulloff included, knew him to be guilty of abduction, theft, assault, fraud, deception, jail-breaking, and murder. But no one could prove that he should be imprisoned beyond the term he had already served. Judge Mason, at the Tioga trial, had spoken of "moral certainty" and declared that he agreed with the jury that the evidence supported that moral certainty. In Rulloff's appeal, Francis Miles Finch had not confronted the issue of moral certainty but had stuck doggedly to one simple idea that proof must be so certain that there was no "rational possibility" of an alternative.

In this struggle between moral certainty and rational possibility, Finch was carrying out his client's instructions. In an undated note to Finch, Rulloff had warned him.

> That cursed word *moral*—mind, I tell you, you must make no terms with, at least so far as the death is concerned. I forewarn you fairly that you are destined to have more trouble with that one word than with any other in the dictionary. If you commit yourself to it, you are gone.

Finch did not. He relied on "rational possibility," and Rulloff was free.

Ed Crapsey closed his account of this chapter of Rulloff's life with high moral dudgeon.

> After a struggle of thirteen years, with a whole people determined to omit no lawful means to wrest from him a life they were convinced he had forfeited by his foul deeds, he had triumphed by what the people in their wrath declared was a technicality of the law, but in fact, by his own shallow cunning in disposal of the bodies of his victims, and by the trustfulness of the people about him in human nature.[61]

5
· · · · · · · ·

This Damn Circus

In May 1860, Rulloff emerged from jail in Pennsylvania free to shape his life anew. If his burglary of Bennett's jewelry store could be mitigated by his need to escape, there was no room whatever for sympathy in what followed. All of Rulloff's dreams of doctoring or lawyering at this point faded into dreamland. Like Goethe's Faust, he could see only a downward spiral into Hell. Later he would tell Ham Freeman: "Every man is, in a measure, the architect of his own fortune or ruin." This profound-seeming sentence was only an adage, another fragment of the quoting world of that era.[1] There was something stale about it; it was merely a cliché. Probably no particular moment marked a turning point when Rulloff ceased to accept responsibility for his own conduct; whenever it had been, by 1860 it was only a remote memory.

Though abandoning medicine and the law, Rulloff had not quite finished with the idea of professoring. After a brief visit to his brother's family, he journeyed south to Jefferson College near Pittsburgh, where he persuaded the faculty that he was a graduate of Oxford.[2]

He then heard that there were teaching opportunities elsewhere, and one professor even advanced him twenty dollars toward his traveling expenses. This sum Rulloff increased by breaking into a jewelry store on his way out of town, and he headed off on foot for the railroad. In the story he told Ham, he persuaded a passing driver to take him along in his buggy, and the man reluctantly agreed. Toward morning the man was arrested for having stolen the horse and buggy, and Rulloff accused the thief of having planted the jewelry in his satchel. The president of Jefferson vouched for Rulloff, and, despite the doubts of local officers, he was sent on his way. In his usual fashion, he fastened the blame for his misfortunes on someone else. "But for the d——d horse thief I might have been a Professor or President of a Southern College. I am the victim, and always have been, of circumstances."[3]

Rulloff had kept in touch with Jane Jarvis, and soon a letter came from her son Al far more kindly disposed to him than the earlier threat. Al needed his help.

To Rulloff's dismay, Al was writing from the jail in Buffalo. He had run into trouble. He had been arrested there and charged with burglary. "He was without friends or money, and the letter concluded by saying: 'I helped you once, and now I want you to help me.'"

Rulloff always placed the blame for his actions on someone else or claimed that a higher motive drove his baser crimes. When he received that letter from Al, he felt under obligation arising from the time of his break from the Ithaca jail, which he described to Ham as a great adventure. By the details he recalled (and fabricated), he turned his narrative into a new love story.

> Plans were laid, friends from abroad were advised . . . surreptitiously. One evening, when the family were nearly all away in the village, Albert came to my cell door. He unlocked and pulled the bolts. He said everything was ready, and that I must go, and make haste. He had some gold and silver pieces which he had collected, and which he insisted upon giving me. It was with difficulty that I could be made to accept them. I was overcome with his kindness, it was so unexpected. I shook hands with him, and bade him good bye, telling him that if he should ever find himself in need of assistance or a friend, to come to me.[4]

How implausible this story sounds! Where would a sixteen-year-old boy "collect" a substantial sum? Why would Rulloff have wanted to take this treasure when he could "command" seemingly unlimited sums from his brother?

Yet Rulloff told the credulous Ham that everything in the decade beginning in 1860 was connected with his promise to Al Jarvis and his devotion to him.

> No one but myself knows how much trouble and anguish the sacred keeping of that pledge has given me. I have been imprisoned; have deprived myself of the necessaries of life; have aban-

doned my studies at times; I have committed crimes; all that I
might keep inviolate that pledge.[5]

So in the fall of 1860, Al Jarvis wrote to Rulloff and redeemed the
pledge.

Rulloff dropped everything and set out for western New York. His
account of his efforts to "keep inviolate that pledge" shows a typical mixture of hand-wringing over his fate and helplessness that he cannot alter
it.

Remembering the obligations I was under to him, I at once
threw up my situation; received what was due me, and started for
Buffalo. Arriving there I found that Jarvis had been caught in the
act of committing a burglary, and that the evidence which could
be brought against him would convict him. By the use of what little money I had with me, the grand jury that sat at the next term
of Court failed to indict him, and he was released.

He came to the hotel where I was, and we had a long talk. I told
him that he had made a bad start, and that he had better try and
get a living in some other way. I said that I had a project in view
whereby I could make money enough to keep us both. I then told
him of the discovery which I had made while in Auburn State
Prison of perfect method in the formation of language, and that I
proposed to write a book which would sell for a large sum, which
I would be glad to share with him; and that until I could complete
and publish my work I could obtain advancements of enough from
men of letters to keep us afloat.

It was finally arranged that Jarvis should go on to New York,
obtain some rooms and fit them up, while I was to go down into
Pennsylvania and procure some money of parties there, and meet
him in New York in about a month. We separated, he taking the
train for New York, over the Central Railroad, and I going to the
place in Pennsylvania where I had told him.

About ten days after I was surprised to receive a letter from
Jarvis, dated at Rochester, telling me that he had got into a hell of
a scrape, and that he wanted me to help him. I had not as yet
obtained the money I had expected to, and the result was I was
compelled to raise some out of a store. I got about $70 in broad
day light without being detected, and immediately came on to

Rochester. Jarvis, with his cussed recklessness had stopped off there on his way to New York, broke in a store and stole $1,600 worth of sewing silk. He had two confederates who had got away with the plunder. I soon found out that he had only been arrested on suspicion, and that they had no direct proof of his complicity in the affair, and I got him clear.

We then went to New York together, rented a cheap suite of rooms, and I began writing on my book. My money soon became exhausted and I had to cast about me for employment. I succeeded in getting a precinct to canvass for a city directory. The money I obtained for this was sufficient to keep us for a while, and before it was gone Jarvis committed a burglary over in Jersey City, and disposed of his share of the goods for some $700. He then insisted that we should change our rooms for something better. I opposed it, telling him that the rooms we had were good enough, and that we were getting along very well, and that we ought to economize our money until I got far enough along with my book to obtain advancements on that.

Jarvis had the better of the argument however, as he had the money, and with his characteristic recklessness and imprudence, went and hired a suite of rooms in a fashionable quarter of the city, for which, with furniture, we had to pay $20 per week. Jarvis' $700 did not last long at this rate, and when it was gone I got copying, &c., from lawyers, and occasionally I was employed to work up the defense in some criminal case. In this manner we managed to live until in August, 1861; we were unable to meet our rent. Jarvis now came to the rescue with a plan for replenishing our depleted exchequer. As usual, when he planned, it was a burglary, and I was assured that it was a safe venture, and sure to pay well.[6]

Jarvis may have been "reckless," as Rulloff twice explains, but he knew how to balance risks with benefits. In Rochester, he had managed to lift sixteen hundred dollars in swag, and that seems, from Rulloff's account, to have been only a third of the take. Some sense of scale is apparent from the fact that in this single burglary, Jarvis, had he not been caught, would have accumulated enough money to pay rent for eighteen month's luxurious living in a Manhattan suite.

Jarvis's most lucrative thefts involved "sewing silk," a product of such value and portability that it made considerable profits, both for dry goods merchants and for parasitic thieves like Jarvis and Rulloff. Silk was the great luxury fabric of the era.[7] If silk was valuable in the late 1850s (when Jarvis began stealing it), it was even more precious after the outbreak of the Civil War.

For thieves, silk was attractive because it could be compressed into bundles and carried through the streets or on trains without attracting attention. Unlike jewelry, silk could not be readily identified, and a thief caught by the police could not be easily associated with a particular robbery. Since many people were involved in the sale and tailoring of silk garments, it was possible to find many buyers for silk of doubtful origin, and thus the wholesale value to the thief was likely to be higher than it would be for other stolen articles.

Late in 1861, Rulloff and his cronies were engaged in a burglary near Poughkeepsie, New York, when their luck turned bad. One difficulty was that they stayed around too long—ten days—and people were vigilant for loitering strangers. Jarvis and the other thief escaped.

> Jarvis done all he could to help me, but as the haul we had made was a small one, he had but little money to work with, and I was committed for burglary, and sentenced to Sing Sing for two years and six months, under the name of James H. Kerron.[8]

Rulloff began his term on November 20, 1861. Older than most of the inmates and far more accomplished, he was known as "Big Jim." The prison officials found him a valuable prisoner:

> [H]e was highly esteemed among the prison officials for his aptitude in several branches of skilled labor, but more especially for his chirographic accomplishments. For this reason he was made book-keeper of the cabinet shop of the prison, and the accounts of that department during the period of his incumbency, looking more like copper-plate engraving than penmanship, remain as striking proofs of his marvelous accuracy and neatness.[9]

In Sing Sing, Rulloff formed a close friendship with another inmate serving time in the cabinet shop, William D. Thornton. "Thornton," like

"Kerron," was an alias, and Thornton was in fact William T. Dexter, known as "Billy." Billy Dexter was serving time for a burglary he had committed in the Bowery.

Crapsey made the friendship into something to celebrate.

In all criminal annals there is no more romantic and singular trinity than that first completed in Sing Sing prison. Separated at times by the imprisonment of first of one and then of another, Rulloff, Jarvis and Dexter always came together again when the sentences had expired, and always to renew their depredations upon mankind. The fellowship of Rulloff and Jarvis, beginning in 1857, and the triumvirate being completed by the addition of Dexter in 1862, it remained thence forward unbroken. There is not the slightest evidence that either of these men ever attempted to betray either of the others, or that their companionship was ever disturbed by even a trivial quarrel, and yet no three men could have stronger points of contrast.

Jarvis and Dexter were indeed alike in years, being young men under twenty-five in 1861, but this was the only thing they had in common. Jarvis was a youth of rare personal beauty, of singularly soft and pleasant manner, of studious and retiring disposition, of considerable mental capacity, fair literary attainments, and honest in his instincts. Dexter, on the other hand, was not agreeable in person or manners, was rough, uncouth, almost without mind, lacking even rudimentary education, and a thief by nature. These two young men differing in all things else, vied with each other in their veneration of and faith in their master, Rulloff, a man twice their age, who used them so plainly for his own purposes that it is probable even their prejudiced perceptions could not disguise the fact. Here, as always, he used his erudition to no better purpose than to obtain him the means of scanty and infamous subsistence, but incited his promises of what he was to do for them in the future by means of his accomplishments, these two youths went on year after year, stealing just enough to keep body and soul together, and meantime buoyed with the hope of that "good time coming," when the world was to fall down and worship Rulloff as the incarnation of earthly knowledge, and they were all to be rich forevermore.[10]

Rulloff himself was equally laudatory in celebrating Al Jarvis.

> Jarvis had a good many noble qualities. He was generous—ready always to give his last cent to any one in want. Kind and obliging, and steadfast as a rock to a friend, and notwithstanding the improvidence, extravagance and utter recklessness with which he would involve himself and friends in difficulty, he was the prince of good fellows.[11]

In a conversation in 1871, Rulloff persuaded Oliver Dyer, a reporter for the *New York Sun,* that Jarvis had been unfailingly generous and personally attractive. From this conversation, Dyer formed the opinion that Al "was perhaps the only being on earth whom Rulloff truly loved."[12]

The far less attractive Billy Dexter completed his prison sentence some months before Rulloff was to be released, and Billy told "Big Jim" that when he was free, he should come to his family's house at 10 Graham Street in Brooklyn. Soon Rulloff joined the Dexter household, and his first enterprise was to perfect a new technique he had invented for coloring photographs. This method was apparently a failure, and Dexter's sister was so outraged by the damage Rulloff had done to her album that she tossed the apparatus and chemicals into the yard, where the chemicals poisoned the neighbor's chickens.

In October 1864, Rulloff and an accomplice were arrested in a small community a few hours by train from New York. The crime was so trivial that it seemed hardly worth prosecuting: They had stolen some harness and a box of cigars. With his usual provoking bravado, he told the lawyer he had engaged to represent him that if he had given his real name, the man would "know it as well as that of his own partner." The two thieves were released when they disclosed the hiding place of their booty and returned it to the owner.[13]

Rulloff's next scheme was a popular one during the last years of the Civil War. Men called to military service could purchase substitutes to go in their place, and Rulloff recruited Billy and John Dexter to step forward as "volunteers." Like many others, they deserted at the earliest opportunity and volunteered again and again. As the carnage of the peninsular battles in Virginia intensified, substitutes could command ever-increasing bounties, and Rulloff was able to support his scholarly leisure through the efforts of the Dexter brothers.[14]

At the end of the war, Billy Dexter soon got himself in another scrape and was sentenced to sixty days in the Kings County Penitentiary. In his absence, Rulloff found a new way to profit from their friendship, and he persuaded Billy's mother to approve a mortgage for five hundred dollars on her house. He led her to believe that the money would be used to spring Billy from prison. As a result of this transaction, Rulloff often spoke grandly of his "properties" in Brooklyn, though he did not have any right to claim ownership.[15]

In the summer of 1865, Rulloff and Jarvis moved to Jersey City and then to Hoboken, where Rulloff set himself up as a teacher of languages. Jarvis occupied himself with pilfering and had "a small success" with a burglary in Newark. Without telling Rulloff of any plans, he suddenly vanished and was gone for three weeks. At the end of that time, Rulloff received a letter from a lawyer in Connecticut telling him that Jarvis was in jail under suspicion of stealing rings from a jewelry store.[16]

At once, Rulloff went to help his protégé. With "unusual foresight," Rulloff told Ham, Al had concealed the stolen rings and they had not been discovered, but when Rulloff arrived, the lawyer had them in his possession. Rulloff saw at once that they were fakes, but nothing daunted him—he went to an adjoining town and sold one for fifty-five dollars. Unfortunately for him, it was soon identified as one of the stolen rings; Rulloff was tried, convicted, and sentenced to sixteen months in Wethersfield prison. No connection between him and the jewelry having been proved, Jarvis went free.

Prison life was increasingly difficult for Rulloff.

> My health was very poor while in this prison. It was at first thought that I was feigning sickness, and I was placed in a damp, dark dungeon, and was kept there for weeks. My eyesight failed me, and nothing but an old pair of boots which I had on kept me from becoming blind. My eyes have always been very weak since. The officers of the prison afterwards saw their mistake, and felt sorry for me, and assisted in procuring my pardon.[17]

The connection between blindness and boots was never made clear.

When he was released in 1866, Rulloff told Jarvis that he would run no more risks and turned to his studies with concentrated devotion. Still he had to have funds to live, and he bought and sold goods from time to time and could not resist making "a *little lift* without detection."

For the most part, however, Rulloff lived a quiet life in New York, and the three thieves were sometimes reduced to such penury that they were obliged to collect for sale or for their own use lumps of coal that had fallen into the gutter from delivery wagons or to glean potatoes in the night from farmers' fields.

Ed Crapsey had a friend who knew of the intimate lives of Rulloff and his companions. In the summer of 1866, Rulloff and Jarvis rented the two front rooms on the second floor of 19 Delancey Street in lower Manhattan. Rulloff was then passing himself off as a language teacher, E. C. Howard, and Jarvis, using the name Charles Thompson, was his pupil in German.[18]

> [B]oth of them would frequently be absent for days together, and when they returned would always have plenty of money, whereas their purses were remarkable only for emptiness just prior to their departure.
>
> Once the other tenant of the floor remarking upon this singularity asked them if they were traveling agents, and both answered in the affirmative with suspicious alacrity. But with the exception of these strange departures and returns, there was nothing to awaken distrust of the lodgers. They were men of the most quiet, inoffensive habits, and addicted in a remarkable degree to sedentary pursuits. They always, when in the city, spent their evenings at home in reading or study, and their frivolities were bounded by occasional games of whist or euchre, in both which games Rulloff was proficient. Sometimes, but still more rarely, liquor of the milder sorts would be brought into the room, and sparingly drank by both, but in this respect both were abstemious far beyond the average of reputable men. If they had any liaisons with frail women, they managed to keep the fact concealed from those who saw almost hourly into their domestic life. They appeared to be model lodgers who were averse to dissipation of all kinds, and certainly never brought their home into disrepute by reeling into it drunk at unseemly hours.
>
> After they had been some months in the house, their domestic circle was increased by the arrival of a one-eyed man, and still later by the coming of two women, to whom the rear rooms on the second floor were given, and who were announced as a sister of

Rulloff and her daughter, which they were not. . . . After these additions there was little if any change in the daily life of the out-laws, and no improprieties in the conduct of any of the inhabitants of the second floor were ever detected.

After they left Delancey Street, a one-eyed man appeared to settle their affairs, not for the first time. Back in May 1857, that same one-eyed, fair-haired man had appeared in Corning, New York, and, using the name James Henry, had attempted to repossess the team and buggy that had been used to speed Rulloff's escape from the Ithaca jail. Now, as then, he was acting on behalf of the Rulofson brothers. He was nor-mally employed in the lumbering enterprise by R. Rulofson. He was James H. Henniger, their half brother.

Ed Crapsey was gallant in protecting the privacy of the two women who spent some weeks with Rulloff and Jarvis at the Delancey Street address. The older woman was not his sister; she was, in fact, Jane Jarvis, who had come to be with her oldest son Al and the man she had loved, Rulloff. With her was her daughter Helen, now eighteen years old, who as a child had played in Rulloff's cell in Ithaca. Helen would shortly marry respectably and set up housekeeping in Harts Falls, New York, not far from Troy. Her mother's intimacy with Rulloff thus con-tinued a decade after their first encounter when Rulloff had been so inconveniently shackled in his cell, but the time together in New York formed them all into something like a family.[19]

Following their departure, Rulloff's absences from the Delancey Street rooms, and his prosperity when he returned, suggest that he had not grown so weary of thieving as he later claimed. Additional income came from his offering legal advice and counsel, and by this means he was engaged in a grander scheme of theft in the company of unusually able thieves. The band with which he associated engaged him to help case a bank in New Hampshire that seemed a likely source of wealth.[20]

At last the bank was cracked. Of course I had nothing directly to do with the burglary. They had some of the best mechanics and machinists in the world with them. I received some of the money. Was suspicioned and arrested. Some of the stolen money and bonds were found on my person, about three thousand dollars only. $80,000 in all was the sum stolen I am told.[21]

I plead guilty and was sent up for ten years, but I was not in prison but a few months, two I think. I received a note one day telling me to do so and so, which was to jump through a door and run while all the prisoners, including myself, were marching to dinner. I did as directed and found on the outside of the prison walls a carriage in waiting, which drove me off. I never asked any questions but I always supposed that the prison officials were bribed to let me off. Of course they were. I had written through one of the keepers to the gang that unless they got me out I would expose the whole thing. The name that I was in prison under there was Shinborn. I was provided with decent clothing, and six hundred dollars in money. I came on to New York.

I met Jarvis. We had a good visit, and did a little business on our own hook. Rewards were offered by the authorities of New Hampshire for my arrest. I was informed of it, and advised to keep out of the way. One day on Broadway I saw a man that I knew to be one of the New Hampshire State Prison officials. I thought he recognized me. I told Jarvis. Jarvis consulted with the gang. He was not one of them, but was known to them. They were *aristocratic thieves*.[22]

Rulloff's next adventure took him westward along the Erie Railroad, the link between New York City and Ithaca and western Pennsylvania; this railroad was a corridor along which most of his crimes were committed. He and his confederates looked for a place that was "a back town" where they might expect to find people of property. This time their destination was Monticello, New York.

I went up on the Erie Railroad and got off at a little station and rode over to Monticello in the stage. It is a rough country, and this was rather a dreary ride, but the free air of these mountains was pleasant and exhilarating to me. I stopped at the hotel for a while, then at a private boarding house, and then went back to the hotel. I placed what money I had, about $400, in the bank at Monticello, and became acquainted with the bank officers, and learned all about the bank, and the habits of its officers.

I wrote for my friends to come on, one or two at a time. After waiting for several days to hear from them I cut down to New

York, and they told me to go back, and watch matters, and advise them when to come on. I went back and remained for some time at Monticello.

At first, Rulloff had stayed at the Monticello House, again using the name James Nelson, but an opportunity too good to pass by presented itself. George F. Bennett, teller at the National Union Bank of Sullivan County, was in search of a tenant, and Rulloff rented rooms in his house.

I gave an oyster supper to which I invited the Sheriff, and Judge [Timothy F.] Bush, and many other of the *nobility* of that little town. They all accepted; they seemed to enjoy my hospitality; they eat and drank every thing I sat before them. I saw afterwards that I was suspected by the bank officers. I could read the countenances of some, especially Sheriff [Benjamin W.] Winner, who is an ignoramus, followed me around a good deal and made himself officious. He has been here once [that is, to the jail in Binghamton] and I suppose he will come again.

The bank was not robbed. The boys came up near there on the railroad. I advised against it for several reasons. One was, I was sick of the business. I had been received in good society there and had been well treated by decent men for the first time in years, and I did not wish to abandon their confidence. I had not the heart to do it. Because I was heartily sick of such business. I was still ambitious of being a gentleman and of being respected by my fellow men.

Rulloff's search for respectability was never fulfilled. If the genial host of that grand oyster supper was so esteemed as a companion, why did Sheriff Winner follow him around the small town? Even the thieves regarded him as a marginal figure, useful as a scout but perilous as a companion because of his habit of getting caught. It was as if a web of circumstance were drawing Rulloff closer and closer to Binghamton, New York.

For some reason, Rulloff suddenly disappeared from Monticello, leaving behind two hundred dollars of the money he had deposited in the National Union Bank. He gave no explanation, but not long thereafter a bag containing burglary tools was found in the haymow of a nearby farm and people assumed it was the property of the mysterious James Nelson. Three years later, when Rulloff was lodged in the Binghamton jail, the cashier of the bank, Israel P. Tremaine, had no difficulty in identifying Rulloff as Nelson.[23]

Rulloff now took marginal jobs, appearing in Binghamton in August 1868 canvassing for a directory, a job that had the added advantage of giving him an inside view of likely targets for robbery. That time, he passed himself off as an immigrant.[24]

I was a book agent *colporteur,* taking names for a State directory, and even maintained the character of a beggar, and had a paper to present stating that I was a poor but worthy German, and had been paralyzed, and I would shake as though I had the *numb palsy.* (Here Rulloff imitated how he would act, and laughed heartily.) In this I learned a good deal, picked up many things, and was introduced to *several cold victuals.* We had a matter fixed up in Binghamton that would have made you all stare, but Jarvis, like a damn fool, spoilt it, and went back to New York in disgust.

"Cold victuals" are foods a beggar could expect to receive; the expression means, metaphorically, hardships. Rulloff's play-acting, forged credentials, and loneliness are all apparent in his story. He was now approaching fifty years old, had spent much of his life in prison, and had few friends. Aside from Jarvis and Dexter, the only people he could count on were his brothers, and they kept him at a distance, though lavishing him with advice. "Don't run any more risks," James Henniger wrote to him; "as long as I have a dollar you are welcome to it."

I was in the habit of receiving, up to July, 1870, small remittances from my relatives in Pennsylvania. They were always very kind to me; as much so as they could be. I was, of course, an outlaw from society, and they knew it. I did not intrude myself upon them any oftener than I could help. I should probably at one time have gone into the country to live, as my brother desired to have me, and pursue my studies, but I wished to be where I could get such books as I wanted, and visit the great public libraries that are to be found in New York city only.[25]

Rural life held little appeal for Rulloff, and he enjoyed the action at the edges of the law. In the summer of 1869, he appeared in Cortland, New York, as a big-city lawyer, James Dalton, in an attempt to spring Billy Dexter from jail. All that he and Billy did there would later be used to convict him, yet again, of murder.

Since their peregrinations took them here and there, Jarvis and Rulloff gave up the Delancey Street rooms and rented at 2 Amity Street in Manhattan. Finally, in 1869, they took rooms in the building owned by the Jacob family at 170 Third Avenue.[26] At that point, Rulloff was using the alias Edward Leurio, and Jarvis passed himself off as Charles G. Curtis. Their landlady's daughter described his life there.

> [H]e lived a very quiet and sober life. We called him a kind of steady old bachelor. He used to play a good deal with the children about here, and they all liked him. Sometimes he gave them pennies, and they used to like to come and see him when he was not studying. He used to show us what he was doing. He would call us up and show us how many words he had translated. He would point with his finger, and say "See there; I have written so much today." Sometimes he would ask our opinion about a word, and say if it didn't mean so and so.[27]

None of his crookedness was apparent to the Jacob family, and they regarded Rulloff as a charming if eccentric tenant. Both Pauline Jacob and her brother Edward were unwavering in expressing their belief that Rulloff was a gentleman. It was obvious that they liked him.

In an interview, Edward Jacob described the last time he saw Rulloff.[28] The interviewer asked what Rulloff said he was going to do.

> Why, he didn't say anything. He went out as usual about eight o'clock in the morning, and the next day the affair took place at Binghamton. We thought it was strange that he did not return, and we went and told his old housekeeper, who lived in Carmine street. She came up, and she was almost frightened to death. The next we heard, the detectives came here to see if some keys found on a drowned man at Binghamton would fit our doors.

Rulloff picked up the thread of the narrative in his long confessional conversations with Ham Freeman. (Maggie Graham was an accomplice of the gang and would do what she could to help them.)

In the latter part of June, he, Dexter, and T—— G—— came out this way. I got a letter from Al, saying they were at Scranton, Pa., and requesting me to send him some things. After staying awhile at Scranton without doing anything, they came to this place and made a good strike in this same Halbert Bros' store. They got a good lot of silks and got away with them without detection. This was in May last. The silks were brought to New York. Some were sold there, and some of them and other silks were peddled off in the country districts by Maggie Graham and different parties. I did not pay much attention to what was going on. I think that the robbery of the Halbert store took place on the night of the 14th of May. The boys on their return were much pleased with their good luck. They said that they had "a pal" in Binghamton who helped them; that he took care of them, and would at any time that they came up here and were sly. They said that there was a fire that night in Binghamton, and that while people were running to that, they got into the store and took the silks. I afterwards learned that two of them went down the river after the robbery, in a boat, with the silks, and landed opposite an island about a mile below the place. The boat was placed, the day previous, where they could see and know where it was.

In early August, Jarvis was roaming the countryside and passed through Binghamton. Halberts' was still a tempting target, and he wrote to Rulloff in New York to say that there was a new shipment of silks just waiting to be lifted. Jarvis invited Rulloff along to act as a lookout and to help carry off the bundles. On Monday morning, August 15, they set out from the Erie Depot in Jersey City.

Rulloff described the prolonged rambles of the incompetent burglars as they waited for the right time to strike.

Arriving at Binghamton at 5 o'clock P. M., Monday, Jarvis and Dexter took charge of all the baggage which we had, which was only one satchel and one good-sized traveling bag, and an umbrella. The satchel belonged to Jarvis and the bag to me. We had our traps in them, tools, etc. I did not put anything in the bag but a shirt and a pair of stockings, and a comb. I was only a passenger. The boys did all the planning and proposed to do all the work. They took the bags over to the Spaulding House and got them checked, so they said. I stayed about the depot, and walked down to the Lewis House, but did not go in. I do not know whether the boys registered their names at the Spaulding House. I did not go in there.

After an hour or so we met at the depot, and walked down the street which leads from the depot to the Court House. We did not walk together, but apart. Jarvis and Dexter were ahead and I followed slowly behind. I thought it was very imprudent, as it was not dark yet, and the streets were full. There was a circus here that evening. Jarvis went into the post office, I do not know what for, then he came down on the canal bridge and went to a saloon on the canal bank. I stood on the canal bridge, looking up the canal, waiting impatiently for Jarvis. He came out with a hard looking chap, whose name I was told was [Martin] Adams, and that he kept the place. Jarvis went down the street, after telling me to go to the Arbor saloon and wait for him.

I went down as far as the American Hotel. There was a large number of people about there, some of whom I took to be circus people, from their style and conversation. I went into the American Hotel, and sat down and pretended to be reading a newspaper. I kept it up before my face, but my eyes saw everything that was going on. Soon I walked over to the river bridge. While standing there Dexter came along alone. I asked him where "Al" was. He said he was with two friends; that they were at a billiard saloon somewhere. I told Dexter for God's sake go and get him, and take me to our rendezvous. Dexter said, pointing with his hand to Halberts' store, "That is the place. We can't do anything here to-night on account of this damn circus."[29]

Binghamton was on the eve of a far more fantastic tale than that told by any circus.

Portrait of
Wm. H. Rulofson.
(California Historical
Society, FN-31299;
used by permission.)

Portrait of
R. Rulofson. (From
Aaron J. Davis, *His-
tory of Clarion
County, Pennsylva-
nia,* 1887], n.p.)

Portrait of E. H. Rulloff. (From Crapsey, *The Man of Two Lives,*
frontispiece. Clements Library, University of Michigan.)

"He attempted to take the Child." In this re-creation drawn in 1871, Rulloff is shown raising the pestle that he will use to kill Harriet. She is shown in a too-elegant parlor wearing a bustle skirt, a fashion that did not become common until a decade after her death. (From *Life, Trial and Execution of Edward H. Rulloff,* facing p. 49. Clements Library, University of Michigan.)

"Convicts Retiring to Their Cells." Auburn was the model for prison architecture across the nation. Here regimentation replaces isolation as a means of punishment. (From James B. Finley, *Memorials of Prison Life* [Cincinnati: L. Swarmstedt and A. Poe, 1854], facing p. 20. Clements Library, University of Michigan.)

Man in stocks. The "shower bath" was an attempt to find a humane punishment in place of flogging. Ice-cold water was dispersed from the floor above through a plate with several openings (not shown here), and it fell heavily in a cascade over the naked prisoner. Far from humane, the mechanism could (and did) result in shock and even death. (From Packard, *Memorandum of a Late Visit to Auburn Prison*, 5.)

ALBERT JARVIS.   WM. T. DEXTER.

Rulloff's Accomplices.
(From *Life, Trial and Execution of E. H. Rulloff,* facing p. 73. Clements Library, University of Michigan.)

Fred A. Merrick. (From Freeman, *The Veil of Secrecy Removed,* facing p. 48. Clements Library, University of Michigan.)

Halberts' store. Fred Merrick was murdered at the head of the stairs at the rear of the store. An iron stool top was used in the attack on the burglars. (From *Combination Atlas of Broome County* [Philadelphia: Everts, Ensign, and Everts, 1876], n.p.)

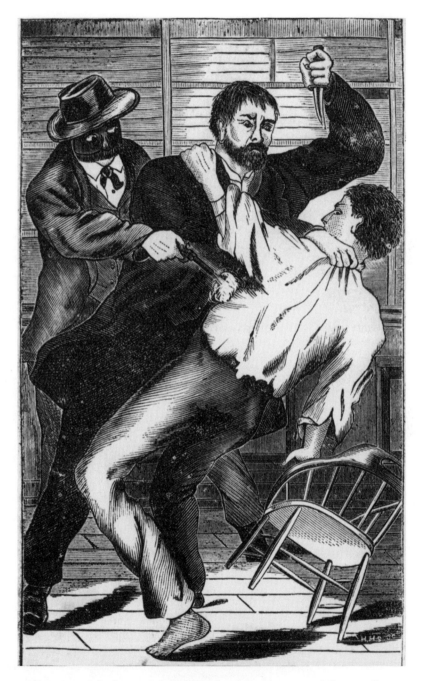

"The Brave Clerk Merrick." In this imaginary version of the murder scene, Rulloff and Jarvis are assaulting the helpless Merrick. (From *Life, Trial and Execution of E. H. Rulloff*, facing p. 6o. Clements Library, University of Michigan.)

JARVIS. DEXTER.

The Drowned Burglars. (From Crapsey, *The Man of Two Lives*, facing p. 60. Clements Library, University of Michigan.)

Broome County Sheriff's Office,

Binghamton, Feb. 27th, 1871.

Sir :

   You are hereby invited to be present at the Execution of EDWARD H. RULLOFF, at the Jail of said County, on the 3d day of March, 1871, at 12 o'clock M.

   Or in case of postponement, of which you will doubt= less learn by the public prints, on the day then fixed.

F. W. MARTIN,

SHERIFF.

To *Hon. Addison Miller*
Justice of Sessions

"Broome County Sheriff's Office." (Division of Rare and Manuscripts, Cornell University Library. Collection number 1677. Reproduced by permission.)

Letter to William B. Sprague. (The Historical Society of Pennsylvania, Gratz 13:39; used by permission.)

"Dismay of Students." (From *Life, Trial and Execution of E. H. Rulloff*, facing p. 65. Clements Library, University of Michigan.)

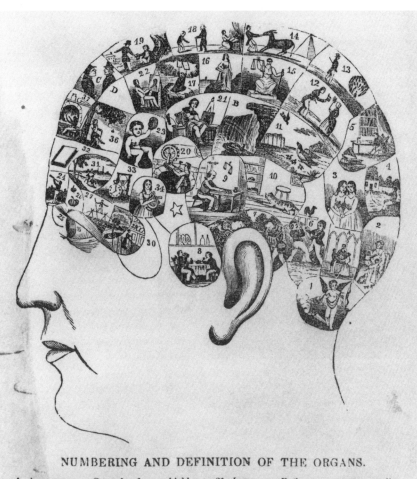

NUMBERING AND DEFINITION OF THE ORGANS.

1. AMATIVENESS, Sexual and connubial love.
2. PHILOPROGENITIVENESS, Parental love.
3. ADHESIVENESS, Friendship—sociability.
A. UNION FOR LIFE, Love of one only.
4. INHABITIVENESS, Love of home.
5. CONTINUITY, One thing at a time.
6. COMBATIVENESS, Resistance—defence.
7. DESTRUCTIVENESS, Executiveness—force.
8. ALIMENTIVENESS, Appetite. hunger.
9. ACQUISITIVENESS, Accumulation.
10. SECRETIVENESS, Policy—management.
11. CAUTIOUSNESS, Prudence, provision.
12 APPROBATIVENESS, Ambition—display.
13. SELF-ESTEEM, Self-respect—dignity.
14. FIRMNESS, Decision—perseverance.
15. CONSCIENTIOUSNESS, Justice—equity.
16. HOPE, Expectation—enterprise.
17. SPIRITUALITY, Intuition--spiritual revery.
18. VENERATION, Devotion—respect.
19. BENEVOLENCE, Kindness—goodness.
20. CONSTRUCTIVNESS Mechanical ingenuity.

21. IDEALITY, Refinement—taste--purity.
B. SUBLIMITY, Love of grandeur.
22. IMITATION, Copying—patterning.
23. MIRTHFULNESS, Jocoseness—wit—fun
24. INDIVIDUALITY, Observation.
25. FORM, Recollection of shape.
26. SIZE, Measuring by the eye.
27. WEIGHT, Balancing--climbing.
28. COLOR, Judgment of colors.
29. ORDER, Method—system—arrangement
30. CALCULATION, Mental arithmetic.
31. LOCALITY, Recollection of places.
32. EVENTUALITY, Memory of facts.
33. TIME, Cognizance of duration.
34. TUNE, MUSIC—melody by ear
35. LANGUAGE, Expression of ideas
36. CAUSALITY. Applying causes to effects
37. COMPARISON, inductive reasoning.
C. HUMAN NATURE. perception of motives
D. AGREEABLENESS, Pleasantness—suav'ts

Numbering and Definition of the Organs. (From O. S. and L. N. Fowler, *Illustrated Self-Instructor* [New York: Fowler and Wells, 1859], frontispiece. Clements Library, University of Michigan.)

Rulloff's death mask. (Used by permission from the Collection of the DeWitt Historical Society of Tompkins County, Ithaca.)

Rulloff's skull. (From Burr, *Medico-Legal Notes*, 77.)

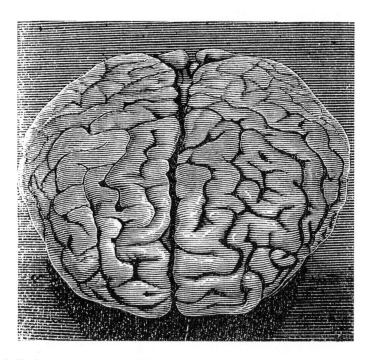

Rulloff's brain in 1871.
(From Burr, *Medico-Legal Notes,* 82.)

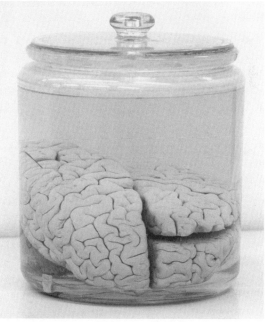

Rulloff's brain in its jar.
(Photographed by Nicola
Kountoupes, October 29,
2002, and used by permission of Cornell University.)

"Edward H. Rulloff." *The Phrenological Journal* presented an imaginary Rulloff drawn to reveal traits of his "organization." (53 [1871]: 162.)

6

·······

Napoleon's Oraculum

A t sunup on Friday, Calvin A. Brewer was walking east across the Chenango River bridge; he was on his way to his job as a clerk in the Binghamton post office. Like everyone else in town, he had heard plenty about the botched burglary at Halberts' store: people knew that two, or perhaps three, of the burglars responsible for Frederick Merrick's death had entered the river not far from the rear entrance to Halberts'. Brewer looked up the river in that direction; about twelve feet away he saw something in the water. It was a corpse, face down in the shallows, among the boulders that covered the river bottom. At first it seemed to float toward him as the coat billowed up around its head.

Another early riser, Arthur T. Thompson, also saw the body. Together they found a rowboat. Thompson, a cartman and strong, took the oars. Squeamish about touching the dead body, Brewer tossed a line with a hooked anchor, and it caught under the coat. Towing the body in the water, they rowed across to the eastern shore, coming to rest just below the bridge. Calvin Brewer went in search of Sheriff Frederick W. Martin.

Just a few minutes after Brewer and Thompson had grappled with one corpse, E. P. Reynolds saw a mysterious object from his bedroom window. He thought at first that it was a log caught on a snag in the river; his wife thought it was perhaps a dead dog. Walking to the store to get something for breakfast, Reynolds heard that a body had been found. He began to suspect that what he had seen was another corpse. He went back to the river and threw stones at it, but it did not move. With his brother-in-law, Jacob Gardinier, he rowed out and they determined that it was, indeed, a second dead body.

Reynolds and Gardinier called to people gathered on the bridge, but no one answered them; the few who paid any attention thought they must be joking. So they then rowed down to the crowd that had collected around the first body. After hearing their news, a young man joined them, and they dragged the second body ashore with the boat chain.

By the time the two bodies had been removed from the water, a crowd of nearly two hundred had assembled. Seeing the two dripping corpses, they began volley after volley of "vehement cheering. . . . Such an outburst of feeling rarely occurs on any occasion. It was not the cheering of gladness, or of ordinary enthusiasm; but the expression of a sense of the justice, administered thus, to the assassins."[1] Here, in this vivid prose, Ham Freeman enters the scene; he was about to begin his most ambitious adventure in journalism. His paper, the *Democratic Leader*, had been first on the scene, and by noon on Friday he had had a free "extra" on the streets to thrill "our eager and excited citizens."[2]

Men carried the corpses into the basement of the undertakers, J. S. Frear and Sons.

The August heat in two days was hastening the decomposition of the bodies, and almost as soon as they were removed from the water, their features began to swell and the faces to turn black.

A local photographer, Seneca Bullock, was called. Since he needed plenty of natural light, he had some men lay the bodies on planks and prop them against the barn outside. Crowds of citizens looked them over, but no one was sure who they were. One newspaper reporter derided the curiosity of the crowd: "a procession, including nearly every citizen, woman, school boy, little girl and small dog, marched by the remains."[3]

From Frear and Sons, the bodies were taken to the basement of the courthouse, where they were stripped naked and embalmed at about 10:30 in the morning by Drs. Charles B. Richards and Daniel S. Burr. In the summer heat, it was difficult to keep the corpses cool, and the doctors arranged that a small sprinkler spray them continuously with water.[4]

Coroner John P. Worthing adjourned the inquest examining the death of Merrick until 7:30 that evening. At one o'clock, a new coroner's jury was selected to examine the bodies discovered in the river. Several people testified that they believed that the larger body was that of Jack Chamberlain, a notorious character from a nearby town; no one was quite so certain about the smaller body. A few days later, the coroner's jury was surprised to receive a message from Scranton written by Jack Chamberlain himself: "Don't bury my body till I come on and see to the funeral."

The *Broome Republican* published a detailed list of the contents of the pockets. The larger man's belongings included a glazier's diamond used to cut glass, a train ticket to Batavia, a pair of gold spectacles, and a gold watch stopped at 2:24. The smaller man was carrying some Confederate money, a train ticket to Batavia, a key to Graham's system of shorthand notation, and a copy of *Napoleon's Oraculum.* In addition, there was the evidence left in Halberts' basement: shoes belonging to someone with a "clump" foot, a well-shaped pair of stylish shoes, a hat, a cap, and a "flaming blue necktie . . . nobody remembers having seen lately."[5]

The *New York Times,* on Thursday, had already published an entirely accurate story under the headline "Desperate Encounter with Burglars at Binghamton—A Clerk Shot Dead in the Struggle."[6]

News of the crime spread with astonishing speed.

Amid the tumult and gossip, a coherent narrative of the drama at Halberts' began to form.

Early on Wednesday morning, after the burglars had fled down the stairs and out the back of the store, Gilbert Burrows, one of Halberts' clerks, rushed into the street to give the alarm. (Gilbert and his friend Fred had been stationed at the back of the store as a precaution against just the sort of burglary that had just occurred.) The first person Gil encountered was a clerk at the American Hotel who had heard shots and come running. Soon the fire bell began to toll, and people came out to see what the matter was. Jennie Pierce, who occupied rooms over the store, looked out the back window and saw men stumbling from the rear of the store toward the river. She was not sure if they got into a boat or entered the water on foot; there were some willow trees along the shore blocking her view.

Sam Robertson, a shoemaker, lived just across the Chenango from Halberts'. His wife was awakened by the gunshots and went to the window. She saw three men entering the river.

One bystander had run to Halberts' and saw Fred Merrick drenched in blood. He hurried across the Chenango bridge to find a doctor. "A man has been killed at Halberts'," he said; "you must come right away." Others followed, some encountering a man walking away from town.

"One of them inquired of me if I knew where the fire was. In my excitement I replied, at Halberts' store."[7] The well-informed stroller was Edward H. Rulloff.

Edwin G. Halbert, the proprietor with his brother Delancey of the store at 9–10 Court Street, was roused from his bed as the alarm spread through Binghamton. They had been too many times the victims of thieves, and he hastened to the store. Gil Burrows gave him an emotional and somewhat confused account of what had happened, but there was no contradicting the fact that Frederick Merrick had been shot in the head and that blood and brains were spattered over the elegant counters where ladies usually examined the costly silks that were the Halberts' specialty.

At daylight, Edwin Halbert sent another clerk to Walton, an isolated village some forty miles east of Binghamton, to inform Merrick's mother of the death of her son. Fred had been an only child. In May 1870, he had gone to Binghamton to take up a clerkship with the Halbert brothers. He had been, Ed Halbert told reporters, an unusually dedicated clerk, "remarkable for his energy and the interest he took in his business."

The public inquiry began with the postmortem inspection of Fred Merrick's corpse. When the doctors had finished, J. S. Frear and his assistants placed the corpse in a handsome casket ordered by Edwin Halbert. At 1:30, Ed and Delancey Halbert placed the casket in front of their store, prayers were said, and an honor guard of merchants and clerks formed to escort the body to the Erie station. Accompanying the body to Walton were Edwin Halbert and two of his clerks.[8]

At the same time, posses of men spread out through town. The police did what they usually did when there was trouble in Binghamton. They arrested Charley Van Valkenburg, a local scapegrace. Ham Freeman let readers know that Charley had been at Quaker Lake a week or two earlier and some tools had been stolen that might have been those used to enter Halberts.

Charley was a regular at Hurley's bordello, and his favorite there was a young woman calling herself Susie French. She was deeply depressed and, just before midnight on Tuesday night, about the time the burglars were entering Halberts, she began to dose herself with morphia. An hour or two later, amid the uproar surrounding Merrick's death, she slipped into unconsciousness. When one of the busy Binghamton doctors finally arrived to tend to her, she had died.[9] Though Charley's parents said he had been home all night, it seemed a good time to put him in jail. "It is natural for them to screen their son," Ham reported, "but their high character gives some credit to their statements."[10]

Thursday evening, a patrol saw a man walking along the railroad tracks and stopped him for questioning, but he declined to submit to interrogation. Two young men, Cyrus Stockwell and Frank Jones, took the lead (and would later seek shares of the reward). With difficulty they followed their fugitive to Chauncey Livingston's place, but the farmer threatened them and told them to be off. At last, they were able to get him to listen to their story of the man who had jumped in front of the oncoming train to elude them. Then, with the help of Livingston's hired man, they found the suspect crouching in the outhouse. Ed Crapsey reported the details.

He carried a small satchel in his hand and, having an umbrella, besides being respectably dressed, if he had not refused to stop when first challenged, had not hidden away, or even had not been so incoherent when first arrested, he might have been permitted to pass.[11]

Stockwell, James, and their friends could not get a straight story out of him. What can a man so respectable as to carry an umbrella have been doing hiding in an outhouse at one o'clock in the morning? And why would he not cooperate? Still, there was nothing yet to link him to the murder in Halberts' store.

With Charley Van Valkenburg and the strange man in custody, the investigation went forward, and there was no shortage of suspicious characters. Down at the depot, the vigilantes found a sleeping man. His face was bruised and he carried a bloody handkerchief.[12]

By the time the bodies were discovered on Friday morning, there were three suspects in custody.

Chief Flynn took them from the jail to view the bodies in the courthouse. The corpses presented a doleful sight in the semigloom of that basement, the eye of the larger corpse having been plucked out by Calvin Brewer's hook anchor.

The mysterious man with the umbrella looked at the bodies with perfect composure. He even asked if he could walk around them for the best and most thorough view. No, he said, he had never seen either one of them.

On Saturday morning, Chief Flynn took the mysterious man to the grand jury room, where Coroner Worthing and District Attorney Peter W. Hopkins presided. They thought he was a rural preacher or maybe a teacher. At first he had said his name was "Charles Augustus." Now he said he was George Williams. Even though it was a warm day, he kept his coat buttoned up to the throat, thus lending a respectable formality to the proceedings. He answered their questions in a calm and even haughty voice. They decided that he had no connection to the burglary and murder.

Then an amazing thing happened. Among the strolling curiosity seekers was Judge Ransom Balcom, whose dissent at Rulloff's Owego trial had anticipated the conclusions of the Court of Appeals in Albany in December 1858. Judge Balcom took one look at the suspect and instantly recognized him. "You are Edward H. Rulloff; you murdered your wife and child in Lansing in 1845."[13]

Turning to the coroner's jury, Judge Balcom warned them: "This man understands his rights better than you do, and will defend them to the last."[14]

Hardly daunted, Rulloff confessed his identity.

"There, gentlemen, you have an explanation of my strange conduct. Knowing of my misfortunes in this portion of New York, you can understand why I was anxious, being here accidentally when a murder was committed, to pass through the city without my identity being known. You know the proverb, gentlemen, about the results of giving a dog a bad name."[15]

Rulloff's citation of a well-known proverb was chillingly apposite: "Give a dog an ill name and he is half hanged."

Coroner Worthing and District Attorney Hopkins were persuaded that Rulloff's strange behavior had an innocent explanation. The jurors thought so too, and he was released. He was free.

Rulloff walked out of the Court House and across the street. Though he had said that he had no money, he managed to buy a cap and soon walked briskly away.

Just after Rulloff's departure, Alonzo C. Matthews, treasurer of Broome County, remembered that Rulloff was missing the great toe on his left foot.

This information explained the odd shape of one of the pairs of shoes—an "Oxford tie"—left in the basement of Halberts' store by the retreating burglars. There were some rags stuffed in the place that missing toe would have occupied.

Rulloff was eagerly followed. Just east of Binghamton, Deputy Robert Brown saw him walking fast—110 steps a minute.

BROWN: "Mr. Rulloff, we've concluded not to let you go just yet."
RULLOFF: "What's up now? What new discoveries have been made?"

Brown made him take off his left boot. Sure enough, the foot was deformed, and Brown marched Rulloff back to town. At the jail he was asked to try on those Oxford ties from Halberts' store. They fit perfectly, and Rulloff laced them up in an idiosyncratic manner that attracted the deputy's attention.[16]

Now Peter Hopkins had a connection between the prisoner and the murder, but it was hardly sufficient evidence to secure an indictment. He needed to identify the two corpses and to link Rulloff with the burglary at Halberts'. Besides the shoes, all he had to go on was the fact that Rulloff and the dead man had in their possession train tickets from New York City to Batavia. It was a small beginning but a start nonetheless. It was time to release Charley Van Valkenburg and the man with the bloody handkerchief.

Hopkins had provided the newspapers with the long list of the contents of the pockets of the two drowned corpses, but not a complete one. In October, he set out for New York and took what he thought would be the choice items: six keys, a letter to one Henry Wilson, and a scrap of paper with the name and address of William Thornton, an attorney in Brooklyn.

Arriving in New York, Hopkins met Captain Henry Hedden and Detective Phillip Reilley of the Fifteenth Police Precinct. Crossing on the ferry to Brooklyn, they went to Thornton's law office. From the photograph of the corpses, Thornton immediately recognized and named Billy Dexter and told where he lived.[17] At the Dexter house at 65 Graham Street in Brooklyn, Hopkins and Detective Reilley found Martha Brady. Cautiously, and without identifying themselves as officers, they questioned her. She looked at the photographs they had brought. One of the drowned burglars, she said, was Billy Dexter. He was always getting into scrapes, she said. "Edward C. Howard" was the shrewd agent for her landlord who usually got Billy out of trouble.

The picture of Rulloff, taken after his capture, was then shown, and she instantly exclaimed, "Why, that's the agent!"[18]

A little more detective work produced Maggie Graham's address: 75 Carmine Street in Manhattan. Hedden and Reilley went together and found a sullen Maggie, on her guard since she had known something of the plan and its failure. She had read the papers, and in September she had received a letter from Rulloff asking her to destroy property that might serve as evidence. Reluctantly, she told the officers that Rulloff had been living at 170 Third Avenue. When they got there, they opened the street door with the key taken from Rulloff's pocket. The Jacob family was astonished.[19]

Now the detectives found a trove of evidence. Burglar's tools, papers, even underwear with a launderer's mark that matched that found on the drawers of one of the corpses. From the Jacob family, they discovered that Maggie Graham had been there (on Rulloff's instructions) to collect some of his belongings. From her they next confiscated his great philological manuscript, but she had thrown Rulloff's other shoes into the street and they had vanished.

Peter Hopkins was exultant. He had what he needed to identify the corpses and to link them to the burglary and the murder. And he had Rulloff trapped.

Almost all the fragments found in the pockets of the corpses could now be pieced together to implicate Rulloff. Jarvis was the larger corpse. Pauline Jacob, the teenage daughter of the household, recognized his watch, blue coat, and spectacles. The ball of twine in his pocket matched the string used to tie the "false faces" around the necks of the burglars. Dexter's pockets were even more productive of evidence, most especially the little fortune-telling book, *Napoleon's Oraculum.*[20]

Rulloff described Dexter as a crude man, nearly illiterate. Yet his pockets were filled with poetry, both clipped from newspapers and handwritten, and scraps of paper with shorthand. (Not "Graham's," as first thought, but a system of Rulloff's own invention.)

Napoleon's Oraculum had been given to Dexter by the son of the jailer in Cortland. (The relation between a deputy's son and a prisoner was, chillingly, an echo of Rulloff's friendship with Al Jarvis in the Ithaca jail.) Its full title was *The Oraculum, or Napoleon Buonoparte's Book of Fate,* which commanded a relatively high price even though it was only a few pages long. As everybody knew, Napoleon had conquered Europe, though he was of humble origin and had had little education. People of similar background could use his "book" in the hope of acquiring his nearly magical aptitude for success.

> The book of which the following is a translation, was obtained from Buonoparte's Cabinet of Curiosities at Leipsic, during the confusion which reigned there after the defeat of the French army. It was held by him as a sacred treasure, and it is said to have been the stimulus of most of his speculations, he being used to consult it on every occasion. The translator has several times consulted it for his own amusement; and, however incredible it may appear, he found the answers to correspond with truth, as they afterwards came to pass. To other matters, besides obtaining a knowledge of any understanding, or any answer to a question you propose, are really curious and useful; and such, it is presumed, are not as to be found in any work in the English language. The whole forming a Cabinet of Curiosities and valuable secrets, which have been approved of by persons of respectable literary character.

The slightly garbled quality of the fourth sentence is likely the result of frequent reprinting of his small volume by various town printers, but the overall impression of this prefatory paragraph is that the system has great power and that both the translator and other persons of "respectable literary character" have found it useful.

The system of consulting allows persons of the meanest capacity to use it readily. First a question is chosen from a list of sixteen. Most of these are of a general character: "Shall I obtain my wish?" or "Does the person love me?" Some, however, seem not to be questions daily confronted: "Shall I recover my property?" or "Will prisoner be released?"

The next step is to make four rows of pencil marks without giving conscious attention to the number of marks in each line. That done, "reckon" the number and, if it be even, represent it as two marks, or if odd, as one. The result will look something like ●● | ● | ●● | ● (with the first and third lines an even number) or • | • | • | • (if all the lines contain odd numbers of marks).

It is then an easy matter to consult the table, where the answers to the question asked will be found adjacent to the selected configuration of marks.

There is no way of knowing if Dexter and his friends consulted the *Oraculum* to predict the success of their burglary. Some of the answers produce uncomfortably specific predictions. For instance, the configuration of marks • | • | • | •• for the question "Will the prisoner be released?" yields the answer: "The prisoner will be released by death only." On the whole, however, the *Oraculum* is weighted in favor of optimism. Of the sixteen answers to "Shall I obtain my wish?" one is ambiguous, five are negative, and ten are affirmative.

If Dexter consulted his book for the question "Success in my undertakings?" he might have been forewarned with the pattern •• | •• | • | •: "Your fortune will shortly be changed into misfortune."

7

A Polly-wog Knee Deep in a Jersey Mud Pool

Peter Hopkins, the district attorney—"the Ajax of the prosecution" in Ham's words—was ready to take the murder to trial after Christmas in 1870. He had an abundance of evidence—none of which he was obliged to disclose to the defendant—and he was sure he could prove that Rulloff, Dexter, and Jarvis were the burglars at Halberts' store, that one of them shot Fred Merrick dead, and that any jury would be persuaded by his evidence and his arguments. Rulloff would hang.

Peter Hopkins was meticulous, methodical, and persuasive. According to Captain Hedden of the New York City Police, "Hopkins is worth more as a detective than all the detectives in my precinct."[1] Attorney-General Marshall B. Champlain, already known throughout the state as an eloquent orator, joined Hopkins. Champlain saw an opportunity to enhance his reputation by prosecuting Rulloff himself.

Determined not to become one more in that string of prosecutors who had failed to bring Rulloff to the gallows, Hopkins hired Lewis Seymour to assist him. Seymour was a former member of Congress and a prominent Binghamton lawyer and politician who could be counted to sway local opinion against Rulloff while Marshall Champlain sought favor in the larger sphere of state politics.

To fund his defense, Rulloff's first idea was to write an autobiography—he knew it would be a big seller among the huge, angry following he had gathered over almost thirty years. Thanks to the good sense and deep pockets of his brothers, he did not have to take this course in order to secure a lawyer. After some discreet inquiries, Rulof Rulofson hired a promising young attorney in Binghamton, George Becker. From the day he was admitted to the New York bar (in May 1860), Becker had defended unpopular clients. Never before had he had a client with such a history of transforming unpopularity into hatred.

Becker persuaded Charles L. Beale, another former congressman, who had practiced mainly in Hudson, New York, to join the defense. Unfortunately for Rulloff, Beale was unable to devote the best of his energies to the case due to ill health and family problems. His long-standing relationship with the judge proved of little help, and Beale was not an effective counselor. But it was the best George Becker could do. As Freeman said, "His effort was the brave, forlorn hope of the mariner at sea, in a leaky vessel, with the night and the tempest closing around him."[2]

After consulting with Rulloff, Becker hit on two theories to demonstrate his innocence. Unfortunately they were not easy to argue at the same time. The first was that there was reasonable doubt that Rulloff had been in Binghamton that Tuesday night and Wednesday morning, let alone in Halberts' store, and there was insufficient evidence to convict him of Merrick's murder. The second strategy was to argue that if he had shot Merrick it was only to prevent a felony in progress, namely Merrick's relentless intent to kill Al Jarvis.

Ham Freeman provided a broad and sympathetic view of the problems Becker faced before and during the trial.

> We know that he undertook the case reluctantly, and that he did not seek it, to the detriment of his health and other business; we know that he was promised support by the brothers, which was but reluctantly given, and his efforts but meagerly seconded; that Rulloff at first misled him as to the material facts of the case; that he concealed from him his place of abode, in New York, until the officers of the law had smelt it out, and gobbled everything there of value to them and injury to Rulloff; that people to whom Rulloff sent his Attorney betrayed his confidence; that he was in every way thwarted in his plans for the preparation of the defense, and at last was disappointed in receiving funds promised, in the counsel he expected to assist him on the trial, and some witnesses subpoenaed did not attend, others cleared out, and another misled him willfully.[3]

Becker's main hope, as the trial unfolded, was to be vigilant for technical errors that might invalidate a conviction. It was no help at all that Rulloff, the would-be lawyer, kept inserting himself into the proceedings.

Equally alert to prevent errors was the judge assigned to the case, Henry Hogeboom, from Hudson, in Columbia County.[4] Early in his career, he had successfully prosecuted "the veiled murderess,"[5] a woman convicted of poisoning two of her neighbors by serving them arsenic in some ale. He was not sympathetic to lawbreakers; he expected miscreants to be punished, and every one of his rulings in Rulloff's case would be against the defendant.

Rulloff's trial opened on Wednesday, January 4, 1871.

The prisoner, EDWARD H. RULLOFF, charged with the double crime of burglary and murder, . . . was brought into Court at 9 o'clock, and took his seat with his back to the large audience, but without having been in the least cowed by the concentrated gaze of the multitude during his walk to it. When he had sat down he looked anxiously around. When Judge HOGEBOOM and associates entered[,] a look of dismay overspread his features, which was a moment later intensified when District-Attorney HOPKINS and Attorney-General CHAMPLAIN came in and took their seats. But the next moment a sudden change swept over his face, which was at once illumed with hope and confidence, as his counsel, Mr. GEORGE BECKER, entered, accompanied by Hon. CHARLES F. BEALE, of Hudson, who had been secured to assist in his defense. With the appearance of these gentlemen, the wearisome duties of the day began.[6]

George Becker requested a postponement, but the judge denied the motion.

Jury selection began the next morning.

Judge HOGEBOOM sensibly remarked that in this age of the world it is impossible to find men of any intelligence who have not read the newspapers and learned something of any important case. Juries worth anything must be got from such classes or not at all, and the rule, therefore, must be that when any one summoned as a juror is found to have no settled opinion of the merits of the case, and believes himself to be without bias or prejudice, he is competent, notwithstanding any opinion he may have previously formed or expressed.[7]

Answers to the questions put to the pool of potential jurors did not reflect well on the citizens of Broome County.

> Many ludicrous answers were given to questions put by Court and counsel by verdant gentlemen. . . . Questions alternately by the Court, Mr. Becker and Mr. Hopkins.
> "Have you formed or expressed an opinion as to the guilt or innocence of the accused?" "Yes, sir!" "Your mind is then made up?" "Oh, no—no it ain't." "Have you got any bias for or against the prisoner?" "Yes, I think I have." "Then you are prejudiced?" "Oh, no, not a bit." "Have you heard of this case?" "Think I have." "Have you read about it?" "Yes, in my newspapers." "What newspapers do you take?" "The Binghamton *Leader* and *Gospel Messenger*." "Well, what did those papers say about the prisoner?" "I don't remember all, but one said he ought to be hung, and 'tother said he hadn't." "So these newspapers left you in doubt?" "Yes, sorter so." "Would you decide on the jury according to the evidence, or mere rumor?" "Mere rumor." "Perhaps you didn't understand; would you decide according to rumor or evidence?" "Wall, I guess both would be *keereck*."[8]

Jurors who had scruples about the death penalty were excluded. The first eleven jurors were drawn from the farms, villages, and hamlets of Broome County.[9] But by five o'clock, the panel was exhausted and only these eleven jurors had been chosen. The twelfth man was obtained with the summoning of three talesmen (or bystanders), and the jury was complete after seven hours.[10] George Becker objected, declaring the selection to be "irregular and illegal," and Judge Hogeboom duly noted his "exception." It was the first of the issues to be taken up later by the Court of Appeals.[11]

Prosecutor Hopkins opened the case by describing the gravity of the crime and promised airtight proof based on these facts: that the two corpses pulled from the Chenango were those of Albert F. Jarvis (alias Charles G. Curtis) and William Dexter (alias William Davenport); that they had been in Halberts' store when Frederick Merrick was murdered; and that Jarvis and Dexter had been confederates and companions of Rulloff's since at least 1867.

Instantly Rulloff half rose from his chair, and, plucking his counsel, Mr. Becker, by the sleeve with spasmodic energy, whispered rapidly in his ear, and before Mr. Hopkins could begin another sentence, Mr. Becker rose and objected to the prosecution going beyond the case on trial. Judge Hogeboom said it was impossible for him to prophesy what the District-Attorney was going to say, or to decide a question before it existed, but he presumed it was the intention to keep within the rule. Mr. Hopkins having thus compelled the defense to show to all the world how little the prisoner could afford a scrutiny of the past, went on to narrate one of the saddest episodes of crime ever told in a court-room.[12]

Hopkins told, with all the lurid detail he could muster, the story of the death of Harriet Schutt Rulloff and her infant daughter Priscilla; Rulloff's imprisonment at Auburn; his indictment for the murder of his child; and his residence in the Tompkins County jail in Ithaca. Poor Al Jarvis had then, he said, been "a prattling, innocent ruddy boy" (though sixteen years old),[13] and he had been led by Rulloff's malevolent influence to his death in the Chenango. Hopkins then presented a piece of damning evidence.

Two facts to prove the presence of the prisoner at the scene of the murder were brought into bold relief, but the most convincing was the shoe found in the store, which exactly fitted the malformed foot of Rulloff, and which Mr. Hopkins claimed would fit no other foot in the State. But beyond this startling fact he said he would prove that the prisoner left the house, No. 170 Third Avenue, on the morning of the 15th of August, wearing the identical pair of shoes found in the store. The second fact was equally conclusive, for it was claimed that in the castaway carpet-bag found in the remote field, was a copy of the New York Times, with an article a column long cut out of it, and that in the desk of the prisoner in Third Avenue, a slip was found which exactly fitted the space, which, being an article on the Prussian policy,[14] which, upon examining an unmutilated copy of the issue of the paper, was found to belong in the space.[15]

When he saw the paper and heard Peter Hopkins's argument, Rulloff became animated.

The shoe fact he had long known, and admitted its force against him, but this newspaper slip was a link in the chain of evidence against him which had been forged without his knowledge.[16]

It was after seven o'clock on the first arduous day of the trial. The vast and exhausted crowd dispersed to home or hotel; the lawyers gathered their papers; Rulloff returned to his cell. Peter Hopkins had triumphed in the court of public opinion, and the first newspaper reports detailed Rulloff's prior murders as if they were proven beyond doubt.

The prosecution called as its first witness Gilbert S. Burrows, the survivor of the two clerks assigned to protect Halberts' store. Hopkins began with simple questions, such as where he was from, his age, the location of the store. Hopkins then led Burrows through a detailed description of the night of the burglary and murder.

Gil had retired at about ten o'clock. About half past two, his sleep was disturbed. When he opened his eyes, he saw three men standing at the foot of the bed where he and Merrick were sleeping. Merrick jumped out of bed, and threatened them with his pistol. Two of the men went downstairs; Merrick threw a stool head down the stairs. The third man threw a chisel and hit Gil, leaving him dazed. The fight continued between the two store clerks and the three burglars. Then the third man shot at Gil and then shot Merrick. Merrick crumpled, apparently killed instantly. The burglars ran away, and then Gil went out and gave the alarm.[17]

In his subsequent confession to Ham Freeman, Rulloff did not dispute the material details of Gil Burrows's testimony; he amplified the basic story.

The idea of the robbery had been to arrive in the evening, snatch the goods in the middle of the night, and depart on the early morning train. As the long August Tuesday wore to a close, Rulloff had been worried about the delay: the three conspirators had been in Binghamton for more than a day. (They had slept in the barn at the county poor home on Monday night.) Now, as Tuesday wore on, they were exposing themselves to danger.

And danger came. Early Tuesday afternoon, Rulloff was recognized by the Superintendent of the Poor, Evander S. Spaulding. Rulloff had been a clerk in the pharmacy in Ithaca, and Spaulding had often traded there.[18]

Although Rulloff urged Al Jarvis to go back to New York, Jarvis was determined to make something out of their trip. Dexter said, "Ed, you must go along with us. Al and I can't do it alone."[19] Rulloff hid on an island in the river, while Jarvis unsuccessfully sought a local friend to assist them.[20] Together they decided to continue with their plans for the burglary. At about midnight they walked to the rear of the store and broke in. (Amazingly, Rulloff claimed to have fallen asleep on some timbers while Dexter drilled holes through the door.) Al dosed the clerks with chloroform, and the thieves began to select bolts of silk.

It was at this point that things began to go wrong. According to Rulloff, Jarvis stumbled over something in the basement and fell heavily, waking the two clerks. Rulloff then claimed that he told them that they wouldn't be hurt, but Merrick attacked them.

> I went towards him, saying, "keep quiet, don't make any noise, and we won't hurt you." He paid no attention to what I had said, but snapped his pistol full at my breast three times. Had it gone off, it would have finished me, for at the time I was not more than four feet from him. When he found that his pistol would not go he threw it down and began clutching at my face. I kept backing away from him, holding my pistol against him, and telling him to keep quiet, that I did not want to do him any harm and would not if he would only keep quiet. Mirick [sic] acted like a perfect demon. He paid no regard to what I had said, but kept following me up, making a noise like a wild beast, but not saying a word. . . .
>
> Had we been disposed to hurt the clerks we could easily have shot them from where we stood; but instead of doing that, which we would have been perfectly justifiable in doing, Jarvis drew his pistol and fired it once or twice into the air, hoping to fright them and make them desist from their inhuman treatment of Dexter.[21]

Rulloff claimed that he fired one shot in the air to scare Merrick, who had Al Jarvis firmly in his grasp. When Merrick wouldn't let go, he fired again and Merrick fell forward over Jarvis.

In Halberts' store, there had been a stunned silence. Rulloff froze in awe. Jarvis, badly injured, rose unsteadily to his feet. Burrows was silent as he felt blood trickling down his face from splinters sprayed from the woodwork to his face by one of the warning shots. Rulloff coolly said,

"Come, Pat, we have done enough."[22] He helped Jarvis out of the store, with Dexter following. Then Jarvis persuaded his friends to cross the river, saying that it was very shallow.

As Rulloff helped Dexter, he suddenly found himself in water over his head. He heard Jarvis splashing.

> Dexter could not swim and struggled at once. He clutched hold of me and come near taking me down with him. I succeeded in freeing myself from him. He sank at once and I do not think he came up again. Jarvis had called for help once or twice, but before I could reach him with a gurgling cry he sank within a few feet of me and I powerless to save him.

Rulloff was adept at expressing his memory of helpless desperation, and Ham knew how to play upon the sensations of his readers.

> "Oh! my God! what a night was that!" (The condemned man here gave way to hysterical grief, rocking backwards and forwards upon his pallet and sobbing like a child.) "Ham, I loved that boy, more than any other human being on the face of this earth, and to see him die right before my face in such a manner, and I unable to save him. My God, it was too bad!" (After becoming more composed, he said:) "How I reached the shore God only knows. I only know that at last I found myself lying upon the bank too exhausted to rise."[23]

This confession, with all the details of circumstance and emotion, would not come until March 1871, when Rulloff's hopes of survival were sinking. At the trial, he did his best to conceal or becloud the story. But all these terrible thoughts flooded his mind as he sat in Judge Hogeboom's courtroom.

Initially, Rulloff was not prepared to admit to any participation whatsoever in the robbery of Halberts' store. Peter Hopkins's opening address to the jury had shaken his confidence, but he still hoped to cast doubt on the identity of the dead burglars and to deny any connection with them. Now Gilbert Burrows was asked to identify the pair of shoes found in the basement of Halberts' store. That shoe was the missing link. Rulloff could not let George Becker shape his defense.

Ignoring his counsel entirely, and stepping forward in a voice slightly quavering with age, but in no way moved to excitement, [Rulloff] stated the rule of common law, that he was not answerable for the acts of others until he had been clearly connected to them.[24]

Lewis Seymour, asserting himself in District Attorney Hopkins's support, then rose to his feet and said that all the details would be connected once the prosecution had been allowed to develop its case. Seymour, the wise and senior lawyer, thus provided the master narrative for the benefit of the jury.

Judge Hogeboom overruled Rulloff's objection, at least for the moment, and Rulloff's questioning continued.

> RULLOFF: "What description did you give of the person you supposed to be me?"
> BURROWS: I described you as a person having on a linen coat, black pants, and also as having gray whiskers, as I saw them coming out from behind the mask.[25]

Rulloff questioned Burrows as to the identity of this man.

> BURROWS: "I saw him square in the face when he went down stairs after he had shot Mirrick and come towards me."
> RULLOFF: "By a good light?"
> BURROWS: "You know what the light was."[26]

Ham Freeman reported: "When this answer was given, there was great applause and uproar in the audience."[27] Judge Hogeboom said nothing until George Becker objected. Only then did he admonish the crowd. Ham was incensed.

> Did it not render the trial rather a farce, a mockery of the justice in this American country, which boasts that every man, black or white, is equal before the law? Grant that Edward H. Rulloff was the most guilty man that ever was charged with crime, still the dignity of the law should not have been allowed to be insulted within the sacred precincts of a Court of Justice, by demonstrations of the popular will.[28]

Rulloff again got to his feet and drew attention to some trivial contradictions between the description Burrows had given of the burglars on Wednesday morning and what he had later said.

Douglass Boardman was called to the stand. Peter Hopkins could have called on many witnesses to identify Rulloff's distinctive handwriting, but none would testify with such effect as Judge Boardman. Before being called to the bench, he had defended Rulloff in Tompkins County in 1856 and braved the anger of the would-be lynch mob. The slip of paper containing the mysterious shorthand writing that had been found in Dexter's pocket was introduced into evidence, and Judge Boardman testified that it was in Rulloff's hand. Other papers found in Rulloff's desk in New York were then added to the prosecution's evidence, and Judge Boardman said that these too had been written by Rulloff.

In the afternoon, the first witness was Joseph Fettrich. A New York lawyer, he testified that he had known Rulloff as "E. C. Howard" and produced the five-hundred-dollar mortgage Rulloff had taken on the Dexter property in Brooklyn. (Douglass Boardman verified that "Howard's" signature was in Rulloff's handwriting.) Rulloff had regularly brought payments to his office, Fettrich said.

William H. Osgoodby, a prominent shorthand writer from Rochester, identified another manuscript written in the same shorthand system as the "key" found in Jarvis's pocket: a lecture on phrenology delivered by Rulloff a quarter century earlier at James Gibbs's schoolhouse in Lansing. This sheaf of papers recalled to everyone's mind those days before Harriet Schutt Rulloff and her baby had disappeared.

Jennie Pierson, who lived in rooms over Halberts' store, testified to having seen the men stumbling from the rear of the extension after the gunfire on the night of August 17 and entering the Chenango.

Binghamton chief of police James Flynn described Rulloff's arrest. The satchel with the clipping from the *New York Times,* he said, had been discovered in a swamp about a mile from Binghamton a few days after the arrest. He gave details of the satchel's contents, mentioning that the *Broome Republican* for August 15 was among the papers it contained.

New York City police captain Henry Hedden testified about the evidence found in Rulloff's rooms, including the scrap of newspaper from the *New York Times,* burglar's tools, and more specimens of shorthand writing. The chief article of evidence was a manuscript believed to have been written by Rulloff.

It was produced in court and was received by Rulloff with unusual emotion. He took it and seemed almost to fondle it. He read it and turned the leaves and seemed to have regained a great treasure. . . . "There is the Proof, your Honor, that my occupation does not send me around the country breaking open stores. There is a book that five hundred men in ten years can not produce."[29]

Rulloff seemed not to have recognized that these densely written pages were not of interest in themselves but only as providing the prosecution with a link between the drowned burglars' pockets and his guilt.

Now Peter Hopkins called witnesses to connect Rulloff and Dexter to prove that Rulloff had impersonated a lawyer and had represented Dexter in Cortland when he had been charged with the theft of some silks. Judge Smith from Cortland identified Dexter from the photograph. John T. Barnes, the jailer in Cortland, identified the ring of keys found in the pocket of the smaller drowned man. These, he said, he had returned to "William Davenport" when lawyer "Dalton" had sprung him from prison just eleven months before. Over objections from George Becker, Barnes identified the smaller corpse in the photograph as "Davenport."

Next Edward Jacob identified Rulloff, though he and his family had known him as "Professor Leurio" and regarded him as a sober and studious tenant. His youthful candor made him an effective witness. Except when Rulloff had been absent to attend the meeting of the American Philological Association in July 1869, he had been living with them almost constantly. "He was very studious and worked hard night and day all the time he was at 170 Third ave. He had a library of about four hundred volumes and his regular work was upon the book we have mentioned."[30]

Edward Jacob was asked to inspect a photograph of the two drowned burglars, and he identified the larger man as "Charles G. Curtis," the man who lived with Rulloff in his family's building in New York. He was given the pair of shoes found in the basement of Halberts' store. They were "Oxford ties." Rulloff usually wore Oxford ties, Edward said.

Again, Rulloff insisted on participating in his defense. In cross-examining Edward Jacob, Rulloff paid close attention to the pair of shoes. Once again, Ed Crapsey was sitting close enough to observe details not easily discerned by others.

His efforts were principally directed to making Jakob state that he had worn boots when last at the house, and at last stepping close up to the witness, and speaking in a voice so low that no one heard him but the person addressed, he asked, "Will you swear I did not have on boots when you saw me last at the house?" to which Jakob answered that he could not so swear, nor could he swear to the contrary.[31]

Like Gil Burrows, Ed Jacob was determined to tell the truth as he knew it and no more. He would not say that the valise and the black frock coat were certainly "Leurio's," only that he had had ones like them.

Hopkins then called witnesses whose medical expertise bore on the crime, Coroner Worthing, who had seen Merrick's body at the scene, and Dr. William Bassett, who had led the team conducting the post-mortem.

Here was an opportunity for the defense to raise doubts, and Charles L. Beale asked Worthing detailed questions about the entry of the bullet, its path through the brain, and the likely time of death.

The reporter for the *Ithaca Journal* grew tired of the proceedings. He thought the jury was bored or bewildered by the medical testimony. "It was all as clear to them as to the reporters, and your correspondent saw just why the bullet killed young Mirick as plainly as he could see a polly-wog knee deep in a Jersey mud pool."[32]

8

·······

They Resembled Dead Persons
Very Closely

On Saturday morning, when court reconvened, Court House Square was ringed with buggies and crowded with people, attracted by stories written by the local reporters and by those from New York City. Though he arrived in Binghamton ten days after the verdict in Rulloff's trial, Oliver Dyer, the reporter for the *New York Sun,* was able to re-create the scene that Saturday.

> The feeling against him before and during the trial was envenomed and universal. The inhabitants of Broome county, in which Binghamton is situated, were determined that he should be hanged, and every breeze that blew toward the court room from Tompkins and Tioga counties, where Ruloff was formerly tried for ancient offenses, was laden with hatred and vengeance toward the prisoner. The excitement was so great in Binghamton that business was to a considerable extent suspended. The Binghamton *Republican,* and the *Leader* also, printed nearly a quadruple daily edition during the trial, and sometimes found the capacity of their presses insufficient to supply the eager public demand for their reports of the proceedings.[1]

Hopkins recalled Edward Jacob to the witness stand. He identified the watch and spectacles found in the pockets of the larger of the drowned burglars, as belonging to the man he had known as Charles G. Curtis. He knew them by the cracks in the corners of both lenses.

On yet another pointless cross-examination, Rulloff elicited the fact that, after Captain Hedden's surprising visit, Ed Jacob had gone to the offices of the *New York Herald* to read the story about the burglary and murder published on August 18. But he had not gone on his own initiative. His parents had received a letter describing Rulloff's "misfortune." It was, he thought, from Jane Jarvis.

Now Hopkins did more to show that the three burglars were frequent companions in New York. The Dexters' tenant, Martha Brady, confirmed the identification of Rulloff as Howard and testified that he had vanished after having collected her rent for August. She confirmed that one of the dead men in the photograph was Billy Dexter.

Pauline Jacob, Ed's sister, then identified "Mr. Leurio" as Rulloff. She identified the letter that had come for "Charles Curtis" with the notation on the outside that it should be opened if he were not there. A worried Jane Jarvis had written to her son. Pauline then identified the undergarments Detective Reilley had confiscated from the belongings left behind at her house. They had a laundry mark, "J. A. No. 3," and Pauline had seen "Curtis" carefully writing those marks with indelible ink. She had wondered, she said, why he used those initials when his name was "Charles G. Curtis."

Though Pauline's sympathy for Rulloff was bravely stated, she also confirmed that Rulloff and Jarvis were intimate companions. She had last seen them leave the house on the morning of August 15. She looked at the "stereoscope" of the drowned men and identified Jarvis as the taller one.

John Dexter identified his brother as the smaller of the two drowned men and said that he had often seen him in Rulloff's company. He recognized the larger as "Curtis." And he identified Rulloff as "Jim Howard." Helen Jarvis Wardwell, Al's sister, testified that she had corresponded with her brother (using his real name) at 170 Third Avenue. Joseph Jarvis, Albert's uncle, and Orlando B. Welch, a clerk at the Ithaca Hotel,[2] confirmed his identity from the photograph.

The former sheriff of Cortland County testified that Rulloff, posing as "Dalton," had come to represent "Davenport." He had offered a bribe of five hundred dollars to let "Davenport" escape.

Rulloff leapt to his feet to object. What possible relevance could such testimony have for the present matter? "Mr. Hopkins said that his object was to show that the prisoner took more interest in Davenport than attorneys usually do in clients, as he was ready to spend money for him."

Rulloff testily replied: "I would do as much for my client as you, provided I had the money of a county at my command," and he ended the episode by remarking, *sotto voce:* "Damn such evidence."[3]

The sheriff's twelve-year-old son told of sending to New York for a copy of *Napoleon's Oraculum* since the bookstores in Cortland did not carry it and Davenport wanted one. He said the copy found in the pocket of the smaller drowned man looked to be the same book.

Now Peter Hopkins brought all of his physical evidence together. Elmer W. Bingham said that he had found the shoes, the bits, and other articles at the rear entrance of Halberts' store. Eugene Simmons, age twelve, testified that he had found a carpetbag in a field under some stumps in August. Henry Simmons, his adoptive father, detailed the contents of the carpetbag, and his description was affirmed by Benajah S. Curran, a lawyer who had been present when it was opened. The drawers found in the satchel—with the marks "No. 1 and No. 2"—corresponded to those worn by the drowned man. Two experts on shoes testified to the probability that the shoe was Rulloff's. Edgar G. Stone testified that he had seen Rulloff in the Lewis House around noon on August 16. He thought that Rulloff might have been a detective sent to watch "a couple of curious hard looking men" hanging around the hotel.

Delancey Halbert described the precautions he and his brother had taken following the robbery the previous May—among them moving the sleeping cots of the two clerks to a more strategic place in the store. He thought that the silks the August burglars had bundled up might have been "ten or fifteen hundred dollars worth."[4]

On Monday, Hopkins dealt with the discrepancies between Rulloff's present appearance and Gilbert Burrows's description, at the coroner's inquest, of the third burglar.

> This evidence was rendered necessary by that complaisance of the sheriff, which had permitted Ruloff to shave off a portion of his beard, and perhaps, dye the remainder, so as to materially change his personal appearance.[5]

When Dr. William Bassett had testified on Friday afternoon, he admitted, under cross-examination, that Merrick might have survived the gunshot wound to the head. To counter the argument that Merrick might have died of natural causes, Hopkins brought Dr. David P. Jackson to the witness stand, who testified that Merrick "exhibited none of the symptoms of a person suffering from heart disease, but he did show all the signs of a person dying from compression of the brain, caused by a pistol-shot wound."[6]

Details about Rulloff's capture and arrest—particularly Rulloff's studied indifference when invited to view the corpses of the two drowned burglars—were provided by Deputy Sheriff Robert Brown. To counter any deception, Brown said, he had placed his hand on Rulloff's chest to see if he could detect any change in respiration or heartbeat. He felt nothing out of the ordinary, no more, he thought, than would be normal for someone looking hard at two sodden and bloated dead bodies. He also testified about the events of the coroner's jury: Rulloff's pretending to be "George Williams"; his sudden identification by Judge Balcom; his release until Alonzo C. Matthews recalled that Rulloff had a deformed left foot; the pursuit and capture.

Dr. Daniel S. Burr testified about the condition of the two drowned men, admitting that a change of eye color after death might account for the discrepancy between the black eyes of the larger corpse and the blue eyes that were remembered by witnesses who knew Al Jarvis. Under cross-examination, he admitted that he had not tried to fit the odd left shoe to either burglar's foot but he had noticed no deformity when he had examined the feet of the corpses.

George Becker had little idea of what to do on Rulloff's behalf. The line of defense that there was doubt that his client had been in Binghamton was shattered, nor was there any question that he had been with his "pals"—the word *pal* in those days meant a criminal's accomplice—in Halberts' store. When Daniel Burr cited a medical authority in support of his opinion that eye color changes after death, Becker tried something extraordinary. He attempted to show that Rulloff had been mistreated while in custody.

Peter Hopkins and the sheriff had wanted to photograph Rulloff, but he had resisted them mightily, distorting his countenance, winking his eyes, and shifting his head. They tried to control him by pinching his ears with blacksmith's tongs, and finally Dr. Dan Burr forcibly drugged him with chloroform. He remained "under" for an hour, and it was then that the photographs were taken.[7] Such testimony did little to project an image of Rulloff as an aged savant mainly concerned with arcane learning. What possible innocent reason could he have for resisting so strenuously the taking of a photograph?

Edward Jacob was called to the stand for a third time to testify that the middle drawer of Rulloff's desk was secured by a lock (and opened with the key found in Rulloff's satchel) and that it was in that drawer that the burglar tools were found. Pauline said that Rulloff's spare boots had been in the closet in her house after he and Jarvis left that Monday morning. Something had become of them between that time and when Peter Hopkins and the police officers arrived in October.

Now all Hopkins had left to do was to present a few additional details. Sheriff Martin reported that Rulloff had cut up his silk stovepipe hat and torn his shirt into tiny pieces and then stuffed them in the toilet the night after his arrest. He remembered Rulloff greeting Gil Burrows sympathetically, saying, "Young man, I am glad to see you; you was very badly used, and I hope you will be able to find out the man who did the depredations."[8] Thomas Johnson, a Binghamton constable, described finding tracks of two men—one wearing rubbers, the other with stocking feet—leading from the rear of Halberts' extension down to the Chenango.

Now Hopkins called upon Phillip Reilley as his last and most dramatic witness. Detective Reilley linked the drowned burglars and much of the physical evidence.

Found a bureau drawer where this key fitted; this key fitted a smaller box; this letter (shown) was found in the small trunk in No. 10 Graham street, letter offered in evidence was as same identified by Judge Boardman as being Rulloff's writing.[9]

That letter, dated 1865 in Rulloff's handwriting, was addressed to William T. Dexter. It clinched the connection between them.

George Becker's discouragement must have turned to despair when Rulloff stood to cross-examine Detective Reilley. Rulloff had first damaged his defense by expressing raptures over his manuscript; now he was happy to lecture the court on improved drill bits using the one found at the back door of Halberts's store as an example. Rulloff could not resist preening when he had a chance to demonstrate his own genius:

[T]he prisoner then with permission explained that the instrument was valuable and interesting as the model of a new invention, but it appeared upon redirect that in the same drawer were two dozen bits which fitted this "model."[10]

Peter Hopkins was entirely satisfied with his case. Credible witnesses had linked every detail. Discrepancies in Gil Burrows's identification of the third burglar hardly mattered now. Absurd conjectures, such as the idea that Merrick had died of a bad heart rather than a bullet in the brain, could be easily dismissed. Dexter and Jarvis had been repeatedly identified by people who knew them well, and both were shown to be Rulloff's companions. Rulloff's cooing over his manuscript or celebrating his invention of drill bits only bound him closer to the evidence and to the murder in Halberts' store. Just to be sure of everything, Hopkins brought Seneca Bullock to the stand to verify that the photographs he had taken of the drowned burglars were accurate. This testimony led to an unexpected wrangle. After describing how the bodies had been arranged, George Becker continued his examination:

"Do you think they had the appearance of having been in water some time?"

BULLOCK: "Yes, sir."

"Was not the clothing on these persons wet?"

BULLOCK: "Yes, sir."

"Did not their faces have a bloated and distorted appearance?"

BULLOCK: "I think they were bloated and discolored in places."

"They didn't look natural?"

BULLOCK: "They looked as natural as could be expected under the circumstances."

"I asked whether they looked natural?"

BULLOCK: "I never saw them previous to that time, and I could not tell you."

"Did they have the natural appearance of dead persons?"

BULLOCK: "They resembled dead persons very closely, I should judge."[11]

This persistent interrogation had no obvious point. The drowned burglars didn't look "natural"; they looked dead, and no arrangement of the bodies in front of the camera would gainsay that fact.

When Seneca Bullock was released from the witness box, the defense team moved to strike his testimony and the photograph. Judge Hogeboom denied the motion.

If the defense could discredit the pictures, it would call into question the string of identifications based upon them from Sheriff Isaac W. Brown in Cortland (who recognized Dexter) to Orlando B. Welch of Ithaca (who recognized Jarvis). But the techniques of photography were entirely familiar to everyone. Rulloff himself had ordered a portrait in Meadville back in 1858, and it had been used to identify him after that theft from P. R. Bennett's jewelry store in Warren.[12] Everyone understood how photographs captured light and shade. Only legal practice had not acknowledged them.[13]

With the conclusion of Seneca Bullock's testimony, Peter Hopkins declared the prosecution at an end. It was shortly after three o'clock on Monday. In just over three days, he had presented forty-one witnesses, and he was sure that he had built a persuasive case. It only remained to discover what defense Rulloff and his lawyers could mount against it.

Despite everything, George Becker maintained the ground that he had laid out in his opening: that Rulloff was nowhere near Binghamton on August 16, 1870, but if he had been there (and had been in Halberts' store) his crime was not murder in the first degree but manslaughter.

[T]he killing of Mirrick, by whoever done, was not murder, but at the worst only manslaughter in the second or third degree, because Mirrick himself, when killed, was in the commission of a felony, in using unnecessary violence upon an intercepted felon, and that the slaying was done to suppress that violence. In declaring what the defense expected to be able to prove, Mr. Becker said that it was almost wholly upon the testimony of J. B. Lewis before the coroner that the prisoner was held. On that occasion Mr. Lewis swore that on the evening of the 16th of August, a man in laboring dress entered his store and asked for the best whiskey without regard to price, which man he held to be Edward H. Ruloff. Since that time, however, and while Ruloff had been in jail, the same man had appeared in his store, and proved to be a drover from the West. Further, Mr. Becker said they would be able to show when the prisoner left New York, and that he went to

Batavia, Buffalo, and other places, so that it was impossible that he should have been in the city of Binghamton on the night of the 16th of August, 1870.[14]

George Becker spoke for an hour and a half before beginning to call his witnesses. Unfortunately for Rulloff, several whom he had expected to appear did not respond, and thus there were no witnesses to support Becker's claim that Rulloff had been in Batavia, Buffalo, or any place other than Binghamton.

Francis L. Farnham testified that between ten and eleven o'clock on the morning after the burglary, Gil Burrows, the principal witness for the prosecution, had told Farnham that he could not identify the burglars. But on cross-examination, Peter Hopkins elicited the fact that Gil had not even been in the store when Farnham claimed he had talked to him there. Rulloff's first witness was a flop and probably a publicity-seeking liar.

The second witness was hardly better. Becker hoped to show that the emotional and frightened Gil was too hysterical to give a coherent account of what had just happened, even in the simplest details, and could not therefore be regarded as reliable when he identified Rulloff as the third burglar. Lyman Clark, the clerk at the American Hotel opposite Halberts' store, said that he was sitting at the door of the hotel when he heard gunfire. Curious, he got up from his chair and was walking briskly toward Halberts' when another shot was fired. Moments later Gil burst from the front door crying "Murder." Chief Flynn, who was sleeping upstairs at the hotel, soon joined them and tried to learn from the excited clerk what had happened. Gil had said, Clark testified, that they would have to go around to the back door to get into the store since the front door was locked. Having just seen him come out the front door, Clark and Flynn tried it, discovered it open, entered, and turned up the gas to find the bloody body of Fred Merrick.

Martha Brady was recalled to the stand. The defense hoped to show that she was motivated by hatred of Rulloff and was lying in her previous testimony. Once again she testified that Rulloff (as "Howard") had collected rents from her, the Dexters, and other tenants of the house. She knew a woman named Haggarty who kept "improper company with men" in her room, and she had caused her to be arrested for "dissolute conduct." She admitted that Rulloff had criticized her for doing so, telling her that he had just managed (in his guise as a lawyer) to get Haggarty released from prison.

George Becker seems to have called whatever witnesses he could see among the crowd in the courtroom. Pauline Jacob told of a boy of three years or so, Stafford Crosby, who regularly visited Rulloff in the summer of 1870 and that she saw him with Maggie Graham too. She thought that Jarvis (or "Curtis" as she knew him) was likely to adopt him since the boy's father had died and his mother decamped. If this testimony had any point at all, it was to show that Rulloff was a peaceful scholar concerned with the welfare of children. But it drew him even closer to Jarvis.

The last three witnesses of the day testified to the reports that Gilbert Burrows had given on the morning of the murder. Virgil Whitney, another guest of the American Hotel, recalled Gil saying that Merrick had been shot by "them drunken Irishmen." He remembered the confusion about the front and the back door. Albert Jewell remembered it too, and so did James Hart. On cross-examination, Hart said Burrows "was no more excited than any one else would have been." He had not seen much "pluck" in the excited clerk.

The conference of the lawyers with Rulloff on Monday evening must have been glum. It seemed unlikely that the witnesses who had failed to appear earlier in the day would be there on Tuesday, and the witnesses who had testified had done little to shake the case presented by the prosecution. George Becker knew they would have just one more day to try to save Rulloff.

In the morning, Becker again tried to discredit Gil's identification of Rulloff as the third burglar. It did not go at all well. No witnesses appeared who would swear that Rulloff was elsewhere.

Thoroughly discomfited by this first effort of the day to prove something favorable to the prisoner, Mr. Becker traveled off into a discussion as to the possible relative position of the burglars and their antagonists during the struggle, as judged from the holes of the pistol shots in the walls, desiring to show that one which struck the wall six feet from the door had been fired from the front door, and not from the head of the stairs, which fact would invalidate Burrows' evidence. When Mr. Lewis E. King was stating emphatically that when himself and Burrows stood before the door of

Rulloff's cell the prisoner unhesitatingly picked out Burrows by the direction of his voice and eyes, a round of applause burst from the audience for the third time during the trial.[15]

The old eminence Charles Beale now intervened on Rulloff's behalf.

[I]n a few eloquent remarks [Beale] referred to these manifestations of popular prejudice, and asked the protection of the Court for the prisoner. Judge Hogeboom, in reply, said that he could apologize for the indignation of an honest public, not, as he believed, against the prisoner, but at the enormous crime; yet this was a Court of Justice, not a popular assemblage, and a place where the auditors were not privileged in any way to participate in the proceedings. He was therefore compelled to reprove these manifestations of public feeling, and to insist that they should not be repeated.[16]

Now George Becker called for the medical witnesses who had earlier appeared, and, though they were not in court, they were expected.

Rulloff took advantage of the lull in the proceedings to move that all the evidence linking him to Jarvis and Dexter be discarded because it did not prove his connection to the burglary.

If it could be proven besides the work on my book I had been engaged in thieving, there might be some proof connecting me with the burglary, but a person engaged on that book cannot be presumed to be engaged on any other work.[17]

Rulloff cited an 1855 case, *People v. Thoms,* that raised the issue of how a conspiracy might be proved. Thoms was a counterfeiter, and the police discovered a fragment of a false bill among the belongings of his wife. Could it be presumed that she was a party to the crime? The judge had said that it could not on the evidence of "fragments of notes" and in the absence of other circumstances. It was right of the lower court, he said, to have excluded it.

Rulloff wished to apply the case in his defense. Just because Dexter had that scrap in his pocket with the key to Rulloff's shorthand system, there was no reason to introduce it as evidence that they had been partners in the burglary. Nor was the 1865 letter among Dexter's belongings in Brooklyn any more compelling in showing that they were in Binghamton together in August 1870. Rulloff might rattle the chain of this evidence, but he could not break it. Letters and receipts did stretch back to 1865, but the most recent, a rent receipt to Martha Brady's husband, was dated May 1, 1870. All were in Rulloff's hand.

Rather than merely ruling on Rulloff's motion,

> Judge Hogeboom speedily interrupted him, and referred to the evidence of Burrows that the prisoner, to the best of his knowledge, was one of the three burglars, and that the evidence of the shoes also connected him with the crime. Ruloff was utterly unabashed by this revelation of the appearance of the opinion of the Court, which was fatal to his hopes, and went on with such calmness and clearness that a stranger could not have supposed that he was arguing for himself.[18]

Charles Beale was appalled. The judge had just treated the essential elements of the prosecution's case as if they were irrefutable facts. Rulloff might be grasping at straws in adducing the Thoms case, but he could hardly be punished for reaching for it.

"Mr. Beales [*sic*] then followed in a masterly, eloquent, and affecting speech in support of the motion."[19] Simply sharing the same dwelling did not imply a conspiracy, he said, and the learned judge had made that point entirely clear in *Thoms*. Edward and Pauline Jacob's testimony demonstrated that many people had access to Rulloff's desk, including themselves. The burglar tools were not discovered until the officers searched the desk in October, and anyone could have put them there. The same was true of that copy of the *New York Times* with the essay about Prussia. Judge Hogeboom said he thought that there was sufficient evidence of complicity between Rulloff and the two burglars to allow these exhibits to be considered by the jury.

In desperation, Beales fell back to the second line of argument—that the killing of Merrick had been only manslaughter since the burglars were acting in self-defense. This would be a matter for the jury, Judge Hogeboom said.

> And further, the Judge referred pointedly to the fact that the two of the men ran back upstairs from the basement, and asked why they did so.[20]

By this time, Dr. Daniel S. Burr had arrived in court and was called to the stand. Rulloff allowed him to inspect his feet, and Burr itemized what he saw in great detail. Rulloff persisted in a lunatic line of questioning: where Peter Hopkins had been satisfied with the word *toe,* Rulloff paraded his learning.

> RULLOFF: Is the protuberance you spoke of on every natural foot, that is the first phalanx you mention; the joint of the left phalanx, that is always a protuberance?
> DANIEL BURR: Yes, sir.
> RULLOFF: Even in Mr. Hopkins' elegant foot?
> DR. BURR: Yes, sir.[21]

This tedious recital of foot trouble was swiftly dealt with by Peter Hopkins on cross-examination: "Where the end of the toe is gone it would fit this shoe?" Burr: "Yes, sir."[22]

Now the defense was in a state of near collapse. Somehow, Becker had discovered one H. A. Hayes, whose qualifications as a witness seem to have been that he too had missing toes, and Becker led him in a discussion of his condition. Hopkins asked him on cross-examination if the shoes in evidence belonged to him. "Those shoes are not mine," Hayes said.

Becker now wanted to bring Drs. Bassett and Thayer to be examined, but they were not present in court. On those grounds, Becker moved that their testimony be excluded in its entirety. His motion was denied.

Becker recalled Edward Jacob to the stand and asked if he had ever seen a pistol among Rulloff's belongings. Edward Jacob said that he had not, but that he had seen cartridges.

Becker had no more witnesses to call. The ones he had examined, wrote the reporter for the *Ithaca Journal,* might equally have testified for the prosecution. The evidentiary part of Rulloff's defense had been a catastrophe.

Now Charles Beale got to his feet. There was nothing in the evidence that he could rely on and little in the law. Consequently, he spoke for three hours mainly about emotion and compassion. Rulloff had been compelled to mount a defense with no money to bring witnesses from afar, while the prosecution had the unlimited resources of the taxpayers at command. There was no denying that Rulloff was acquainted with Dexter and Jarvis, and he did not try to refute the idea. Yet, he said, the testimony of Gilbert Burrows was so inconsistent and unsure that it could hardly be relied upon in judging what had happened in Halberts' store. Gil had been in a frenzy, afraid for his own life, and shocked by the bloody death of his friend. All that Burrows had said, both at the coroner's jury was doubtful, inconsistent, and unreliable. He did not blame the young man for his high feelings and scattered memories, but he urged that Rulloff not be sent to his death on such testimony.

Beale described Rulloff's scholarly endeavors in New York, the affection felt for him by Edward and Pauline Jacob, his kindness toward that pitiful orphan child, Stafford Crosby. It was absurd that such a man would engage in petty crimes. Someone had put those burglar's tools in Rulloff's desk, Beale hinted darkly; someone bent on finding proofs of criminal habits in an innocent man. The shoe might have been worn by anyone, he declared. These were the principal links in the chain of evidence, and none of them were entirely credible; taken together they could not put the matter beyond a reasonable doubt.

Having dismissed the evidence, Beale now turned to the law. There had been no premeditation in Merrick's killing, even if Gil Burrows's story was taken at face value. The burglars felt no malice toward Merrick, and he was shot only as a means of saving Jarvis and Dexter from death.

The more he talked, the more Beale drifted away from the evidence and the law. Outbursts from the public made a sham of courtroom decorum, he said. The many women present were animated by a "morbid curiosity," and they were no better than the "unrefined women of old" who cried out for death in the bullrings of Spain or the gladiatorial combats of ancient Rome.[23]

> His speech as a forensic effort was admirable, but as an argument it was without value. Mr. Beales [sic] seemed to feel the hopelessness of his cause, for he concluded with the beautiful allegory of the creation of man at the prayer of Mercy; and, picturing the lonely, friendless, penniless prisoner at the bar, asked the jury to temper justice with mercy.[24]

At nine o'clock on Wednesday morning, the judge invited the prosecution to present its closing. Attorney-General Champlain had prepared himself for rhetorical exertions. The front rows of the benches were filled with reporters poised to take down his words and telegraph them across the state and even the nation. It was a wonderful opportunity for a rising politician.

Brushing aside his own celebrity as an attorney and fame as a state official, Champlain reminded the jury and the wider public that he was just a plain lawyer doing the people's business. He would summarize the law and the facts, since that was all that needed to be done.

Rulloff had not been the victim of the rigors of the law but a beneficiary of its concern for justice, however slight the doubt might be. In a sheering reference to Rulloff's Canadian birth, Champlain said he would not have enjoyed the freedom to conduct his own defense or to be allowed to question witnesses "in the country from which this man came as an exile."

America was a great country, famed for justice, and its citizens paragons of virtue. Champlain reproved Charles Beale for comparing the women present in the court to the bloodthirsty spectators at the Roman coliseum.

> The learned counsel is mistaken in the sentiment that brings the ladies here. They are not animated by such brutal and unnatural instincts; they come in search, rather, of objects over which their sensibilities may expand themselves and their sympathies weep. Although by their presence here they may have partaken, somewhat, of that aroused public indignation at the enormity of this crime, and the desire to have it ferreted out and punished, they partake, in a large degree, of the anxiety to see, as described by the counsel, one of the most extraordinary men of this age.[25]

Champlain summarized the evidence and the law in a straightforward narrative, omitting, of course, any inconsistencies in Gilbert Burrows's identification of Rulloff, the possibility of shots coming from the front of Halberts' store, or the likelihood that Frederick Merrick had died as a consequence of heart failure brought on by fear.

Burglars do not enter stores, he said, with the sole purpose of stealing valuables; they are animated also by "another latent, guiltier, slumbering, conditional intent, that if they are resisted or detected, that they slay the person who thus resists, or attempts to detect them."[26] The three burglars were not, then, merely thieves, but murderers with their intention held in reserve against necessity. Consequently, Merrick's murder was implicitly premeditated, and, hence, the only proper verdict was guilty of murder in the first degree. And since the murder was carried out as part of a "confederation and a conspiracy" to murder, it did not matter who fired the fatal shot.

Champlain reviewed the evidence that Rulloff, Jarvis, and Dexter were old pals, and he told the story of the burglary in chronological order, from the departure of the three from New York on Monday to the arrest of Rulloff early Friday morning. What was the evidence that they were in Binghamton on August 16? The fact of the drowned burglars being in the Chenango for "two or three days" was evidence enough for the presence of Jarvis and Dexter. But could the jury be certain that the corpses in the river were indeed Jarvis and Dexter? Here Champlain itemized the clothing they wore, the contents of their pockets, and the satchel found under some brush. He mentioned the undergarments and recalled Pauline Jacob's testimony about seeing "Curtis" mark them with initials. He produced the spectacles found in Jarvis's pocket and reminded the jurors that his sister Helen had put them on before identifying them as his. Dexter's clothing and the contents of his pockets were also surveyed, especially the keys that opened the Dexters' door in Brooklyn. He gave particular notice to Dexter's "Fortune Teller," the *Oraculum*.

Anticipating the question that would form the basis of the appeal, Champlain turned to the photographs that had been used to confirm the identities of Jarvis and Dexter. Isaac Brown, the former sheriff of Cortland County, had recognized "Davenport" by examining that photograph of the drowned burglars with a magnifying glass. Could the photograph be regarded as reliable?

Here Champlain did not state the question in so bald a form, asserting merely: "Thus art and invention is made a mighty auxiliary in the investigation, detection and punishment of crime—'Alas! that star-eyed science should wander there, / To bring us back the tidings of despair.'"[27] (These lines are from Thomas Campbell's *The Pleasures of Hope,* a long poetical disquisition interrogating sorrow, disappointment, and mystery. All these, Campbell asserts, contain within them, however indistinct it may appear, some trace of "hope.") Soaring from poetry to polemic, Champlain declared photography to be a kind of divine gift. Science does not explore the heavens and find mere vacancy but in some profound way transmits a message of optimism. In other words, photography has nothing to do with "deception" and everything to do with "truth"; thus it had become a "mighty auxiliary" to the search for solutions to mysteries.

But what about Rulloff? There were the burglar's tools found in his desk, and Champlain recalled Rulloff's delight in describing them to the court. The drill bits found in that desk matched the ones at the back door of Halberts', and the room in which they had been left had been locked from the time of Rulloff's disappearance until it was opened by the officers in October. (Champlain ignored the evidence that Maggie Graham had entered it in the meantime.) As to Rulloff's presence in Binghamton, there was the testimony of Evander Spaulding, who had seen him on the afternoon of August 16.

J. B. Lewis had identified Rulloff as well, recalling the man who purchased liquor from him that same Tuesday evening. Champlain suggested that the supposed "drover from the west" who turned up when Rulloff was in jail might well have been an accomplice who dressed as Rulloff and, after the event, came to Lewis's place of business merely to confuse him. This supposed ruse, he said, had failed, and Lewis had confidently testified that the man he had seen was Rulloff.

Champlain dramatically traced Rulloff to the fetid darkness of Chauncey Livingston's outhouse.

> [H]e thought he saw in his outhouse, which was in plain view a few rods away, a deeper shadow than natural; and as the pupils of his eyes were dilated by the darkness and his vision became stronger, he went there and discovered the prisoner hid, and, he has described to you, the evidences of guilt that he exhibited.[28]

The shoes found in Halberts' store came in for scrutiny, and Rulloff's mutilation of his shirtfront and hat as a failed attempt to conceal incriminating evidence. Rulloff's shirt was stained with Merrick's blood. He described Rulloff's unfeeling indifference when asked to view the two drowned burglars. He was, Champlain said, responsible for their deaths: "Who placed these ill-fated youths on that rude bier?"[29]

Champlain described the murder in the most dramatic terms.

> Ruloff placed his brutal hand upon the neck of Myrick, turned the head and fired the shot which carried the ball into Myrick's brain. The poise was steady, the aim was deadly. Here is deliberation; here is unity of action and intent, co-operation of mind and deed.[30]

"Premeditation," the very key to the charge of first-degree murder, was here present, he said; all that the law requires is a moment of premeditation, and, as he told the story, Rulloff behaved deliberately and thoughtfully. The idea that Rulloff turned Merrick's head slightly was an embellishment Champlain made to the testimony, and that hypothetical slight adjustment of Merrick's head was the key to his case.

Could the jury believe Burrows's testimony and his identification of Rulloff as the shooter? Champlain presented the callow Burrows as the very type of truthfulness.

> Gentlemen, the reason I believe the testimony of Burrows is, because I cannot disbelieve it. If Burrows was what he is not, if he was brought here from some slum, some den of pollution, covered all over with sin and shame, and had sworn to this relation, I should have to believe it. Every fact and every circumstance in this case throws a concentrated ray of light upon the scene, and points to this man as the leader in the plot, and present in its execution.[31]

Now Champlain directed attention to Rulloff himself. He speculated that had he directed his talents to the service of society he would have risen to the highest ranks and would have contributed immeasurably to it. He could have been "a benefactor of his race": Instead he had defied society and attempted to destroy it.

Nearly two hours had passed and he promised that he was close to his conclusion. He spoke again of the glorious United States, the nation where Rulloff had sought refuge from monarchy. How did Rulloff repay the generosity of the country that had received him? By attacking the body politic.

> That country, thus wounded, through her aroused magistracy, turns upon him, and, though he were an intellectual giant, binds his limbs with chains, brings him to the bar of public justice, and demands that he be sent to the scaffold. We demand this verdict in the name of society, whose peace he has violated; in the name of the public law, which he has offended; in the name of the memory of this pure and spotless youth, sacrificed in the faithful discharge of a high trust; in the name of every obligation, public, private, moral and religious, that you should let no consideration turn aside the uplifted arm of the law from falling on the guilty head.[32]

9
········

The Doom of Death

Marshall Champlain, having reached the height of his address, slowly subsided, doubtless feeling entirely content with his performance. There had been no need of a long speech, he had thought, since the evidence and the law were so persuasively linked, and he had satisfied himself (and the jury) with speaking for just under two hours. The densely packed crowd was satisfied too.

Judge Henry Hogeboom now commenced his charge to the jury.

> *Gentlemen of the Jury:*—We have now arrived at the close of this protracted investigation, and the fate of the prisoner is about to be committed to your hands. The testimony has all been taken. You have listened to it with patience and attention. The arguments of counsel have been heard. The court is about to submit to you a few remarks in regard to the law and the facts of the case, and then the solemn duty will remain to you to pass upon the life or death of the prisoner. He has been indicted for the murder of Frederick A. Mirrick, on the seventeenth day of August last, in the store of the Halberts, in the city of Binghamton, and it will belong to you to determine the fact as to whether he is guilty of that crime or not.[1]

Two differences between legal procedure in the 1870s and those of today are immediately apparent. Judge Hogeboom did not allow opposing counsel to brief him on instructions to the jury. Instead, he pressed forward with the charge and anticipated "exceptions" to be offered once he had finished. The judge also felt obligated to give his own view of "the law and the facts of the case," showing how one interacted with the other and what weight the jurors might wish to give to them.

In the usual way, he stated the definitions of *murder* and *manslaughter*. First-degree murder, he said, requires premeditation but no fixed duration between the "perfected design" and the assault. Second-degree murder occurs "in the heat of passion" and involves "circumstances as to constitute excusable or justifiable homicide."

Deliberating about a human life was serious and solemn business, particularly in this case, he said. But Judge Hogeboom's recital of the facts was laden with judgments and conclusions.

> You will scarcely have any doubt that the discharge of this pistol shot was the cause of his death. It seems to me very idle to say that he might have had a heart disease, or he might have had a very delicate constitution, or a nervous organization; nothing of that kind is in proof. We have here an apparent and sufficient cause for death. We must treat these subjects in a practical light. We must take the facts as they come to us.[2]

The judge urged the jury not to be "frightened at mere possibilities" but to use common sense. The "practical light" thrown on the circumstances had, implicitly, only one explanation: Rulloff was the third burglar. Gilbert Burrows's testimony linked them. "Who was this man?" the judge asked.

> Was it the prisoner at the bar? Burrows thinks it was. He is the only living witness produced upon this occasion who survives to tell all of that transaction. Mirrick has gone to his last account. The prisoner, if he was present, has not been sworn, and Burrows is the only person who relates the incidents of that night. He says that the third burglar in his opinion was the prisoner.[3]

Judge Hogeboom raised the question of why Rulloff had not appeared as a witness on his own behalf. George Becker rose to his feet to object, but Judge Hogeboom motioned him to sit down. Only later would he allow Becker to speak.

Bolstering Champlain's eloquent identification of the third burglar, Judge Hogeboom declared that only two people living could describe what had happened in Halberts' store. Burrows, he said, "had the best opportunities for observation and for knowing that face, of any living man, except the prisoner himself, if he were there, and he gives you the results of his observations."[4] The clause "if he were there" is buried deep in the grammar that alleges that there were two living witnesses: Burrows and the third burglar, the one with the gray chin-whiskers. Was Burrows right in identifying Rulloff? Witnesses, he allowed, are sometimes mistaken in identifying persons they have seen. It was up to the jury to decide if Burrows had been mistaken.

Judge Hogeboom then discussed the physical evidence upon which the jury might base a verdict: Dexter's shoes found at the back door of Halberts' store, the cap belonging to Jarvis. But the most important piece of evidence were those Oxford ties.

There were two pairs of shoes at the foot of the stairs, doubtless taken off to prevent noise when this transaction was going on. One pair of these shoes is claimed to belong to the prisoner at the bar. This seems to me a most important item of evidence; for, if they did belong to the prisoner at the bar, what must be the inference you are to draw from that circumstance? Now, it is sufficiently established, you will probably conclude, that he wore, formerly, such a pair of shoes—in 1869, at Cortland, and in 1870, at New York, where he lived—that he was more or less in the habit of wearing such a pair of shoes; that they were somewhat peculiar in their form, either originally made so, or acquiring that peculiar form from the character of the feet. The indentations at the toe of one of the shoes, and the protuberance at another part of it, is claimed to fit exactly the foot of the prisoner, and to have been tried on by him, and fitting him as the witnesses state. To whom do these shoes belong? If they were the prisoner's, what is the inference? If they were not the prisoner's, whose were they? Is there any other person to whom they are proved to belong? If they were not the prisoner's, where are the prisoner's shoes? Are they in New York? They are not. What has become of them? If these belong to the prisoner, the question is answered: they are here produced before you. Since August 15, these shoes have not been seen in the city of New York. Since August 16 or 17, at least, the prisoner has been here. Where are the prisoner's shoes, if not here? That is the question for you to answer. That is a very important element in the investigation of this crime.[5]

These facts and these inferences are entirely reasonable, but no modern judge would feel free to select these facts and draw these inferences. The shoes might well fit Rulloff's feet, but was he the only person imaginable whom they might fit? How could one be certain that Rulloff's Oxford ties were no longer in New York City?

Having given great weight to the most persuasive piece of physical evidence, Judge Hogeboom then recounted the stories of those who recognized Rulloff on August 16: Spaulding and Lewis. He raised no doubts about the identifications given by these two, but only asked the question: "What was he doing here?"[6] Dexter and Jarvis were certainly in Binghamton; their drowned bodies proved that fact. And he asked, rhetorically, once again: "Was Rulloff here?" Certainly, he said, Rulloff was seen skulking around Binghamton, trying to avoid "public observation."[7]

With this, one of the newspaper reporters jotted down another of those bouquets of grammatical fragments that gave so vivid an impression of the events.

> You can scarcely doubt that there were three men; and on the very night following this burglary, Rulloff was arrested. About twelve o'clock at night, he was commanded to stop—refusing to do so—endeavouring to escape—retreating to an outhouse— avoiding observation—detected—arrested—taken to this place and examined—refusing to disclose his name, or giving a false one—sometimes George Williams, sometimes Leurio, sometimes Howard, sometimes Dalton, sometimes Charles Augustus, now Edward H. Rulloff. He refused to give an account of himself. Why, in the dead of night, was he traveling away from this place? What was this man of scholastic pursuits and domestic and retired habits, doing here upon that occasion?[8]

Judge Hogeboom's early success as a prosecutor was everywhere apparent in his charge, and Marshall Champlain must have been pleased to hear oratory that echoed his own in condemning Rulloff.

Returning to the question of Rulloff's deceptions on being arrested, the judge raised again the issue that he had neither testified under oath nor provided some explanation of the events cast in so damning a light by the prosecution.

> It is true the prisoner is not bound to be sworn. It is true, the prosecution is bound to make out their own case, and must satisfy

you by evidence on their own part; but all of these things you have a right to consider, and draw your own inferences from them.[9]

Here he seems to invite the jurors to draw inferences from Rulloff's failure to give sworn testimony in his own defense.

Now Judge Hogeboom returned to the chronology of the crime: the departure of Rulloff, Jarvis, and Dexter from New York; the witnesses who identified the bodies from the photograph taken by Seneca Bullock; the clothing known to be theirs; the newspaper clipping found in the carpetbag in the swamp and the corresponding remainder of the page discovered in Rulloff's desk; the burglars' tools; the keys found in Jarvis's pocket when his corpse was pulled from the Chenango, the duplicate set found in his satchel; the doors at 170 Third Avenue, New York, containing the locks they opened.

This long recital disposed of the question of Rulloff's whereabouts. Of course, he might have been elsewhere, but Judge Hogeboom did not feel obliged to add more than a question mark to the evidence that placed him and his companions in Binghamton and in Halberts' store.

At last, the judge turned to the second line of defense put forward on Rulloff's behalf—that if he were in the store, his crime constituted only manslaughter, not murder in the first degree. He quoted the law: "Every person who shall unnecessarily kill another while resisting an attempt by such other person to commit any felony, shall be deemed guilty of manslaughter in the second degree."[10] The felony in question was attempted murder: Merrick's deliberate and intentional effort to kill Albert F. Jarvis.

This line of argument produced no sympathy in the judge's mind.

> Burglars who appear at the bedside of sleeping clerks are not entitled to the most careful handling of their persons lest some injury be done to them. It was proper for the clerks to protect their own lives. It was proper for them to protect the property of their principals; and it is for you to say whether it was not proper for them to judge from appearances as to the ulterior purposes of these men, found under such circumstances in this store at night.[11]

To reach a conclusion that Merrick's murder was an incidental consequence of the law-abiding burglar's attempt to prevent a felony, the jury would first have to conclude that the clerks themselves were felons. How this would be possible is hard to imagine. Merrick had been presented by the newspapers and by the prosecution as a paragon, scrupulous in the discharge of his duty and assiduous in protecting the property entrusted to him. Burrows, though rattled and confused as he burst from the store, was similarly virtuous. The two honest youths could hardly be seen as felons. Judge Hogeboom called them "manly and faithful sentinels."[12]

Rulloff's case was a small instance of a larger idea that animated nineteenth-century America: that good would triumph over evil. This idea was fully developed as Judge Hogeboom drew toward his conclusion.

> With these facts and circumstances thus developed in evidence to lead your minds to a particular result, they furnish but another illustration of the great truth, that "truth is mighty and will ultimately prevail." She may be for a time defeated and overcome— she may be obscured by the clouds of ignorance, of sophistry and of falsehood, but she will ultimately assert her supremacy, and shine forth in the undiminished brightness of her nature; coming from God as her source—returning to him as her ultimate aim, she meanwhile walks majestic and serene in all the pathways of human action; bringing light out of darkness, and order out of confusion, and sooner or later asserts her irresistible power in all the transactions of men.[13]

Judge Hogeboom concluded by reminding the jury that "mathematical certainty is unattainable." He repeated with great emphasis the words *reasonable doubt,* and drew the jury's thoughts to the consequences of acquittal.

> If in this investigation that conclusion is favorable to the prisoner, it will be your appropriate and pleasing duty to discharge him from imprisonment, and leave him to the admonitions of his own conscience, and to the impressive lessons of this hour.[14]

What pangs of "conscience" should Rulloff feel? Surely if he were innocent, his conscience would hardly be troubled at all. And what would those "impressive lessons of this hour" be? Surely that by dint of his own genius he had weaseled out of yet another crime.

Judge Hogeboom did not draw the jury's thoughts to the principal consequence of conviction: that Rulloff would be hanged.

> If, after the same patient attention to, and solemn consideration of the testimony, you shall be obliged to bring your minds to a different result, and declare his guilt, I have no doubt you will do it with the same solemnity—the same fearlessness—the same impartiality, which should characterize in all cases the actions of men placed under the solemn responsibility under which you act.
>
> In this confidence, gentlemen, I commit this case to you for its final disposition.[15]

There was a solemn silence in the court when Judge Hogeboom spoke these words. His charge had taken about an hour.[16]

Peter Hopkins had been keeping careful notes as the judge spoke. His associate, Lewis Seymour, took the opportunity to have the judge repeat the elements of the charge most supportive of the prosecution: that there was no defined interval between intention and deed required for premeditation. Only seconds might separate a deliberate from a spontaneous act.

Rulloff's lawyers provided the grounds for a charge less than first-degree murder.

> That if the person who fired the shot fired it not to take life, or with malice, or a premeditated design to take life, but simply to rescue his companion—and the jury may infer this from the shots fired over the heads of Mirrick and his adversary, and lodged in the wall—if they infer it was fired by the one who shot Mirrick, then the jury should not find a verdict of murder in the first degree.[17]

Judge Hogeboom then addressed the jurors and agreed that they might find circumstances to mitigate the violence of "the person," "the one who shot Mirrick." Here was a narrow path by which Rulloff might escape the gallows, and Becker and Beale did their best to point it out to the jury. The judge patiently explained.

> You must find a premeditated design to effect death. You must find something more than a mere attempt to rescue, before you

can convict of murder in the first degree. I have given you the rules which should govern your action upon this subject and I have no occasion to change.[18]

Now it became vividly clear why Marshall Champlain had introduced that entirely hypothetical adjustment of Merrick's head just before the shot was fired. That moment, that "instant," was enough to sustain a verdict of first-degree murder. But there was no evidence whatsoever that the shooter had placed a "brutal hand upon the neck of Myrick, turned the head and fired the shot." These were merely Champlain's oratorical fictions.

Now an elderly and infirm Charles Beale argued on Rulloff's behalf. He went tenaciously forward in developing the idea of the unnamed shooter as a rescuer, and the judge allowed him to do so. Over and over again, Beale presented the idea with an increasing emphasis on the rectitude of the burglars in the face of the violence of the clerks.

That in itself, their return for this purpose was lawful and right. It was, in fact, an act of duty to assist and rescue their comrade, and it became criminal only by the excess of violence employed on their part in suppressing the violence of Mirrick and of Burrows.[19]

Charles Beale had abandoned any attempt to raise doubts about where Rulloff had been on that August morning. Now his only hope was to persuade the jury to find him guilty of a lesser charge, one that did not lead to the gallows.

Finally proceedings drew to an end. Everything was said if not done.

It was nearly one o'clock, and the jurors were granted a midday meal. They were taken from the courtroom under the protection of three officers. Rulloff was returned to jail. "The halls of the Court House," Ham reported, "and the path to the jail has every day been lined by people, all eager to have a sight of the notorious criminal."[20]

To the spectators, it seemed reasonable that the jury would take a decent interval to reach a verdict, and no one grudged them a dinner at the expense of the public. But as two o'clock came and then three, people began to worry that the obvious decision would not be made.

Hiram Mosher, a merchant and well-known auctioneer in Binghamton, had his hands full as foreman of the jury. Almost immediately after they were sequestered, the first ballot was taken. When the slips of paper were counted, everybody agreed that Rulloff was guilty of something. But what?

On the second ballot, eight voted in favor of a guilty verdict on the charge of first-degree murder—that Rulloff had formed a deadly intention when he turned Merrick's head and fired the shot. But three jurors were in favor of the charge of second-degree murder. One juror was apparently convinced that Rulloff's shot was an attempt to save his former pupil from Merrick's deadly embrace, and he voted for manslaughter.

They continued their discussion before agreeing to vote a third time. Now the majority in favor of the first-degree verdict was nine, but three stuck to the lesser charges.

On the fourth ballot, the vote shifted to ten to two. On the fifth ballot, eleven to one.

Inside the jury room the majority was even more confident that the first-degree verdict would prevail, but outside there was a growing fear that Rulloff would be freed. Weeks before, Will Schutt had boasted that a posse of two hundred men was prepared to come from Tompkins County to take justice into their own hands if the jury should fail to find Rulloff guilty. Word had spread that the minister of the First Presbyterian Church in Binghamton had "advocated in guarded terms the right of the citizens to take vengeance into their own hands in case the ministers of justice failed to carry out the people's wishes in the case of Rulloff." Newspapers competed vigorously in spreading such rumors.

George Becker had heard the rumors of a lynch mob too. He informed Sheriff Martin of the danger, and the sheriff, his deputies, Mr. Becker, and his clerks armed themselves to protect the prisoner.

Finally, the jury took a sixth ballot. The verdict was unanimous after four and a half hours of deliberation.[21]

Most spectators who had found places to sit in the morning had remained in the courtroom. The first indication that something was about to happen was when Sheriff Martin began to clear spectators from the seats where the jury would sit.

Judge Hogeboom asked the sheriff if the jury was about to return, and he confirmed that they were. The lawyers arrived, Rulloff was brought back from the jail, and the jury filed in. It was six o'clock. There were few lights in the courtroom. The atmosphere was gloomy and filled with tension.

Joseph L. Johnson, Judge Hogeboom's clerk, asked the foreman, Hiram Mosher,

"How say you: do you find the prisoner at the bar guilty of the murder whereof he stands indicted; or not guilty?"

MOSHER: "We find the prisoner guilty."

JUDGE: "Guilty of what?"

MOSHER: "Guilty of Murder in the first degree."[22]

There was a burst of applause from the spectators. Judge Hogeboom promptly suppressed it and had little difficulty in doing so since the emotion expressed by the outburst combined relief with a solemn sense that Rulloff would now certainly be put to death.

Clerk Johnson polled the jury. Each man answered "Guilty."

According to Ed Crapsey, Rulloff himself sank back into his chair, "seemingly for the first time overpowered and exhausted."[23] The reporter for the *Ithaca Journal,* though, declared that "he assumed the appearance of one entirely unconcerned, and unaware of the nature of the verdict."[24] Other reporters noted Rulloff's "imperturbable coolness," his "stolid and indifferent" manner as he heard the verdict.

Becker moved for a stay of the proceedings so that the verdict might be appealed on legal points. To allow him to consult with Congressman Beale, who was unwell and had not returned to court that evening, Judge Hogeboom granted the stay until the next day. Arguments could be made in the morning on this motion, and then he would sentence Rulloff.

Ed Crapsey regularly embellished his narrative with remarks on Rulloff's aplomb: "He recovered himself, however, almost immediately, and in a few minutes was led back to his prison, undismayed by the words of doom, walking with a firm tread and uncowed demeanor."[25]

On Friday, January 12, Court House Square was crowded with curious spectators. A rumor spread that Rulloff's friends had broken him out of jail, and he had escaped. The solemn parade from the jail to the courthouse quelled any such fears. Among the lawyers and deputies, there was Rulloff.[26]

Promptly at ten o'clock, Judge Hogeboom entered his courtroom. In support of his motion to postpone, George Becker argued that, since the Court of Appeals would next sit in Albany beginning February 7, there would not be time to prepare the briefs on the many exceptions that had been entered in the course of testimony. Peter Hopkins disagreed but thought that no harm would be done to the prisoner if the execution were set for a time after the Court of Appeals had convened.

If some further delay were imposed by the Court of Appeals, that would serve the ends of justice.

Appeal first; hang second. Only in the hysteria of the conviction would such a sequence need to be recited.

Judge Hogeboom agreed. More than a week had been devoted to this case, he said. The jury was clear in its verdict, and he saw no reason for that the case should not be promptly concluded.

> The Court then directed Rulloff to stand up. The prisoner arose quickly, with a nervous start, and looked into the face of the Judge with a steady gaze. It was not the gaze of a man embarrassed, or abashed, or yet afraid, nor did the look of the prisoner indicate a bold defiance.
>
> It was rather a mixture of the stolidity of the Mongolian, and the sensitiveness of the Teuton, with very little of the consciousness often exhibited under similar circumstances, by persons born and reared in this country. (Rulloff is said to be a native of the Province of New Brunswick.)[27]

Judge Hogeboom asked Rulloff if there was anything he had to say as to why he should not have the sentence of death pronounced upon him.

Rulloff's reply was a model of grammatical evasion. In his answer, he buried as deeply as he could any hint of agency. "It is not deemed desirable to say anything at present."[28] Who *deemed*? Who *desired*? Who would *say*? And when would a better occasion for such an explanation arise if not "at present"? Rulloff did not elaborate on this odd sentence.

Judge Hogeboom began his declaration with a celebration of the farmers and mechanics who had constituted the jury.

> Edward H. Rulloff. The judicial investigation which has occupied the continuous attention of this Court for several days past, and in which you have been the central object of interest, has been brought to a close. You have been tried for the willful murder of Frederick A. Mirrick, on the 17th of August last. A jury was most carefully selected, after great deliberation and patience, which brought into the panel a body of men seldom surpassed for apparent intelligence and fairness. They have bestowed upon the case the most patient attention, and have apparently brought to its final disposition a conscientious consideration of all the facts and

circumstances bearing upon its ultimate result. The cause has been conducted on both sides with great learning and ability.

You have been defended by counsel of distinguished talent and eloquence, and you have yourself, to a considerable extent, personally participated in the legal discussions and examinations incident to the conduct of the case. Whatever you may think or know of the propriety of the final results, you must feel assured that there has been no lack of ability or earnestness displayed in your defense.

After a week of the most deliberate and careful investigation on the part of those concerned in the conduct of this case, the jury have pronounced you guilty of murder in the first degree. That verdict stands, for the present at least, as the judgment of the Court, and must be followed by the sentence of the law. That sentence is now our duty to pronounce.

We do not desire to add a single unnecessary pang to the painful sensibilities of this hour. The throng of bitter memories, which crowd upon the anguished head at such a moment are of themselves well nigh enough to overwhelm and crush it.

It is, however, not improper to remark, even at such a time, that the killing of Mirrick was perpetuated under circumstances of peculiar atrocity, and though he is beyond the reach of human sympathy, we do not deem it amiss to record in this public manner our sense of his noble and unfaltering fidelity to the interests committed to his care. Nor do we deem it proper to recur to your past history. We only know of it as it is registered in the judicial annals of our State, and to some slight extent in common tradition.

If there be anything in it to stir up painful memories, they are doubtless indelibly impressed upon your mind. The commission of crime carries its own punishment with it, and the agonies of remorse and the sting of a guilty conscience can no more be permanently expelled from the human heart than the vital current which courses through it.

These are things of the past. "Let the dead bury the dead." It is not the past, but to the future your thoughts should be directed. The past is irrevocable. No earthly power can reverse its history. The future may have a gleam of hope even for the outlaw and the felon. To that future we counsel you to devote the remaining hours of your life.

If we have committed no mistake, they [that is, the remaining hours of Rulloff's life] must necessarily be few—all too few, even if rightly employed and not curtailed by the inexorable demands of justice, to make fitting atonement for the misdeeds of the past. Let the remnant of your life be devoted to that task. There is mercy in Heaven for the penitent and the contrite. We may not be able to bestow it here. But in that final tribunal, whose judgments cannot be reversed, and from whose decisions no appeal can be taken, the secrets of all hearts shall be made known; the untold history of all lives shall be revealed, and our doom forever sealed.

It does not belong to us to assume the functions of the ministry of religion, and we therefore refrain from further comment or suggestion. It is no pleasant duty which the law imposes upon us. But it is nevertheless a duty, and we cannot shrink from its performance.

We are commissioned and required to pronounce upon you the doom of death. The sentence of the law is that you be remanded to the county prison, where you have been incarcerated; that you be there confined—and that on the third day of March next, between the hours of 10 o'clock in the forenoon and 2 o'clock in the afternoon, within the walls of that prison, or within a yard or enclosure adjoining thereto, you be hung by the neck until you are dead.

And may God have mercy on your soul.[29]

That was the end. Spectators rose in murmured silence, and the courtroom quickly emptied.

Now the newspapers were full of stories of Rulloff the Murderer, and both facts and imagination conspired to make his life a fable. Though the jury had found him guilty of one murder, that of Merrick, it was easy to enlarge the number of his crimes and to transform him from a failed burglar to a fabled grotesque, "a monster of unequalled monstrosity," one Binghamtonian said. Harriet and Priscilla were his victims, of course. What Judge Hogeboom called "the common tradition" had defined them so, and the jury had been invited to consider those deaths a quarter century earlier as virtually certain instances of Rulloff's murderous career. Then there was Will Schutt's wife Amelia and daughter Amille. If five were not a number large enough to satisfy the craving for corpses, the deaths of Al Jarvis and Billy Davenport could be added too, as reporters speculated that Rulloff had deliberately drowned them to remove impediments to his own escape.

Ed Crapsey unearthed some old news. On the night of February 14, 1865, three burglars had invaded a silk trimmings factory on Thirty-fourth Street in New York, and the watchman, Philip Kraemer, had been so badly bludgeoned that he died soon thereafter. The fact that Rulloff was in jail in Wethersfield, Connecticut, at the time was perhaps not then known to Crapsey, but he did discover that in 1869 Rulloff, using the name E. C. Howard, had brought some silks to that very factory to be dyed. Crapsey was circumspect, attributing the murder of Kraemer to Rulloff only in the "minds of many."[30]

Counting Kraemer brought the total of Rulloff's victims to eight.

Only in the twentieth century was the feeling of guilt made the foundation of much mental illness and the explanation for many kinds of odd behavior. Rulloff's repeated blunders in his crimes were inexplicable to the nineteenth century, and no contemporary observer would have thought to search Rulloff's youth for their origin—either in some event connected with the death of his father or in the repressive home life provided by his mother and grandmother. Instead, the explanation must lie in his "nature," his race, or his "blood," even in the mark of Cain upon his brow. It might be that he was a "Mongolian" or perhaps a "Teuton." Somewhere lay the key to the mystery. No one doubted that it could be solved if only Rulloff would confess and open his dark heart for inspection.

Newspaper speculation concluded that he would not do so and that the details of his motives and of his other crimes would go with him to the gallows. If his character were to be discovered, he would have to face the certainty of death squarely and fully, and this he would not reasonably do until all legal recourse had been exhausted. Uncertainty, energized by speculation, stimulated sensational and national publicity. The week following the verdict, the *National Police Gazette* made Rulloff the murderer of the month with vivid woodcuts of the crime and grim portraits of the principals.[31] Rulloff was about to become an international celebrity.

At the same time, George Becker began to write feverishly. From Judge Hogeboom's court, his next step would be at the general term of the Supreme Court in Albany. Claims for which there had been no evidence at trial could not be argued on appeal, so the promised alibis placing Rulloff in Batavia or Buffalo or any place but Binghamton could not be presented.

While Becker was engaged in the appeal, Oliver Dyer arrived in Binghamton. Knowing that Rulloff was unwilling to talk to journalists, he persuaded George Becker's young assistant, Newell Whitney, to provide him with an entrée to Rulloff.

Mr. Whitney advanced to the cell door, shook hands through the grate, and immediately engaged him in conversation. The prisoner sat on the foot of his bed, close to the open iron work door, in which was fastened a small hand-lamp; on a stool in front was a manuscript, evidently laid aside that instant. The small sharp eyes of Rulloff were so intently occupied scanning the face of the counsel, that I passed unobserved behind the latter and took my position directly opposite the door, with Rulloff's figure and face in full view, the latter fronting obliquely to my left. Here I watched and listened for several minutes. The prisoner cross questioned the counsel sharply upon the progress of the appeal, laying much stress upon some points prepared by himself, and wished mainly to know if their importance had been fully appreciated and considered in the action thus far taken in the appeal. When this was firmly settled in his mind, he said in confidence that the Court could not do otherwise than grant his appeal, and when the counsel expressed the belief that an impression would be created in his behalf that would benefit him in a new trial, he said in a laughing and exultant manner, "I would not give twenty-five cents for all the sympathy or feeling that could be invoked for me if I can only be allowed full swing to carry on the defense." He is willing if a new trial be granted, to plead guilty to murder in the second degree, and this is the point of his appeal, that he is guilty of no higher crime. While conversing with the counsel he seemed perfectly sane, self-possessed, and sensible, but of course intensely in earnest.[32]

While the published story in the *Sun* was "conscientious," it was far from "impartial." It provided grounds for believing that Rulloff had been railroaded by the passions roused against him, and many metropolitan readers of the paper met Rulloff for the first time in Dyer's report. They were ready to believe that the rubes of Binghamton had committed an injustice.

Since George Becker was still raising doubts about the evidence, it was hardly helpful to have a major newspaper publish Rulloff's apparent willingness, if given a chance, to plead guilty to murder at less than the first degree. But if Dyer betrayed him on the legal side of his case, he did much to arouse interest in Rulloff's theory of language, an aspect of the case soon to reach national prominence. This theory, he wrote,

> when understood rightly, contains much that is attractive, and would, were it divested of the prejudice its author's career attaches to it, attain a certain degree of popularity among curious students of words, if not with more advanced philologists.[33]

It was an angle on the story that the *Sun* would shortly pursue in much more detail.

Just a few days later, George Becker and Charles Beale appeared on Rulloff's behalf in Albany, opposed once again by Peter Hopkins.

In his brief, Becker did his best to reverse the sympathetic portrait of Merrick and Burrows. In the first wave of the assault, Becker said, Burrows had entirely disabled Dexter so he was no longer able to resist but was prostrate on the floor of Halberts' store. So violent was Burrows's attack that he had testified that his blows to Billy's head with a box chisel were "hard enough to kill any body but an Irishman or a nigger." (These were precisely the words used by Burrows in his testimony.) Like Merrick, Burrows had reached immediately and effectually for Dexter's testicles and thus held him "foul" while hitting him with the chisel. Burrows had testified, and there was nothing to contradict him, that Dexter "could not have got away without help." The feisty clerk, as he proudly declared, knew how to hoe his own row when it came to a fight.

As the two other burglars retreated down the stairs, Merrick called upon Burrows to "despatch" Dexter, and, just to ensure that the helpless man would play no further role in the combat, Merrick struck him with a metal stool top so hard that he "forced one of his eyes from its socket." Burrows thought that they had spent five or ten minutes in their effort to subdue Dexter. At some point in the struggle, he had said, Dexter had "hollered" to his companions for help.

Al Jarvis ran up and attempted a rescue, but Fred Merrick was not to be outdone by his fellow clerk in violence. Becker recounted what had already been luridly reported by the papers: Jarvis was bent back over the counter, and Merrick had one hand at his throat and the other grasping his testicles. Jarvis, Becker's brief declared, was "entirely at his mercy and in his power."

At last the third burglar came to a belated rescue, ascending the stairs and firing three warning shots from his pistol. Burrows, struck by flying splinters from the stair railing, believed himself shot and fell back, but Merrick was undeterred by the gunfire and continued to inflict agonizing pain on Jarvis. The third burglar then shot Merrick in the head, perhaps from a distance of three inches, perhaps further. (Dispute over the presence or absence of powder burns on Merrick's hair was never quite settled. Whether his death was immediate or delayed by as much as an hour was never resolved by the evidence.)

Portraying the clerks as violent brutes who fought foul was Rulloff's best line of defense, and Becker made every effort to portray Merrick and Burrows as crazed maniacs whose bloodthirstiness could be sated only with the deaths of Dexter and Jarvis. Here was nothing like "noble and unfaltering fidelity." Here was a whirlwind of murderous violence.

Becker then turned to less passionate issues. Every "exception" entered by Rulloff and his counsel at trial was carefully summarized: the selection of a talesman for the jury; the failure of Drs. Bassett and Thayer to appear when Becker called them to testify in Rulloff's defense; the admissibility of the evidence brought from Rulloff's desk in New York; the dispute over Seneca Bullock's photograph of the drowned burglars; the nuances of Judge Hogeboom's charge, particularly whether he had invited the jurors to hold against him Rulloff's decision not to give sworn testimony. One by one these matters were considered, and George Becker's attempts to have them declared "errors" failed time after time.

The main hope for Rulloff lay in the argument that when the two clerks awoke, the tables were turned, and the burglars stopped being felons and began to be victims. But the judges of the supreme court were not swayed. The supreme court embraced Judge Hogeboom's view that armed burglars are implicit murderers and will kill wantonly to achieve their ends. If Merrick and Burrows had been successful in "despatching" all three burglars, they would have been hailed as heroes and guardians of the Halbert brothers' property.

Oliver Dyer's story in the *Sun* encouraged the opinion that Rulloff had been unfairly treated, and George Becker was willing to use the press to gain more sympathy for his client. He let it be known that "day to day" in the course of the trial he had received death threats. The doctors who had conducted the autopsy on Merrick's corpse had been afraid to appear for cross-examination. The people of Broome County were hysterical: "The people cried out as in the days of old, 'Crucify him! Crucify him!' and they seemingly would take no other answer but one that satisfied their demand."[34]

On February 21, having deliberated after two days of arguments, the supreme court affirmed Judge Hogeboom's conduct of the trial and allowed the verdict of the jury to stand. March 3 remained the date for the hanging, and Sheriff Martin ordered printed invitations for those to be privileged to watch it.

Newell Whitney, Becker's young associate, and the faithful Ham Freeman broke the news to Rulloff.

> The Binghamton *Leader* says that its editor, in company with Mr. Whitney, of Rulloff's counsel, visited him in his cell on Wednesday [February 22], and found him as usual reclining on his couch, and engaged in reading. He had not before heard the decision of the Court, and his counsel for the first time informed him. He exhibited no visible emotion, but received the report with that same coolness, and maintained during an hour's conversation that calm self-possession which has ever characterized him since his arrest. He expresses the fullest confidence in the justice of his position, and that the Courts will yet release him.[35]

George Becker was not ready to give up either. As soon as the court had made known its decision, he asked one of its judges, Josiah T. Miller, to issue yet one more "writ of error." Judge Miller declined on the grounds that the Court of Appeals was in session and Becker's request should be directed to that tribunal. So Becker speedily did, and the presiding judge assigned the matter to Judge Martin Grover. Judge Grover too denied the writ. Still Becker persisted in his efforts, and finally Chief Judge Sanford E. Church directed that he be heard again by one of his colleagues, Judge Charles A. Rapallo, in New York City.

Ham Freeman applauded the decision.

> Accordingly counsel appeared before Judge Rapallo, in New York City, and the application and arguments were patiently

heard. Judge Rapallo very wisely decided to grant the application. He thought that in a case of so much importance, where there was even a doubt as to the correctness of the legal decisions upon the trial, that the prisoner should have the privilege accorded to every one of laying his case before the highest judicial tribunal in the State. Some people were foolish enough to find fault with this decision of the learned Judge, and one of our exchanges [that is, a newspaper Ham received in return for sending the *Leader*], printed away up in the wilds of St. Lawrence County, demanded that he be *impeached.* Yet we believe that Judge Rapallo still continues to be a member of the Court, and that no articles of impeachment have, as yet, been proffered, notwithstanding the fury of its blood-thirsty back-woods editor.[36]

On February 28, at noon, Peter Hopkins, Charles Beale, and George Becker appeared at Judge Rapallo's residence, 17 West Thirty-first Street. George Becker argued familiar points: the question of the photograph, the admission into evidence of the burglar's tools found in the Jacobs' house, the violence against Rulloff's two companions. He added, further, that the hatred against Rulloff in Binghamton had made it impossible for him to gain a fair trial there. Peter Hopkins countered that the supreme court had already heard all these arguments, and Judge Rapallo allowed that the jury had settled the issues of substance in its deliberations.

Nonetheless, Judge Rapallo saw an opportunity for rulings by the Court of Appeals that would settle some questions that might be raised in further litigation, particularly in fixing the law on the use of photographic evidence, which he declared was "entirely novel in criminal practice and of great importance generally." He said he had "not the least doubt" that the jury had reached the right decision, but these legal issues needed to be settled.[37]

With Judge Rapallo's signed opinion in his pocket, George Becker took the night train to Albany. There, early Wednesday morning, he went to the clerk of the Court of Appeals and obtained his signature and the seal of the court. Now Judge Rapallo's paper had legal force, and Becker immediately took the train for Binghamton, where he filed the writ with the county clerk and delivered a notice of it to Sheriff Martin. At five o'clock in the evening, George Becker sat down, exhausted, to breakfast.

Judge Rapallo's decision disturbed the expected course of events, and many people were fearful that Rulloff might again go free on a legal technicality. In Ithaca the Schutts and their friends were especially worried. The *Ithaca Journal* tried to be reassuring, expressing a view that echoed that paper's response to the lynch mob of 1859.

> We have no fear that Rulloff will, after all, escape his just punishment. Those so fearing are lacking confidence in the security and correctness of our laws. The very remarks of Judge Rapallo in granting the writ of error must dispel all hope on the part of Rulloff. All that he can possibly gain is a few days time. And that the law gives him. Let us all bow before its majesty and sustain its decisions.
>
> We all in this community believe Rulloff guilty. Judge Rapallo in granting the writ of error, also proclaims his belief in his guilt. Whatever our individual views may happen to be as to the propriety of hanging for murder, there seems to be very few who are not ready in Rulloff's case to confess their acquiescence in that extreme punishment. But we trust all are willing, when they reflect, to await patiently while the case is duly tested by all the forms and safeguards of the constitution and the law—relying upon the sufficiency and power of the law and courts to detect crime and punish the criminal.[38]

There was not much time for Becker to meet the inflexible deadline set by Judge Rapallo. But thirteen days were enough for him to prepare his papers, and he was assisted again by Charles Beale and now by a lawyer new to the case, R. E. Andrews of Hudson. Marshall Champlain, perhaps alarmed that Rulloff's case had not already been settled and the prisoner hanged, returned to help Peter Hopkins. On March 13, all the lawyers were ready to argue the case.

No new issues were raised in the many eloquent hours spent in rehearsing the facts and the issues of the appeal. The judges were further presented with the huge trial record and all of the documents that had accumulated since the appeals had begun.

On March 28, the Court of Appeals issued its decision.

> There was no error of substance committed upon the trial; and the judgment must be affirmed, and the proceedings remitted to

the court below, to proceed upon the conviction and pronounce sentence of death as prescribed by law.[39]

It must have pleased Judge Hogeboom that the judges pointed to aspects of his charge to the jury that were even more favorable to Rulloff's defense than were strictly required. Judge Hogeboom's decisions on the indictment, the photograph, the ratchet drill, and all the rest were affirmed. Most important of all, the question of the murderous intentions of Merrick and Burrows was set aside. Citizens protecting property entrusted to their charge will not "be made to change places" with "the admitted felon."

Ham Freeman raised the question of whether or not Rulloff had been given a fair hearing.

> The Court afterwards unanimously sustained the verdict and decisions of the *Courts below*. Judge William F. Allen wrote the opinion, which was unanimously adopted. Notwithstanding that Rulloff had many fine-spun, hair-splitting theories in his favor, and his counsel presented some new and nice questions, the Court did not deem it worthwhile or expedient to interfere with the course of justice. Perhaps if there had been great doubt as to Rulloff's innocence, and if he had always borne a previously good character, then the technicalities might have availed, and the Court might *then* have granted a new trial; but they were not going to let this old offender off *on a quibble*. We do not vouch for the truth of it, but it is said one of the judges proposed, after the case was argued, *to hang Rulloff first and examine his case afterwards.*

Yet again, Rulloff would have to be sentenced to death, and the court assigned the task to the supreme court in Elmira and scheduled April 4 for the proceeding.

Ham asserted once again Rulloff's stoical response to his "troubles."

> He received the news of the defeat in the Court of Appeals with apparent indifference, and immediately set to work to devise other ways and means to escape from the meshes of the law.[40]

Now, perhaps at last, Rulloff would unveil the mystery of his life. Ed Crapsey in the *New York Times* was especially hopeful.

Next to relieving society of his presence, RULLOFF could render the public no greater service than by devoting the brief space of life that remains to him, to the writing of a truthful sketch of his checkered career. If he could, in the near presence of death, but lay aside the charlatan, and resume the manhood he so grossly perverted, we might have a narrative of talents misdirected and opportunities abused that would be no less interesting as a psychological study than valuable as a text for moral illustration.[41]

Rulloff was not yet ready to write his confessional autobiography, and George Becker was not yet ready to concede defeat. Before the sentencing scheduled for Elmira in April, they pursued two strategies. The first was to obtain commutation, or at least further delay, by proclaiming the value of Rulloff's linguistic discoveries. The second was to pursue yet once more avenues of legal appeal.

No one took Rulloff's legal arguments seriously, but there were larger issues to be considered. A few believed that his philological work might be sufficiently valuable to warrant a delay in the hanging; some thought it likely that Rulloff was crazy and therefore executing him would be wrong. Plenty of people thought as Peter Hopkins did: hanging was uncivilized and unworthy of a modern society, but it was important to hang Rulloff first and discuss the matter afterward. A tiny minority felt that the appetite for Rulloff's execution was just the right moment to renew the debate on capital punishment.

The first influential statement on the question had appeared in Horace Greeley's newspaper, the *New York Tribune*. His paper was the most respected of the New York dailies, and what appeared on its editorial page was always taken seriously. The editorial, widely presumed to have been written by Greeley himself, was published on April 25 and titled "What Should Be Done with Ruloff?"

> In the prison at Binghamton there is a man waiting death who is too curious an intellectual problem to be wasted on the gallows. He is one of the most industrious and devoted scholars our busy generation has given birth to. While other men of equal mental powers have been applying all their energies to the acquisition of money, this austere student has lived remote from the world, bending every faculty of his being to the work of philological inquiry. His mind has dwelt so fixedly upon this absorbing theme

that the usual morbid condition consequent upon too powerful and continued tension has resulted, and the man has gone mad. . . . He could not take precious time from his studies to go into business and make a living, as other men might do. He had no capital to support him, or to labor for him in any reputable business. He was driven logically into crime by his love of learning. By using the vulgar criminal who fell in his way, to accomplish his burglaries, he lost no hours of work, he incurred no useless expenditure of leisure and energy.

Greeley explained that robbery was, for Rulloff, merely a means to an end: "He murdered the shopkeeper in the interest of philology."

A man in this disordered state of mind is dangerous to the public peace, and should not be permitted to remain at large. But nothing is to be gained by killing him. He should be treated like any other violent madman, and confined under close and merciful surveillance. With his great power of application and method, he might be made of great use in the administration of a prison or an insane asylum, and a liberal portion of his time should be allowed him to develop his scheme of universal philology.[42]

In Ithaca, John Selkreg, who had been campaigning for Rulloff's execution for nearly twenty years, expressed shock.

It is hardly conceivable that the *Tribune* can be in earnest. In any event it cannot impose its vagaries upon any one who is conversant with the case, and Rulloff will not be allowed to escape his final punishment through any device as contemptibly "thin" as this.[43]

Selkreg was a Republican; Greeley's position was surprising to other Republicans as well (in 1871 Greeley was campaigning for the Republican nomination for president). Even more surprising was a letter appearing the following week in the *Tribune:* "A Substitute for Rulloff."

Sir: I believe in capital punishment. I believe that when a murder has been done it should be answered for with blood. I have all my life been taught to feel in this way, and the fetters of education are strong. The fact that the death law is rendered

almost inoperative by its very severity does not alter my belief in
its righteousness. . . .

Feeling as I do, I am not sorry that Rulloff is to be hanged, but
I am sincerely sorry that he himself has made it necessary that his
vast capabilities for usefulness should be lost to the world. In this,
mine and the public's is a common regret. For it is plain that in
the person of Rulloff one of the most marvelous intellects that any
age has produced is about to be sacrificed, and that, too, while half
the mystery of its strange powers is yet a secret. Here is a man
who has never entered the doors of a college or a university, and
yet, by the sheer might of his innate gifts has made himself such a
colossus in abstruse learning that the ablest of our scholars are but
pigmies in his presence. . . . Every learned man who enters
Rulloff's presence leaves it amazed and confounded by his prodi-
gious capabilities and attainments. . . . But what if the law could
be satisfied, and the gifted criminal still be saved. If a life be
offered up on the gallows to atone for the murder Ruloff did, will
that suffice? If so, give me the proofs, for, in all earnestness and
truth, I aver that in such a case I will instantly bring forward a
man who, in the interests of learning and science, will *take
Rulloff's crime upon himself,* and *submit to be hanged in Rulloff's
place.* I can, and will do this thing; and I propose this matter, and
make this offer in good faith. You know me, and know my address.
                    —April 29, 1871 SAMUEL LANGHORNE

Modern readers will at once detect that this letter is a composition of
Samuel Langhorne Clemens, "Mark Twain." That authorship must also
have been widely known in 1871. Twain and his family were summering
at Elmira, and, if Twain did not get a glimpse of Rulloff, he was certainly aware of the dramatic events of that day as the crowds thronged
to the courthouse to see him brought, finally, to justice.

Twain sent his letter to Whitelaw Reid at the *Tribune* with an accompanying note.

Friend Reid:
I have written this thing for an *object*—which is, to make people *talk* about & look at, & presently ENTERTAIN the idea of
commuting Rulloff's penalty.
The last paragraph (as magnificently absurd as it is,) is what I

depend on to start the *talk* at every breakfast table in the land—
& then the talk will drift into all the different ramifications of this
case & first thing they know, they will discover that a regret is
growing up in their souls that the man is going to be hung. If the
talk gets started once, that is sufficient—they'll *all* talk, pretty
soon, & then the *acting* will come easily & naturally.

The last paragraph of the article is bully. Silly as it is, nobody
can read it without a startle, or without having to stop & *think,*
before deciding whether the thing is possible or not.

Now if you don't want this or can't print it now, I wish you
would re-mail it to me, for I want to print it somewhere. Don't
comment on it, unless you'd like to back up this brave Redeemer
for Science.

      Ys

        Clemens[44]

While this and other letters to the press did little for Rulloff, they did
have some impact on discussions of capital punishment. In June, after
the hanging, this idea that his life might have been prolonged in the
interest of philology was raised again. *Appleton's Journal* devoted a column of indignation to it.

This notion, entertained by a few people only, and which was
quite as thoroughly ridiculed here as it deserved, has called forth
in a London paper a long article, in which we are told that "any
thing more *bizarre,* more grotesquely suggestive of the intellectual confusion of American society, of the way in which over there
all moral beliefs are drifting toward the unknown, has not recently
arrived." This is another instance of the common practice of seiz-
ing upon one or two expressions of opinion and treating them as
indications of general convictions.[45]

Appleton's received this transatlantic slur on American morality with
considerable resentment. The thought that Rulloff should be spared,
even if only for a short time, was absurd, and it was transparently clear
to the author of the piece that hanging was a great deterrent to murderers. In any case, Rulloff's trial did not raise issues of morality but
ones of force: the social need to exert power in the interests of self-
preservation. *Appleton's* had no wish to allow Britons (or anyone else)
to accuse the republic of moral "drift."

10

•••••••

The Soft Coo of Love

Though the trial had been well publicized, news of Merrick's murder and Rulloff's conviction did not reach much beyond eastern New York. All that was about to change.

First, in mid-January, A. B. Richmond wrote a long and circumstantial account of Rulloff's sojourn in Meadville, mentioning his arcane learning and meticulous craftsmanship. This recollection first appeared in the *Meadville Republican* and was soon reprinted in other papers.

Then, on January 25, the *New York Sun* devoted most of its front page to the case. The headline—"The Modern Eugene Arum"—recalled the story of an anguished schoolmaster who suffered through years of respectability until it was discovered that he had murdered a student. The equation linked Rulloff to Arum and Jarvis to the student, and the poem by Henry Alford was ready made for Rulloff's condition: "The guilt-worn student, skilled without avail / In ancient lore."[1]

The author of this article, Oliver Dyer, was well known for his interest in linguistic matters, particularly the reasons behind English spelling. Before the Civil War, he had been a shorthand reporter in the U.S. Senate. Afterward, he became celebrated as a New York journalist. Seeing the case as an intersection of philology and sensation, he took the train to Binghamton.

While waiting in George Becker's office the week after Rulloff had been sentenced, Dyer read an article on language that Rulloff had written for Ham Freeman's *Leader* and decided that the condemned man was onto something.

> That subject having been a hobby with us for many years, we were able to see that Rulloff had really been at work in that field, and

165

that his claims to extraordinary results, though perhaps exaggerated, actually had a basis of original discovery and philosophical insight.[2]

Rulloff had been turning away reporters since his sentence, but Becker thought that he might be willing to talk about language with Dyer. Rulloff authorized Dyer to view his manuscript and agreed to discuss it, but said he would answer no other questions.

On the way to the jail, Becker and Dyer stopped at Halberts' store. Burrows was also eager to talk to the famous big-city reporter, and he showed him the scene of the crime including the bullet marks in the railing and on the walls. By this time, Burrows had become a practiced teller of the dramatic story, and Dyer was favorably impressed. Next, they spent a few minutes in the bank vault, where Rulloff's manuscripts were deposited as surety for payment of his legal fees. After this edifying detour, they went on to the jail.

Subsequent interviewers would describe Rulloff's prison in ways that suggested at least basic comforts. What Dyer found was considerably less pleasant.

> The cell seems to have a sufficient grip of the prisoner to hold him fast whatever plans of escape he may be maturing or conjecturing. We were introduced to Rulloff by Mr. Becker, and as he held a small kerosene lamp, so as to throw the light upon us, with his left hand, he extended his right through the opening in his iron door for a friendly shake. As near as we could judge in the dim, religious light of the jail,[3] Rulloff is about five feet eight inches in height, slight but compact in build, and strung with tough and elastic sinews. Grizzled streaks show in his hair and close-cropped beard, but his manner and voice give no token of age or failing powers. He was in his shirt sleeves. His keen hazel eyes looked swollen and bloodshot, the result, as he said, of writing constantly by an insufficient light. It was then 3 o'clock in the afternoon, and the corridor in front of his cell was too dark to read or write without a lamp, and his cell itself was dark as night beyond the limited space which was feebly lighted by his kerosene burner.

Rulloff was delighted at his interest in the manuscripts. Dyer asked why he had undertaken this work.

RULLOFF: "I wanted to make something of myself. I wanted to get at the origin of art and science, and begin at the beginning, and I thought that was the way to do it."

DYER: "You had a passion, perhaps, for the study of language?"

RULLOFF: "No, it was not that. My first idea was to make a man of myself. I began when I was about sixteen. I was a clerk then, and when I got through at the store about 6 o'clock in the evening, I used to go to my room and study till midnight, and sometimes till one, two, or three o'clock in the morning. . . ."

DYER: "But I want to get at a starting point. You know there are two fundamental and opposing theories as to the origin of language. One of those theories is, that language, more or less complete, was bestowed upon man at the time of his creation, by the Creator. The other theory is that language was originated and gradually developed by man just as music, mathematics, or any other art or science was. One of these theories is the true one. Which of them do you accept?"

RULLOFF: "My theory is that language has been developed and constructed by man. God does not give us our mortar ready mixed. He gives us the sand and the water and limestone, the elements of which mortar is made, and leaves us to find out how to burn our limestone into lime, and how to mix our mortar. It is the same in every other case. It is the same in language. God gives us our organs of speech, but leaves us to find out how to use them and how to mix our consonants and vowels into words, and how out of words to construct our language."

DYER: "Very well. Now we have a starting point. You adopt the development theory as to the origin of language. How far back on that track do you start? Do you hold that the human race existed for an indefinite period of time without any spoken language at all, and from pantomime and a few inarticulate grunts finally worked their way up to articulate and intelligent speech?"

RULLOFF: "I can't say as to that. I know that articulation is an art, and could not have been brought to any high degree of development without antecedent intellectual activity."

DYER: "Do you adopt the phonetic theory of vocal and linguistic development? That is, do you hold, with the phoneticians, that the same emotions or passions were originally expressed by the same elementary sounds, whether articulate or inarticulate, and by all races alike?"

RULLOFF: "Perhaps they were. That may be so. A man in love, when looking upon his sweetheart, if unable yet to articulate and express his feelings in words, would of course be confined, in the expression of them, to mere grunts of admiration or affection; and there can be no doubt that such a man would give altogether a different tone and character to his grunts from what a man who was looking upon a rival whom he hated, and wanted to strangle, would give to his. In fact, that is so, even now. Who does not know that the soft coo of love, though inarticulate, is wholly different from and impossible to be mistaken for the deadly growl of hate, which is also inarticulate. In the spontaneous expression of those two passions—love and hate— why should not the voice differ as much as the countenance? When an untutored creature, not yet arrived at the development of speech, attempts to give inarticulate expression to his passions, why should not his voice in the one case correspond to the smile of love, and in the other to the scowl of hate?"

What was remarkable to Dyer, and to his readers, was Rulloff's claim that language had been "constructed" by human beings. It was neither divine nor natural but almost entirely and self-consciously cultural. And furthermore, the inventors of language had left clues to their handiwork. As Rulloff admitted, some features might be natural: The coo of love; the growl of hate. But the complexity of human language lay in the code. Its genetic constituents were the four liquid sounds: *l, m, n,* and *r.*

RULLOFF: "They combine readily with other consonants in the formation of the roots of words, and these roots are all-important. The possibility of the construction of an artistic and scientific language rests upon roots susceptible of change without loss of identity. Stick a pin there. Make that emphatic: *Roots susceptible of change without loss of identity.* The whole thing depends on having such roots of words. Such roots are entirely unknown to modern philologists. I have discovered them, and if I had time could revolutionize the study of language, and make it a new and living thing. It is, of course, impossible to develop my system here, in such a place as this, and under the circumstances of this interview, in such a manner as to convince you of its infallibleness. A few examples may be given off-hand, which will point the inquiring mind in the direction of the goal. It is a principle in the formation of a philosophical language that things which are opposites in meaning, are named from the same roots, in which the elements are reversed. Take the words *stir* and *rest* for example, the meanings of which are opposites. In *stir,* the root is composed of *s, t, r;* in *rest* these are reversed—*r, s, t.* Things relatively large and small are also named from the same roots. But it is impossible to illustrate this subject in a proper manner in an interview like this."

DYER: "How have you managed to pursue your researches and studies in this manner?"

RULLOFF: "I can't answer that question. I don't know. I seem to have been driven on by an over-ruling power. I have cried, sir, over this thing. It has almost crazed me. Sometimes I have been in despair over it."

DYER: "Why did you cry over it?"

RULLOFF: "To think that fate should lead me into so many com-plications and perplexities which interfered with my prosecu-tion of the work. But when interrupted and annoyed and defeated in purpose so that, as I said, I have cried over it—and I am not ashamed to confess it—I have finally rallied and gone at it again; and when again disastrously interfered with, and driven almost to despair again, I have rallied to the work once more, and so have gone on with it, year after year."[4]

This interview was filled with familiar Rullovian anguish. He had been interrupted and annoyed in his intellectual work through no fault of his own. Only the necessity of robbing stores and the tedium of a prison cell—complications and perplexities—kept him from his work. But he had risen above these setbacks.

In so doing, he was assisted by various acts of kindness from people who did not seek to publicize their sympathy for him. A Binghamton lawyer, James A. Winslow, lent him philological volumes, and his cell seems to have been abundantly supplied with reference works. These included Liddell and Scott's dictionary of Greek, Ethan Allen Andrews's dictionary of Latin, a *Homeric Lexicon,* and Edward J. Ver-non's *Guide to the Anglo-Saxon Tongue.* There were other works noticed by visitors as well: Robley Duglison's *Dictionary of Medical Science,* for instance, a Bible, and Foxe's *Book of Martyrs.*[5]

Though he would later complain about Dyer, Rulloff must have been immensely pleased by the long article so prominently published in the highly regarded *Sun.* The weekly philological essays in Ham's *Leader* made him locally famous, but Dyer's article brought him to the attention of a far wider public.

Not all this attention was enthusiastic or even respectful. Writing in *The Galaxy,* Richard Grant White, well-known for his essays on words and word origins, declared: "We fear comparative philology is likely to make an addition to the long list of good things that have been overridden and run into the ground." One source of this dismaying development was the tendency of scholars to speak of their work as a *science* instead of one of the supreme developments of the humanities. With the respect granted to "scientists," the gullible public was drawn to ill-found speculation and ridiculous conclusions. Such was the allurement of Rulloff.

> The latest and extremest (if the reader will pardon the double superlative—we have seen *supremest* in poetry) is that of the murderer Rulloff. This old sinner sent a local paper to columns of rubbish, which the learned editor publishes as "of interest to scholars."[6]

With such sneering condemnation, it is surprising that Rulloff found any sympathies for his views. Yet there was a thirst for easy knowledge of ancient languages, and White went out of his way to ridicule any belief that a "system" would unlock the mysteries.

Publicity brought a letter from Julius Seelye, and Rulloff replied to his kindly letter that he remembered him "with a very unusual regard" and pleaded with him to give to his philological principles "such an amount of thought as will enable you fairly to see their application."[7] Seelye did devote attention to Rulloff's ideas, and he retrieved the detailed critique of a Greek passage Rulloff had written in the prison in Auburn back in March 1857 and showed it to his colleague, Richard H. Mather, the professor of Greek and German at Amherst. Mather later said that Rulloff's essay on a passage from Plato made him "warmly interested." Himself a native of Binghamton, Mather welcomed the opportunity to return home, and he journeyed to the jail to seek an audience with the author of this critique.

Knowing that there was some skepticism about his abilities, Rulloff asked Mather to test him on his knowledge of Greek, claiming that his interest had begun in boyhood and that all his knowledge had been acquired by "honest work." He had never had the opportunity to study languages in college or university, and he had labored to learn them, he said.

Rulloff invited Mather to pick a text on which he might be examined. Mather selected a Socratic dialogue, one in which "the sentiments of Socrates with reference to God and duty in their purity and exaltation approach so nearly to Biblical revelation." These portions Rulloff quoted with ready fluency, and he went on to recite from memory portions of the *Iliad* and of the plays of Socrates. Mather was satisfied that he was in the company of a finished Greek scholar.

The conversation then turned to textual interpretation. In his commentary, Rulloff showed depth of understanding that Mather found even more surprising.

> He did it with such subtlety and discrimination and elegance as to show that his critical study of these nicer points was even more remarkable than his powers of memory: in fact I should say that subtlety of analysis and reasoning was the marked characteristic of his mind.

Remarkably, Rulloff seemed oblivious to the death sentence. A learned conversation more appropriate to a classroom was taking place in a death cell.

> He urged me to come with several [philologists], and take time to see whether his theory is true. He asked my pardon for the apparent dogmatism of the statement, but said he felt convinced that this theory of language was a special revelation to him, and that perhaps a hundred years might elapse ere it would be known again, and then added significantly, "And, you know that whatever is done must be done quickly."[8]

Rulloff's literary memory was not limited to the ancient Greeks, and his quotation, however approximate, from *Macbeth* connected Shakespeare's fictional murderer with real life. Here is yet another in the long sequence of literary allusions that empowered the discourse of the day.[9]

In the course of their conversation, Mather told Rulloff that Seelye would not regard it as "an obtrusion" if Rulloff were to communicate the gist of his theory. Before nightfall, Rulloff had written eighteen pages of etymological speculation and sent them off to Amherst. Imagine his disappointment when he read the next day this report of their conversation.

VISITED BY PROFESSOR MATHER

Rev. Professor R. H. Mather, of Harvard College [*sic*], had an interview with Rulloff this morning, on the subject of his book. Professor Mather pronounced some of his translations as excellent, but he could not comprehend the theory of his book.[10]

For Mather, this man was deeply troubling because in him learning and morality had parted company.

He is certainly an enigma, and offers in himself a powerful argument against the theory that education is alone sufficient to lead to true manhood. Those who would throw out moral and Biblical teachings from our systems of culture, have a difficult task to harmonize their theory with such a character as this.

Rulloff was an affront to the prevailing value system. How could someone able to read Greek—including New Testament Greek—not be swayed by the divine wisdom flowing through the texts? How could a person whose ideas were shaped by poetry be so evil? In the same way, the lunacy commission would shortly be curious about his religious faith and, particularly, his religious upbringing. Somehow the good influence of his zealous Christian parents had not taken.

Mather's opinion, as reported in the newspapers, filled Rulloff with despair. Anyone could give "excellent translations," but it was his grand theory that he wished to have celebrated. If the learned professor could not "comprehend it," it might not be important. When he next wrote to Seelye, Rulloff pasted the brief notice of Mather's visit to the final page and hoped for something better.

My best respects to Prof. Mather if you please, and say to him I would be glad to furnish him the means of making a more favorable report than the following, which, as it now stands, is regarded as a mere *euphemism*—instead of saying that my discovery is all humbug.[11]

Musing over the injustice of it all, Rulloff came up with a new idea. He would appeal to the governor for a delay of his sentence long enough for him to finish his great philological work.

On April 13 he asked Ham Freeman to convene "a committee of some gentlemen learned in the languages" and have them call on him in the jail.

> The burthen of his mind then was that he had made a great discovery in the science of philology; that the world did not understand or appreciate what a great man he was; that if understood, the world would wish, and the Governor would allow, him to live to complete it, and then, said he, "my mission on earth is performed; when my great book on philology is completed, and placed before the world, I shall be ready to die, and I don't care a d——n how soon."[12]

Ham Freeman and George Becker scoured the town in search of people who knew something "of Latin, Greek, German, Hindoo, Dutch, or Irish." It took nearly two weeks to assemble the delegation; people were afraid of being "drawn in. Some ten gentlemen called with Mr. Becker, and spent two hours with Rulloff, listening to his expositions of his philological labors."[13]

Rulloff tried to explain his theory, but his illustrious visitors did not agree with it. He then asked them to sign a petition urging the governor to delay the execution. One by one they refused.[14] When word got out about this extraordinary interview, the "practical people" of Binghamton began to mock Rulloff as "the philological drudge."[15] Nothing daunted, Rulloff wrote again to Seelye and described the interview, emphasizing the responses that seemed sympathetic to his views. Hoping that Seelye would add his name to the petition, he even enclosed two three-cent stamps so that the influential professor might write directly to the governor.[16]

In his diary, the Reverend Edward Taylor gave an account of this remarkable interview, and George Becker's appeal to him as he left the jail.

Becker, his counsel, tried me again on the steps, but I was firm. Prof. Farnham sd. he watched Ruloff & he was trying to mesmerize me. T. more I thought of it, t. more indignant I became. He is a crafty scamp, writes Greek beautifully; knows many etymological facts, but no system or principle about it.[17]

The other "savans," as the newspapers called the visitors, agreed. Next Becker drew up a petition for the appointment of a Commission of Lunacy and gained an appointment with Governor John Hoffman. Responsive to local opinion (and statewide publicity), the governor saw no harm in appointing a committee. Rulloff had never wanted to be regarded as insane; he very much wanted to be regarded as a brilliant philologist.

Rulloff was not alone in believing that he was on the brink of an important discovery. Oliver Dyer's article had provided details of Rulloff's manuscript, including a quotation in the first paragraph in the introduction. Here Rulloff had quoted James Burnett, the eighteenth-century philosopher and Scottish law lord.

If it can be shown why the roots of a language should be such or such sounds, rather than others, it is evident that if the language be a complete work of art, its roots will be of that kind.

Monboddo 2.209.

Rulloff's invocation of Monboddo—the judicial title by which Burnett was usually known—was enough to give his theorizing serious underpinnings. In 1773, Monboddo had argued that "natural" human beings would never produce the creative powers of language, and he offered the orangutan as an example of a creature with fully human capabilities but no such language. Monboddo declared that human language was created by "artifice," not "nature," and that Greek was the most perfect of languages.[18] For Monboddo, Sanskrit was merely a corrupt dialect and hardly worth the attention that was beginning to be paid to it at the end of the eighteenth century. In this, as in other ideas, Rulloff heartily embraced Monboddo and thus put himself outside the main line of linguistic doctrine that had been evolving in the nineteenth century—that there was an "Aryan" parent language and Sanskrit was the most revealing of its ancient qualities. But the ideas he developed under Monboddo's influence were not, in the 1860s, "humbug" or lunatic, but only old-fashioned.

All at once Dyer had given Rulloff's philological speculations a respectable line of descent and forced readers to take him far more seriously than ever before. In his *New York Tribune,* Horace Greeley urged Governor Hoffman to postpone the execution until Rulloff could complete his work; Rulloff "is too curious an intellectual problem to be wasted on the gallows," Greeley wrote in answer to the headlined question: "What should be done with Rulloff?"[19] In a similarly sympathetic vein, an anonymous letter to the *New York Herald,* published too late to effect its purpose, said that "It would be gratifying to me to see Governor Hoffman afford him a respite of six weeks or three months, that the world may have the benefits of this man's efforts."[20]

Others were not quite so ready to raise such profound questions about the benefits of deep learning. Instead they alleged that Rulloff was a fraud, and his knowledge a pretense designed to win sympathy he did not deserve.

Writing for the *American Journal of Insanity,* George C. Sawyer reported his own visit to the Binghamton jail. In presenting his findings to the medical community, Sawyer wrote,

It is in the interest of science to analyze a character presenting extraordinary traits seldom seen in conjunction, while it is in the interest of society to show a wicked man, as he really was, to strip from him the vail [*sic*] of deception, and to show him as a horrible life-long criminal, and to exhibit him, as, even in respect to his philological claims, largely a deceiver, as he was a pretender.[21]

On May 13, the week before the execution, Sawyer, accompanied by Dr. Judson Boardman Andrews (assistant physician at the New York State Lunatic Asylum in Utica), visited Rulloff, well aware that Professor Mather had formed the opinion that Rulloff's "acquirements in the department of the classical languages were considerable." Sawyer formed a different impression. Rulloff was silent when asked about "some of the common-places of the classics."

"We judged that the different result we attained from that of some other visitors, was to be ascribed to our setting before him what we wished him to do, instead of allowing him to discourse as he pleased," Sawyer reported.[22]

For them, the crucial test came in a conversation about a letter Rulloff had received written in Greek, composed, he surmised, to test his knowledge and requiring an answer in that language. Producing the letter, he began to translate "but stopped in the middle of the letter, declaring with scorn that a certain sentence made no sense, in fact could not be translated." This sentence Sawyer offered, in Greek, to his readers.

> We translated the passage, and referred to the corresponding Latin idiom. Rulloff merely assented, and excused himself for not having paid more attention to the letter previously, owing to more important matters, and to his feeble health.

None of the participants seem to have thought it bizarre to be quizzing a condemned man just days from his execution about the nuances of ancient idioms. Rulloff's inability to translate a small passage, though he read the rest of the letter "readily enough," revealed to Sawyer that Rulloff was a dissembler and a "pretender" to knowledge of the classics.

Sawyer did not make clear just what role Dr. Andrews played in this examination. Andrews had been a regimental surgeon during the war and was, at time of the visit, assistant to Dr. Gray at Utica. Since Gray had already declared Rulloff to be sane, Andrews's motive may have been merely that of a curious onlooker, though his education at Yale almost certainly included at least some Greek. But Andrews did not offer his views to the public. Sawyer was the principal critic of Rulloff's learning, and he was a tenacious and skeptical interrogator.

In his essay, Sawyer dismissed Rulloff as a fake. Since Dr. Gray was the very active editor of this journal, Sawyer's reply was not only an endorsement of Gray's diagnosis of Rulloff but in addition a blast at Dr. William A. Hammond and the more sympathetic view of Rulloff presented in Hammond's *Journal of Psychological Medicine*.[23] Sawyer thought Rulloff knew little Greek and adduced his failure to translate the letter he had received as evidence of his superficiality. Though nearly every visitor had marveled at Rulloff's skill in writing Greek, Sawyer sneered that he omitted the accents and breath marks and had no profound insight except in those few examples where he had the texts down by heart.

Sawyer did not say just how long he thought it ought to take for a scholar learned in languages to arrive at a philological theory, nor did he find interesting the speculations that, if not a genius, Rulloff was crazy.

He stands forth as one more, and a conspicuous example of the utter worthlessness of high intellectual endowments, severed from moral culture. Some one has speculated as to how much evil a man perfectly developed intellectually, and thoroughly unscrupulous, might accomplish. Rulloff approaches to the type of such a moral monster.[24]

Just as the victors write the history of wars, so the scientists whose method prevails are able to declare their competing forebears quacks. What is significant in Rulloff's philological endeavors is not so much that he pursued a dead end, but that he was headed in a direction that seemed promising enough to some of his contemporaries who were regarded as persons of "high mental endowments."

Sawyer correctly understood that Rulloff's ideas about the evolution of language began with those of Charles Kraitsir. One of those émigré scholars so fascinating to Boston intellectuals, Kraitsir took Boston by storm in the 1840s. Emerson wrote to his brother that "the best teacher of language in existence" was Dr. Kraitsir, and Elizabeth Peabody—an important figure in Emerson's circle—became a strong advocate of his linguistic views, sponsoring lectures in her bookshop and publishing three pamphlets based on them. What made the Boston intellectuals of the time fall for Kraitsir's views was their extreme abstraction and frequent invocation of a connection between language and nature. Emerson had already declared that language was "fossil poetry," and Kraitsir promised to look at the fossils of contemporary languages and derive from them a picture of life in its original and natural state.

Rulloff had divided sounds into three categories: liquids, mutables, and vowels. His triple division, in principle if not in the precise specifics, was similar to Kraitsir's. As Kraitsir explained his theory, it was nature that had ordained the nature of language.

> There are three classes of sounds in consequence of the harmony between our organs and the several categories, into which nature is divided in our conception. . . . Gutturality, labiality, and dentality, floating in the element of euphony, and corresponding to the ideas men have of things material and moral, make up language.[25]

Even in the heyday of speculative etymology, Kraitsir's word histories were breathtaking. Explaining how "the first men" gave a natural expression to the word *line,* Kraitsir showed how the idea of "living and moving" emerged through a series of words beginning with the letter *L.*

Kraitsir was hardly alone in the opinion, embraced by Rulloff, that a prehistoric perfect language had been dispersed and altered (as a consequence of Babel) into the historical and imperfect languages known to modern observers. A homegrown American savant, Stephen Pearl Andrews, had come up with similar ideas in his book *Discoveries in Chinese; or, The Symbolism of the Primitive Characters of the Chinese System of Writing.* Andrews exemplified his system of analysis by treating all the Chinese characters containing the brushstrokes for *tree* as having something in common with each other. In other words, there was what Rulloff would call a "method" in the development of Chinese, and study of such clusters would reveal the evolution of thought through the "secret meaning" of *tree.*

[T]he attempt will be to found etymology upon a new science, which I denominate IDEOLOGY—the Philosophical and Historical Evolution of Human Thought, *which has underlaid and inspired the development of human language, and is therefore logically precedent to it.*[26]

Such an approach was welcomed by those who believed in an Adamic perfect language, as well as the more secularly Romantic view of language as the expression of transcendent thought. For Andrews, it was obvious that the character representing "the east" should show "the sun rising through the trees."

If Andrews's imaginings or Kraitsir's invocation of sounds "floating in the element of euphony" strike a modern reader as absurd, the legitimate line of descent of modern philology is almost as odd. William Dwight Whitney, who graduated from both Williams and Yale Colleges, spent time as a bank clerk while perfecting his languages. He then embarked for three years philological study in German universities. By 1864, Whitney had achieved sufficient prominence to be invited to lecture at the Smithsonian Institution, and the publication of these lectures, *Language and the Study of Language,*[27] gave him an international reputation that would lead to his views becoming the foundation for twentieth-century "structuralism" in philology.

Whitney emphasized that the connection between word and referent was arbitrary and conventional, that the evolution of languages and language families was orderly and mechanical. Individuals had little to do with the development of language except insofar as they were part of a community in which innovation spread from one person to another through democratic social processes. One language (or kind of language) was not inherently superior to another. These principles served to secularize philology and remove from it the spiritual and mystical elements that had animated Kraitsir, Andrews, and others of their kind.

Whitney's towering genius was formed not through solitary study but by often-combative interaction with other scholars in person and in print and by his work on two important dictionaries of midcentury, the great Sanskrit dictionary being assembled in St. Petersburg and Chauncey Goodrich's revision of Noah Webster's English. Whitney thoroughly deserved the high esteem in which he was almost universally held.

A modern reader is likely to suspect that Whitney's brilliant lectures swept all competing views from the scene and rendered notions like Rulloff's absurd. But that was not the case. Demystifying language was not a popular project, nor did Whitney's views of the independence of language and race find a ready audience. "Race and blood," he declared, "had nothing to do directly with determining our language."[28] That statement alone was heresy in a time when the Pan-Aryan theorists were proclaiming racial and linguistic superiority. There was no place in Whitney's views for the triumph of one inherently superior language over an inferior one. It was clear, however, that Whitney was to be given serious attention, and he was invited to expand his six Smithsonian lectures in a longer series of new lectures presented at the Lowell Institution in Boston.

During the same season, lecture-goers could also hear eleven talks on a related subject presented by Peter Lesley, secretary of the American Philosophical Society in Philadelphia. He titled them *Man's Origin and Destiny, Sketched from the Platform of the Sciences*.

Declaring Kraitsir's ideas ridiculous, Lesley asserted that "comparative philology is one of the most beautiful and attractive of all the modern sciences."[29] But he demurred when it came to Whitney's claim that prehistory of humankind can best be studied through the languages that can be reconstructed through the comparative and historical method. Impersonal evolution ignored human intervention in language, Lesley said. Summarizing Whitney's claim in his Smithsonian lectures of the prior year, Lesley declared baldly, "I do not believe it."[30]

The great mistake made by the new school of linguistics, Lesley thought, was in giving insufficient attention to the role of "actual invention," the process by which an organized group of human beings create and sustain innovation in language by conscious efforts. "Philologists of Professor Whitney's school busy themselves entirely about the men and women, but forget all about the priests."[31] Rulloff shared this idea with Lesley, that language could be formed by human agency. Rulloff's key to the secret lay in the way words were sounded; for Lesley, it was the way words looked. His priests wrote down what they saw in the form of an alphabet: "The letter A is simply a pyramid or mountain with a line drawn across it," he asserted, and thus derived a metaphorical connection between *Alp* 'a mountain,' an *Arm* lifted in prayer, and *ElephAnt* 'the mountain beast of Asia with the howdah on his back.'[32] With such opinions being given respectful attention, it was hard for ordinary people to distinguish the savants from the lunatics.

Secret societies flourished in nineteenth-century America, and both of Rulloff's brothers were members of Masonic orders. For these brotherhoods, ritual and lore were central, and the idea that ancient priests might have encoded secret messages in language seemed obvious, since the rites of these orders dealt in considerable detail with codes and secrets. In Rulloff's day, oral tradition was highly regarded, and it was entirely plausible to the members of such groups that some "secret order" might have preserved mystical knowledge from the remote past.

In 1849, while Whitney toiled with the rudiments of Sanskrit, Rulloff was engaged in similar intellectual pursuits in Auburn Prison. Both Whitney and Rulloff were disciplined scholars. Though Sawyer might denigrate his Greek, Rulloff impressed others with his knowledge. In 1850–52, William Waite, Seelye's fellow student at the theological seminary in Auburn, made regular visits to the prison with the chaplain. Among the most memorable of the prisoners he met was Rulloff, and he showed Rulloff an essay he had written on a passage in Greek from the New Testament. They had lively discussions.

> A little fluid-lamp used to be hanging at the grating of his cell-door, a special favor conceded to his well-known love of study. He would always come briskly up to the door for a talk; was quick in perception, impatient to reply, and had a habit of setting his head on one side, with a deep, scrutinizing look, while addressed, that gave one the impression of his intention to make a pounce the

moment the sentence was finished. Often he caught the word out of the speaker's mouth, and poured forth a voluble reply of his own. His language was good, with a dash of sarcasm, and what he knew, he appeared to have well in hand.[33]

Waite did not keep the commentary Rulloff had written in response to his essay, but he recalled the flavor of it.

> I remember that he objected, on some frivolous ground, to nearly every one of my positions, controverted all my grammatical authorities, but, of the Scriptural passage in question, had such excessively refined grammatical views, *that he utterly declined to venture on any rendering or exegesis of his own.*[34]

In philological matters in his younger days, as in legal ones, Rulloff prided himself as vigorous disputant, ready to dismantle the theories of others though sometimes chary about asserting full-scale theories of his own. It was at this time that Rulloff composed his critique of Tayler Lewis's edition of Plato that had so impressed Julius Seelye.[35]

As Rulloff's execution approached, even Tayler Lewis, then nearly seventy years old, remembered Rulloff's commentary on his 1844 book, *Plato against the Atheists.* Lewis was a deeply learned professor of Greek at Union College and had the broad interests not uncommon among the learned in his day.[36]

Apparently, George Becker in his tireless defense of his client had drawn the old scholar's attention to Rulloff's plight. Lewis did not wish to address the philological researches, declaring in a letter to the *New York Times* that he "could not endorse [them] because I know nothing about them beyond a short statement, which I could not fully understand." Yet he said that he felt "a deep sympathy" for Rulloff, and his argument for sparing his life was not philological but legal. It had been wrong, he said, to tax Rulloff with the guilt assumed by the "common tradition."

> It is contrary to pure justice that any former crimes, for which he has paid the law's full penalty, should now operate against him in his application for mercy. The present case should be judged on its own merits, with a consideration as unprejudiced and impartial as would be given to that of any other man who stands before the

law, either wholly innocent, or, by due process of law, discharged of his crimes.[37]

Lewis was baffled by Rulloff's theory of language. But that was irrelevant. Rulloff's knowledge of Greek was irrelevant: He had been unfairly treated.

During his last weeks in prison, Rulloff filled in some of the details of his mature philologizing. Process rather than product was uppermost in his talk, and he emphasized that he had done hard and serious work and had carried it out in straightened circumstances.

Rulloff had had no learned companions with whom to discuss his theories, though tutoring young New Yorkers preparing their German for college occasionally interrupted his solitary studies. Yet Jarvis and Dexter had been convinced that the brilliant Rulloff was about to make a discovery that would make them rich, and they were willing to risk arrest to allow him the leisure to visit libraries, particularly the Eclectic Library in Irving Place in lower Manhattan. Ed Crapsey presented these disciples as humble underlings of philology.

> The meager needs of his abstemious life were meantime supplied by rural burglaries committed by Jarvis and Dexter; for there is no evidence that Rulloff was engaged personally in any crimes during 1869, or in 1870, until August. His two young confederates never desired his company on their lawless expeditions, because of his clumsiness and the fatality of detection which seemed to attend him everywhere. There was therefore an agreement mutually satisfactory, that he should devote himself uninterruptedly to the philological department of their mutual labors, excepting such demands as should be made upon his time by the disposal of the booty. For Rulloff was suspicious even of his devoted disciples, and always insisting upon himself turning their stolen goods into money, thereby kept the finance within his own control.[38]

Rulloff's public debut as a philological theorizer came in June 1869. Somehow he wangled an invitation to the meeting of the American Ethnological Society, then gathering at various members' houses in Manhattan. Someone suggested that he might wish to offer his proposal to the inaugural meeting of the American Philological Association planned for later in the summer.

After one of the Ethnological Society meetings, Rulloff joined a journalist for the ride downtown, and he did his best to get some notice of
his theory in the paper. The reporter politely declined, noting that "the
typographical resources of a daily paper did not permit the proper illustration and explanation of his valuable paper."

> Mr. Leurio was very active in bringing his discovery to the per-
> sonal notice of most, if not all, persons of linguistic attainments in
> this City [New York] and vicinity. He was especially assiduous in
> laying it before the professors of languages in this City and else-
> where, extending his visits for this purpose as far as to New-Haven.

So that spring of 1869 was recollected, two years later, by George Fisk
Comfort.[39]

Almost certainly the philologist Rulloff visited in New Haven was
William Dwight Whitney, the most famous American philologist of the
day. Having been inspired to his own career by the German philolo-
gists, Whitney worked to expand and implement their theoretical views.
Rulloff, though he knew this work, dismissed it as merely mechanical.
Like Lesley, Rulloff thought their views lacked mystery and spirituality.
Like Whitney, G. F. Comfort was prominent and certainly well
qualified to judge "Leurio's" discovery.

Comfort had immersed himself in German science, though his own
special field of interest was art and archaeology.[40] On his return from
study in Europe, Comfort had become chair of aesthetics and modern
languages at Allegheny College in Meadville just a few years after
Rulloff's temporary residence there. In 1868 he accepted an appointment as professor of Christian archaeology at Drew Theological Seminary in Madison, New Jersey, and commuted there from his home in
New York City. He was among the best known of the New York cadre
of "persons of linguistic attainments." To his chagrin, Rulloff bent Comfort's ear with his view of language. Comfort was not sympathetic.

> But one opinion as to the scientific value of this so-called "dis-
> covery" was formed by all to whom Mr. Leurio explained it. Not
> only did he disregard all the established principles in the science
> of language, but he utterly ignored the individual facts upon
> which those principles are based. . . .

His earnestness and persistence seemed to remove him from the class of ordinary charlatans. The only explanation of his case seemed to be that he was a monomaniac on the subject of his discovery.

About the 1st of July, Mr. Leurio issued a circular, in which he described his manuscript as containing the most remarkable discovery of the age, and offering it for sale at the modest price of $500,000.[41]

The circular was publicized in the New York newspapers and made startling claims about the "method in the formation of language." It promised a manuscript "of peculiar interest, disclosing a beautiful and unsuspected method in language spoken and read by millions of our race."[42]

The circular was received with considerable astonishment. Recollecting this document shortly after Rulloff had been convicted of Merrick's murder, an editorialist in *The Nation* made a statement as true today as it was in 1871: "A very wild lunatic, indeed, it would be who should hope to get five hundred thousand dollars from any assembly of philologists of the United States."[43]

Comfort and others from New York City must not have been pleased when Rulloff appeared at the Mill Street Congregational Church in Poughkeepsie on July 1, 1870, and enrolled himself as a founder-member of the American Philological Association.

Rulloff recalled that meeting for Ham Freeman and presented himself, once again, as a victim of circumstances.

> I was a stranger, personally to every one there, but by persistent effort, at last succeeded in getting a committee appointed to examine my work. Now, then, mark what reception the grandest discovery of this or any other age met with: A committee of three had been appointed—one of them a young man, evidently fresh from some College, where his conceit had been developed more than anything else, came and sat down beside me in the Convention, and said that he was *Chairman* of the committee on my work. . . . He talked with me for an hour, perhaps, long enough to convince me, at least, that he knew absolutely nothing of Philology, and then left me to make a report adverse to my book. I haven't attended any Philological Conventions since.
>
> I was chagrined and disappointed that I did not get a fair hear-

ing at Poughkeepsie. . . . I was dressed respectably but plain, and they probably took me for some poor enthusiast, and perhaps for a shyster or impostor.

At any rate I was treated very cavalierly, but I was not discouraged. I was resolved to make the learned men of the world appreciate and acknowledge the merit of my method, and with that end in view I returned to New York.

Far from being fobbed off by the scholars, Rulloff was given a courteous and serious hearing. Those appointed to evaluate his "discovery" were among the most eminent of those present.[44]

Comfort gave a somewhat different and far less sympathetic account of these events.

> He managed to secure the appointment of a committee to examine into the merits of his manuscript. He was also indefatigable in calling the attention of the members of the Association to his new system. But upon all of the linguists there assembled from every part of the country he made the same impression as he had upon those in this City.
>
> The report of the Committee was unfavorable, as might be expected. At this the mild and gentle Mr. Leurio disappeared. In his place appeared the violent, abusive and profane Mr. Leurio.[45]

Rulloff's "method" was absurd, but no more improbable than some of the ideas proposed by respectable scholars in respectable places—Lesley's priest-inventors of the alphabet had not been laughed off the rostrum of the Lowell Institute.

On January 16, 1871, just days following his conviction, Rulloff wrote a long treatise describing his assumptions about "method in the formation of language." His model of language invoked the sacred. It stood in stark contrast to Whitney's secular model, in which words and referents were connected only by arbitrary convention. Rulloff discerned, and promised to reveal, hidden truth.

> In language formed upon this plan, words are not merely arbitrary signs. They are signs, each of which is specially and appropriately significant. Their significance depends upon certain artistic relations, everywhere pervading their structure.[46]

Rulloff shrewdly combined the ineffable and the practical. His "method" would reveal truth hidden by the ancient priest-scholars and at the same time have practical application, since every schoolchild would become a philologist by application of the simple principles of analyzing liquids, mutables, and vowels. For Rulloff languages had been constructed and maintained by this priesthood; in modern times everyone could be initiated and ordained through his "method."

Rulloff described himself as none other than the long-awaited messiah of philology foretold by Isaiah in the image of the "man of sorrows." Rulloff's sorrows were simply more evidence of the culmination of biblical prophecy in his life and learning.

In maintaining a natural and artistic connection between word and referent, Rulloff was in effect recapitulating the Genesis account of naming-day in Eden when Adam conferred upon his world the words that belonged to each creature and thing within it. Rulloff did not, however, invoke the Tower of Babel and its destruction to explain the diversity of human languages, but rather supposed that the priest-scholars, in cooperation with poets, maintained the natural connection of words with their meanings. What caused language to change and become more diverse was change in the culture of those using it.

Thus Rulloff's ideas combined familiar biblical Christianity with more secular knowledge of antiquity, both spiced with the mysteries of the brotherhoods. As Darwin had swept away magical thinking in *Origin of Species,* so Whitney had discarded myths of language. Natural selection described the success of chance mutants by environmental causes; linguistic change, in Whitney's view, resulted from similarly arbitrary accidents. Rulloff boldly declared that languages had nothing arbitrary about them.

It is amazing that this unknown murderer shackled to his cell in a provincial American town could command so much attention, but writers across the nation felt obliged to engage him in debate. In the lead article in the *American Educational Monthly* of April 1871, the whole story of Rulloff's life was once again told. It was not a sympathetic portrait.

Here is a man of great philological pretensions, undeniably endowed with extraordinary abilities, possessed of varied acquirements, and who has, with an almost morbid activity, collected an immense mass of information in various branches of learning, yet a being heartless, soulless, a perfect Mephistopheles, who has gone through a long and checkered career of black and unredeemed villainy.[47]

Like Oliver Dyer, the author saw the weakness in Rulloff's argument. What sort of language had been spoken *before* the priests commenced to "form" a new means of expression?

This astounding theory does not explain under what forms men conveyed their thoughts previous to this priestly *hocus pocus*, and in what way this powerful and learned caste induced the plain, practical people of the lower classes to attach any intelligible meaning to their arbitrary combinations. The formidable problem of how men reached that advanced stage of society necessary to the existence of so learned and ingenious a priesthood without first having a well-defined language, is left equally without elucidation.[48]

As the day of Rulloff's execution approached, the lunacy commissioners questioned him on this very point.

Was the original alphabet of the Greek language, in your view, formed from arbitrary signs and the language thus built up, or was it derived from some other language and subsequently perfected?

To a modern philologist, both halves of this question seem absurd. What could it possibly mean to speak of a language being "built up" through its alphabet? And what did it mean to "perfect" a language? For many intellectuals of his day and for Rulloff, however, the question drew upon well-settled assumptions about the relation of writing and speech: written language was primary and spoken language subsidiary to it; some languages (like Greek) were "perfected" and others "degenerate" or "unrefined." Rulloff had no difficulty in answering the commissioners' question.

A. "Hardly arbitrary, because that excludes choice. There was method in its formation. Each letter was indicative."
Q. "Do you mean that the Greek is an original language? If not, from what was it derived?"

A. "The phraseology of Homer is worked up wonderfully and is greatly enriched from that of the early Greek writers. The letter 'r' was not found in the earlier Greek. In writings up to that time that letter was not necessary, but when Bacchus came out of Melia and bacchanalian life, with its orgies, revelry and carnivals began, it then became necessary to use hitherto unknown letters to describe the new conditions of life."[49]

Long known as the "dog letter" (from its sound-resemblance to canine growling), *r* was easily enough connected to the bestial life expressed in drunken orgies and rip-roaring carnivals.

Some time after their visit, Rulloff seems to have reconsidered his historical sketch. If Bacchus had introduced orgies and thus changed language forever, orgies ought still to be routine matters of social practice. The magical letter *r* continued, but revelry was no longer so popular. Somehow the fact that the world did not continue to wallow in carnivals had to be explained, and in his petition for clemency to Governor Hoffman, Rulloff put a rather different twist on the cultural transformation wrought by the letter *r*.

With the return of Bacchus from India, the letter R was brought into Greece, and was there employed in the application of language. The introduction of that letter was one of the most important events in the history of the human race. Few single occurrences have done more to awaken intellectual activity or cultivate artistic perceptions. To the introduction of that letter was ascribable, in great part, the enrichment of an ancient language; and with the same remote fact, in a manner which is truly wonderful, but which can not be mistaken, are connected leading ideas in the formation of the English language; particular letters in every sentence we employ, and the types of numerous words which are still peculiarities of the language we are now speaking.[50]

Somehow the energy poured into orgies and carnivals had been shifted to intellectual activity and artistic expression. Just how the priests managed this transformation could be easily explained by the simple expedient of postponing the hanging and giving Rulloff more time to work it out. Rulloff had not quite answered the lunacy commissioners' question about the "original language," the one where there had been no need for *r*. But he was prepared to address all his energies to it if he were given time.

> The phraseology of Homer is as perfect and as fresh now as when written, and will be for all time. Yet I do not believe that such a person as Homer ever lived. He was the center of a system which was perfected under that name. I believe, with others, that no one man was the author of all that is ascribed to Homer.[51]

Instead of asking about that alluring and mysterious *r* in Homer, the commissioners drifted into asking Rulloff if he thought Shakespeare was the author of all the works with which he was credited. The two doctors never explained exactly how this sequence of questions might bear upon sanity.

As long as he held to the high ground of abstraction and speculation, Rulloff deserved at least as much attention for his views on language as Peter Lesley had received. It was when he got down to cases that he got himself in real trouble.

One such example emerged in an interview with the reporter from the *New York Herald*. In proclaiming yet once again the loss to humanity if he should die without having fully laid out his "method," Rulloff had said, "I could go on for hours; but what is the use?"

> For the first time there was a look in his eye, as it gazed upon the grating as if the iron were entering into his soul. His lips remained compressed, but did not quiver.
>
> The good-natured District Attorney came to his relief with the Query:—"What is the derivation of love?"
>
> RULLOFF (quickly)—"'Voluptas,' which indicates both love and lust. I have an article in type, which will appear this week [in Ham Freeman's newspaper], on Ovid's 'Metamorphoses.' I show them to be a perfect philological study; as, for instance, with Æolus, from the names of whose parents all words relating to mind are taken. You are aware that the word 'favio' gave much trouble to the ancients as to its derivation. Well, I have found it, and you will say how simple it is; but will you conceive the study necessary to acquire familiarity enough with the language to trace the analogy? It comes from 'plaudo.' Take the 'p' away and you have 'laudo,' the first conveys satisfaction, the second praises. 'Favio,' then, is a

gentle shade, i. e. favor, and easily derivable by softening from 'plaudo.'"[52]

This stunning series of etymological deductions once again silenced Rulloff's hearers. What could it possibly mean to "take away" the *p* from *plaudo* and to derive therefrom *laudo*? It was the same principle by which Rulloff had explained the relation between *awe* and *daunt* by saying that the latter was simply the former with some consonants attached to it and that *love* and *lust* were related to *voluptas* by the fact that all three words shared some of the same letters.

Most of the reporters and philological visitors were mystified and bewildered by Rulloff's "derivations," but most of them also believed that there might, perhaps, be "something" to his theories. Among the German-influenced intellectuals, the endeavor to philologize myth and legend was an entirely respectable occupation. Thus Rulloff's claim that "all the words relating to mind" could be connected to the mythic god of the winds was not, on its face, utterly absurd. Rulloff's idea was, once again, akin to Lesley's notions, and Lesley had declared that "a general Arkite mythology governed the fancy of men and therefore shaped all their attempts at expressing their religious and historical ideas, both in architecture and in mythology."[53] For Rulloff and Lesley, these mythologies could be teased out of modern spoken languages by alphabetical prestidigitation.

Only George Sawyer seems to have pressed Rulloff really hard on his etymologies, and Sawyer's summary of them is entirely compatible with the long articles Rulloff published in Ham's newspaper.

Taking up one of his manuscripts he pointed to the following "καρ-βαν." This, he said, is the key to the system, which I did not invent but discover. Here we have the perfect root, from which all modern languages of any culture are derived, through the Greek. The perfect root is double, each root being triliteral, containing a vowel, a liquid, and a mutable. The perfect root has always these elements, but the perfect root is seldom apparent as such.

But to form words, the liquids may be interchanged among themselves, or with the mutables, and *vice versa*. The vowels usually interchange with each other, but by no definite rule that can at present be determined.

From *amictus,* clothing, is derived directly, *tunica,* tunic, and this affords, he said, a beautiful illustration of his method. Thus we take from the first word the letters *t, u, n, i, c, a.* These all being found here, the *n* of the second is plainly substituted for the *m* of the first, both being liquids. Yet, at first, he had said that *amictus* itself was nearly a perfect root, with a mutable substituted for one liquid, and the *a* merely prefixed.

Upon my asking whether the final *a* of *tunica* represented this initial *a* of *amictus,* or was an ending, and not a part of the root, he answered unconcernedly, "Oh! it may be one or the other, I am not sure of that. You must remember my system is not perfected, and must pardon any little inaccuracies of mine."[54]

Sawyer felt obliged to tell his readers that not even "the merest tyro in etymology" would simply toss the letters of one word into a hat and draw them out into the shape of another.

When asked by what law these seemingly arbitrary changes are made, we were told that the "necessity of the case" was the guide. He showed us many lists of words, all formed, as he explained, by his method, sometimes tracing a root through the Greek, Latin, English, and German, in what seemed an utterly arbitrary way. He stated, as a special adjunct of his plan, the discovery that one word may be derived from another by writing it backward. Thus from the Greek ερεφω we derive the Latin *operio.* . . .

Indeed, we failed to discover that he had any conception of the aims of philology, as a science. He did not seem to have information enough to understand what are the points upon which modern philologists are at work. When it was suggested to him how much had been accomplished in the study of cognate languages by a comparison of forms of later development in the Greek and Latin, with, in some cases, earlier forms in the Sanscrit, he said he had nothing to do with Sanscrit, that he meant, with a smile, no disrespect to that language, but it had nothing to do with his method. That the Sanscrit was earlier in any of its forms than the Greek, he said was stuff. When asked whether the relation between the Latin and Greek was that of brother and sister, he said the Greek was undoubtedly the parent of all Latin forms.[55]

One of Rulloff's last etymologies was composed in response to a question from Sawyer during that two-hour interview in his cell. Sawyer had asked him to explain *"squab,* a young pigeon." (*Squab* is usually taken to be of Scandinavian origin, and Rulloff claimed to know "all the languages of Europe" *except* the Scandinavian languages.) The line of descent Rulloff proposed in a letter to Sawyer written the day before his execution was: *palumba, columba, cuab, squab.* This sequence is as mysterious and as eccentric as Rulloff's other etymologies. *Palumba* is, indeed, a Latin word used for several kinds of birds; unrelated to that word, except in Rulloff's liberal notion of substituting one consonant for another, is *columba* 'dove.' The process by which *columba* becomes *cuab* is a purely Rullovian transformation in which "letters" that are not wanted in the result are discarded from the source to produce an "intermediate" form. This "origin" Rulloff "respectfully" submitted in the letter to Sawyer: *cuab* obviously becomes *squab.*[56]

While his lengthy essay on Rulloff did not appear until 1872, Sawyer almost immediately summarized his views in a newspaper essay. Ham Freeman gave Rulloff's response.

> This article met Rulloff's eye the evening before his execution, and one of the last things which he said to Mr. Becker was to denounce it, and to point out the injustice of it, saying that these gentlemen were with him but a short time, and that it was impossible that they should have comprehended his method in such a brief time.[57]

Here Rulloff was unable to distinguish being misunderstood from being wrong.

"Truly," Ham wrote sadly, "the ruling passion is strongest in death."[58]

Three days before his death, he wrote a final letter to Julius Seelye. In it he regretted the "circumstances" that had prevented them from becoming "the warmest and most intimate of friends." He said he could see no evidence of a benevolent purpose in the universe—a theme of their correspondence twenty years before—and declared, "My position is wholly and entirely unjust." Nonetheless it was time to bring things to a close. He said his papers would be sent to Tayler Lewis in Schenectady and then, if Seelye wished, they would be forwarded to him. Then, at last, the papers should be sent to his brother in Strattanville, Pennsylvania. He included a dollar to cover the cost of postage.

The pride that made Milton's Satan so obvious a comparison to those who thought about Rulloff was apparent in this final letter to Seelye: "In the whole history of the human race," Rulloff asserted, "no more remarkable instance of blind and stupid malignity can any where be shown than that which closes its eyes to the value of my discovery."[59]

At the end of his life, Rulloff left behind a letter he had composed in Greek. The reporter for the *New York Herald* wrote on May 19 that it was being translated.[60]

Nobody bothered to keep track of what it said.

11
●●●●●●●

I Wish They Would Hurry
This Thing Up

In Elmira, when Rulloff had yet one more time been sentenced to hang, Mark Twain was finishing up the manuscript that would be published later that year: *Roughing It*. He wrote the dedication with Rulloff on his mind.

> *To the Late Cain*
> This Book is Dedicated:
> Not on account of respect for his memory, for it merits little respect; not on account of sympathy with him, for his bloody deed placed him without the pale of sympathy, strictly speaking: but out of a mere humane commiseration for him in that it was his misfortune to live in a dark age that knew not the beneficent Insanity Plea.[1]

Later Twain thought better of the idea and made a different dedication of the book, but this draft written just days before Rulloff's execution shows the intensity of Twain's feelings.

Only a few days remained until Rulloff was to hang. Press coverage was intense, as was interest from townspeople. In the afternoon two days before the hanging, the sheriff was preparing to supervise the tests for the gallows, and a "respectable man," who asked if he could inspect the apparatus, approached him. Decorum and restraint were beginning to fail.

> The morbid infection has even extended to the female sex. Two ladies, in no wise young enough to do a giddy thing, accompanied by three small children, presented themselves at the Sheriff's

house, adjoining the prison, and craved to see the interesting philological murderer. While the perplexed Sheriff Martin was staring, open-mouthed, at the unfeminine request, the applicants swept past him and had looked on the wretched man through the grate of his dungeon. They were quickly shown a side door.[2]

But the whole affair threatened to end in a circus, and just at that point the burlesque came to town.

Scenes of darkness and light made for journalistic drama: darkness in Rulloff's cell as the hours wound toward Thursday and the execution; brightness as the performers prepared the limelight for their performance. The reporter for the *Herald* further provided a vivid picture.

> To appreciate the scene in the grim intensity, picture yourself a corridor in a prison, with two iron grated doors looking out upon it. Behind each of these doors is a sort of pen, with cells opening out on it. In one of these, to accommodate Rulloff, his bed is placed in the corner of the pen near the iron grated door. In daytime it is dark enough. Last night, was seen by the flicker of one candle the form of a man seated on a stool and crouched over a board upon his knees. Upon the board was a sheet of paper, upon which he was writing rapidly. Heaped around were lexicons, glossaries, dictionaries, &c. This was Rulloff. He did not look up as his visitors stood before the grating.[3]

Dozens of reporters, from the metropolitan dailies and from the rural weeklies, descended on Binghamton. They jostled for a view of the condemned man and, for those sufficiently persevering or famous, interviews with him and the principal figures in the drama, especially Sheriff Martin and George Becker. As a consequence of this intense coverage, the last days of Rulloff's life were minutely detailed. The clank of his leg irons was to echo through newspapers across the continent.

On Tuesday morning, the Western Union boy delivered a telegram to the jail, where Becker and Newell Whitney were talking with Rulloff. Becker read it.

> Rulloff cannot be saved. All efforts will prove useless. I thank God I have done my duty as I understand it, and regardless of the consequences.
>
> E. H. Freeman

He passed the telegram to Rulloff, who said, using the words of yet another outcast, Ishmael: "All the world is against me." (Ham had turned from journalism to advocacy and had gone to New York to seek a postponement from the governor's appointments secretary).

A second telegram brought official word that Governor Hoffman would not intervene. Becker asked Rulloff if he should continue his appeals: "I should be glad to go to New York by the night train." It was time, Rulloff thought, to "die game."

> No, let her rip. I shall be remembered long after Governor Hoffman is forgotten. He will be remembered only as a scheming politician; I as the author of one of the grandest theories on the formation of languages. You and I, Becker, are the two greatest men of the age. I am great on philology and you are of great weight.[4]

His ghastly joking was not funny, and he was ungrateful to boot. He told Becker that he regretted having given him as much of his life story as he had, and he feared that Becker would write a book about him. The idea that someone would write a biography filled with untruths preyed on Rulloff's mind.[5]

On Tuesday evening, the Wallace Sisters Burlesque prepared for an extravagant performance. As part of a regular tour of provincial cities, the troupe had attracted an enthusiastic following. Notices in the papers that nothing bawdy would be performed were merely an enticement, and a good deal of exposed female flesh could be counted on since all the performers but one were women, and he was a female impersonator.[6]

The main entertainment of the evening was to be a performance of John Brougham's *Po-ca-hon-tas*, or, to add the extravagantly full subtitle, *An Original Aboriginal Erratic Operatic Semi-Civilized and Demi-Savage Extravaganza, being a Per-Version of Ye Trew and Wonder-refulle Hystorie of Ye Rennownned Princes, Po-ca-hon-tas*. Full of incongruities (like Powatan singing a song in an Irish brogue), ridiculous rhymes, and extravagant wordplay, it was a sure-fire hit. Everyone knew the story of Captain Smith and his rescue by the beautiful Indian maiden, and the romanticized spectacle offered wonderful opportunities for high jinks. The Wallace Sisters were rollicking along when they reached the exchange between the Indian king and Smith.

KING: You shan't be long! prepare yourself! but stay!
    You'd rather not be hanged, I think you say!
SMITH: I'm really fearful it would be a drop
    Too much for me![7]

With Rulloff on their minds, the liquorish joke was too much for the audience: "A full audience was enjoying the multiple jokes that sparkle through [the play], when suddenly the laughing ceased, and the house was still."[8]

Early Wednesday afternoon, Rulloff ate his last meal. Reporters noted wryly that he had been feeding morsels of his food to a rat that lived in the jail, and that animal appeared promptly when Rulloff's dinner was delivered to the cell. In the first of many farewells, Rulloff smiled and told the rat that he would have no more food from him.

At three o'clock he requested George Becker to call on him immediately. Becker responded without delay. Rulloff received him with great cordiality, apologized for his earlier criticisms, and thanked him for his efforts in a "desperate case." He said that his trial and the subsequent legal proceedings had been "a farce and a mockery of justice."

Not long after Becker departed, Sheriff Martin visited Rulloff and asked him delicately what should be done with his body. It was the first of a series of such inquiries from well-intentioned persons wishing to have all the events of the next day clearly planned. On this occasion, Rulloff replied: "You can do what you damn please with it."

As a precaution against suicide, the sheriff removed the kerosene lamp from the cell, leaving only a candle to illuminate the darkness.

Still preoccupied with the idea that he would be anatomized in posthumous biographies, Rulloff set about erasing the paper record that he had so abundantly gathered around him. He burned all the papers in his cell, but he could not get at the manuscript Becker had deposited at the bank.[9]

After the destruction of his papers, Rulloff grew more cheerful. He was animated and chatted with the three deputies assigned to watch him for signs of suicide. At half past nine, he lay down to sleep, but it was only a nap. At eleven o'clock he turned to his dictionaries.

Shortly after midnight, the *Tribune* reporter visited Rulloff.

He sat before me, the gas in his cell flaring out a light bright as noonday, his meaningless small brown eyes dancing good nature.

"My works," he continued, "have not met with proper apprecia-
tion—particularly when you recall the charlatan theories that gain
credence now-a-days. I have done that which shall make this
epoch illustrious to other generations, but I go to my grave unrec-
ognized and unrewarded. A work of beauty—a triumph of genius
must have educated recognition. For instance, an Indian takes
more readily to a highly-colored daub than to the most delicately-
tinted and exquisitely finished painting—so with this lingual science which I have brought to completion. Learned idiots make
ridicule of it, while ignorant alike of its fundamental truths and the
beautiful and symmetrical principle involved. My system has
rationalized the complex system of primitive derivation and roots,
and can be used for every known tongue. "If I could have had
time"—absently looking about the cell and clasping his neck with
significant anguish—"you know." The sentence died out in an
inarticulate guttural.[10]

He continued to claim that Burrows's unreliable testimony invalidated
the proceedings. The governor was a low politician with no interest in
justice. Rulloff's mood swung wildly between bitterness and humor.

Then, in the early hours of Thursday morning, Sheriff Root of Tompkins County entered Rulloff's cell, hoping to learn at last about Harriet
and Priscilla. At first Rulloff seemed open to the topic. "Things about
here will be all hurly-burly tomorrow, and I had better do all my talking
tonight."[11] Despite being willing to pay the five-thousand-dollar fee that
Rulloff had once demanded for a truthful account of his life, Sheriff
Root departed none the wiser. Rulloff still feared that the fabulists in
the press corps would embellish his life story with all sorts of ghastly
fabrications, but he held tight to his remaining secrets.

As the night wore on toward dawn, Rulloff continued to joke and
swear, and observers regarded him with horror. In an elaborate jape, he
tore up slips of paper and said they were checks drawn on a bank. "The
bank is open boys, go and draw your money. I think you [referring to the
inside guard] are better looking than the others and won't need so much
to carry on business."

He seemed restless, and walked the limits of his apartment,
laughing and joking with the two men who watched with him
inside his cell. Soon he sat down on the couch and stared at the

walls, watching the daylight breaking through the grates. A loud crowing of cocks roused him from his reverie, and he asked facetiously what the rooster had to crow for at that unseasonable hour.[12]

Rulloff continued to talk animatedly with the two deputies charged with watching him, Thomas Johnson and Austin B. Stillson. Both of them had journeyed with him to Elmira, and they had come to know him well during the nine months he spent in the Binghamton jail. In the small, male world of the jail, Rulloff and his watchers developed intimacy if not friendship. Reporters thought that the bawdy jokes Rulloff told that night were a sign of his mental depravity, but they were more likely part of a pattern of male banter long before established.

> He was now left alone to the company of Thomas Johnson, the watchman, and resumed his search at the dictionary. What a picture! This man, on the verge of eternity, quibbling with words as though it was some little half-hour, like that before a pleasant dinner party, but really a *mauvaise quart d'heure de Rabelais* of the most terrible nature, with the grim figure of death stretching his awful wings over his unknown future. The hours rolled on, one, two, and still Rulloff chatted, read, told stories, in which levity, blasphemy, and obscenity were the features. Then he turned to mapping out mathematical puzzles and showing them to his astonished watchmen, who looked on him with open mouth and eyes as either a prodigy or a monster, they could not tell which. . . .
>
> This mood presently changed, and, turning suddenly upon the Deputy Sheriff, he cried vivaciously, "I ought to make some great discovery this morning. The paper I gave yesterday contains the basis of all my science."
>
> At length the watchman broke the silence by remarking, "Edward, your business matters in this world ought to be pretty nearly fixed."
>
> Rulloff started up and said, thoughtfully, "Yes, I guess they are." He was thoughtful for a minute, and then he broke forth once more into his levity and obscenity.[13]

Even though his book on Rulloff had been published two months earlier, Ed Crapsey still had articles to write for the *New York Times*. Deep in the night, he badgered Rulloff for more, while the *Herald* reporter scribbled a venomous portrait of the "dapper" reporter.

It was now three o'clock, and at this point a reporter, who, in his indecent, pitiful anxiety to obtain the shadow of one item for his blanket sheet, stood in front of Rulloff's cell for half an hour pestering him with questions upon the doomed man's unfinished book. After finding that Rulloff would not give him any information of the morbid sort the reporter relieved the man at death's door by going away. Not content with this, the anxious, pitiful creature got in and crouched behind the sheet iron door of the cell and remained there for some time afterwards, eavesdropping congenially.[14]

It seemed as if every minute of the long night would be documented for the curiosity of the national public, and the Western Union office bustled with activity as reporters sent their stories out over the wires.

Four o'clock sounded and the man continued his anecdotes.

"Edward," said the watchman, "did you murder that man, Mirrick, or not?"

"I did not. It was Al Jarvis who did it. Stand up and I'll show you how it happened. It was all Mirrick's fault."

Here he went through a pantomime, showing the relative positions of the two young dry-goods clerks, his two accomplices, Jarvis and Dexter, and himself. His demonstration, without going into unpleasant details, tallied with his statement on the trial but conflicts not only with the testimony of the surviving clerk, Burrows, but with itself, he, in fact averring that Jarvis fired the fatal shot while grasped from behind by the murdered man, Mirrick.

The reporter did not want to dwell on the unpleasant detail that Merrick was crushing Jarvis's testicles while holding him face down over the counter.

The impossibility of Rulloff's explanation will be seen in the fact that Mirrick was shot in the back of the head. Rulloff reverted to his books again, and while thus engaged six o'clock boomed out on the dawning day, which was to be the last that would ever dawn for Rulloff. The deep sound fell on his ears, and he started up with a look of anxiety.

"What o'clock is that, Thomas?"

"Six."

"Ha! time is growing shorter!' His whole manner changed, and beads of perspiration stood upon his forehead. The shackles had been removed, and he paced up and down the corridor greatly agitated. The watchman now asked him a question:

"Are you satisfied that you are going to die in a just cause for a crime you have committed?"

Rulloff replied quickly, with a scowl, "No, not by a damned sight!"

"Have you ever given a true history of your life, Edward?"

Rulloff: "The history of my life will be told in my book."

Again he sat down to his books, as if in them he could find the charm against thought, prospective or retrospective. But this time it failed. The lexicons would be sometimes upside down, and he passed from one to the other nervously. Again he started to his feet and gave way to the thoughts that forced themselves in with an increasing pertinacity, as the blessed daylight forced its reluctant way through the thick window bars into the charnel semi-darkness of his dungeon.

Purple prose bedazzled with adjectives and metaphors found an eager readership: "blessed daylight" forcing "its reluctant way into the charnel semi-darkness." No reporter worth his lexicon would have written, "Dawn came."

How long this hopeless agony would have lasted can only be conjectured, but another watchman asked him for his autograph to save him from any distressing thoughts.

"Here's a book, Stillson," said Rulloff; "take this instead."

The book was a little religious *brochure* for prison circulation, entitled "The Cross in the Cell," which had been sent him by a pious old lady.

"Won't you write your name in it?"

"It's a book, Stillson, that I never believed in and never ordered. I won't. Here's a copy of my shorthand."[15]

Just after six o'clock the sheriff came to shift Rulloff to a strong room in his house. No band of Rulloff's friends would break in and find him there.

Alone with his guard, one of the ways that Rulloff passed the time was by "playing horse."

> He would walk rapidly across the floor. The guard would shout, "Whoa! there, whoa, sir!" Then Mr. Rulloff, the great philologist, etc., would kick up his heels and neigh in imitation of a horse.[16]

Murderers went to the gallows nearly every day, somewhere in America. Few of them were so minutely observed. Nothing should elude the curious public.

Thursday was a festive day in Binghamton. It was a spring day suited for a picnic or a "feast of horror."

> The morning of the execution dawned bright and beautiful. With the earliest rays of light the citizens of the town in which a human being was to be hanged were astir, and by 7 o'clock the streets were alive with an eager, impatient multitude, hungry for the feast of horror that was promised. At this early hour the broad, open space surrounding the jail began to fill with people of all ages, classes, and conditions. The surrounding country for miles away emptied its population into the city at an early hour, all anxious to breathe the atmosphere that was pregnant with the horrible execution.
>
> Countrymen in whole families came early in their various vehicles, and clamored for available positions in the neighborhood of the place of execution. The early trains on all the railroads brought swarms of similarly greedy horror-seekers. By 8 o'clock dense throngs of men, women, and children surrounded the jail, and by 10 o'clock the multitude could be numbered by thousands. It was, of course, known to each and all of these that it was absolutely impossible to get even a partial view of the execution, or even to hear anything that might be said attending the shocking scene; yet they struggled desperately for the positions nearest to the jail building, and urged their preemption claims of standing space with all the pertinacity of squatter sovereigns. Meanwhile the streets and shops of the town were crowded with people, who were anxious to see what could be seen, though they might not see

the execution, or turn their pleasure trip into one of business, and do their spring shopping while the opportunity offered. Thus the storekeepers drove a thriving business, while the peripatetic venders of nostrums and quackery found an abundant harvest. Altogether, it was a great day for Binghamton. It was the greatest holiday the town has had for a long time, and replenished its coffers in no small degree.

Surveying the people gathered on Court House Square, Rulloff called them a "damn pretty rabble for such an occasion."[17]

Two of Rulloff's brothers-in-law, Eph and Aaron Schutt, had made the trip from Ithaca. Long convinced that Rulloff had murdered their sister and her child, they hoped that he would provide details, even help them locate the bodies. Rulloff, once again, disappointed them.[18]

Becker and Whitney were his next visitors, and together they awaited Ham's arrival. He was on his way home from New York on the night train.

BECKER: Edward, I suppose you still think that you are a martyr to the cause of science and education.

RULLOFF: Yes. The world has not appreciated and has misunderstood me. If my life could be preserved, I could be of great service to the cause of education, but such is my luck. What can't be cured must be endured.

RULLOFF: Have you heard from my brother?

BECKER: Yes; I have just received a letter from him.

The letter was handed to the prisoner. It was dated at a station on the Erie Railway, May 13, and postmarked May 17. It was a kind letter, exhibiting deep interest in the condemned man's behalf, and had evidently been sadly delayed in its transmission.[19]

It became obvious to all that Rulloff's brother would not arrive to bid him farewell.

Becker then asked Rulloff what should be done with his remains.

I don't wish my remains to be desecrated. If buried in the Potter's Field, they will probably be disturbed by some hyena. Can't they be placed in a vault somewhere to await the action of my friends, if I have any?

Becker agreed to try to carry out Rulloff's wishes.

Rulloff asked Becker the time. "Ah, we have an hour more of it."[20]

At 10:20, Rulloff saw the crowd from the window: "What are all these people doing here?"

> BECKER: "Well, I suppose they have a morbid desire to see a murder committed."

He then turned from the window and sat down beside Mr. Becker. Taking hold of that gentleman's watch chain, he began toying playfully with it. The chain is a long gold guard chain on which are hung several trinkets. Fumbling a miniature compass attached to the chain as a charm, he said:

"I suppose that is to take your bearings if you get lost. Well, keep your head clear and take care of yourself and you need no other bearings. You have a bright future before you."[21]

Another reporter saw a more sinister purpose in Rulloff's toying with Becker's watch chain.

> It was plain that he was meditating some desperate effort and not the less earnestly that his latent endeavor had been defeated. While his counsel sat talking to him in a low tone, he approached him, and, looking wistfully in his eyes, ran his fingers slowly down the links of a long gold chain that encircled the gentleman's neck, and, with a quick secret movement, plunged his hands in his vest pocket, as though in search of some means of ridding himself of life. He turned away, with a face livid with rage and fear, and sank gloomily on the edge of the bed, muttering indistinguishable imprecations.[22]

At 10:35, while Rulloff was talking with Becker, a breathless Ham Freeman entered the second floor of the jail and was received "very affectionately." As was always his practice, Rulloff shook him eagerly by the hand and Ham felt better.

> We plucked up courage, and entered into conversation with him for some ten minutes, during which he condemned the action of the Governor for failing to see the merits of his work, and said the world would yet feel the great worth of his method. As our inter-

view drew to a close, he earnestly thanked me for the interest I had taken in his case and efforts in his behalf, and hoped I never would have occasion to regret my course towards him. He then took me by the hand and gave a hearty shake, accompanied with an affectionate kiss, and implored of the writer to stand firm, as he certainly should on the gallows.[23]

Sheriff Martin's worry that his famous prisoner would commit suicide was well grounded, and Rulloff may well have looked to George Becker to supply him with a knife or other means of easy death. Certainly he had negotiated with Ham Freeman about ways to evade the noose.

He had requested me to provide him with a lancet, and with fifteen grains of *sulfate of morphia,* so that he would be prepared to COMMIT SUICIDE in case his counsel were not successful in saving his life. I had never promised that I would, and did not say I would not. He was afterwards very angry with myself and others, after all hope was gone, because he did not have his poison or lancet. He indirectly alluded to it more than once. He had several plans for me to give it to him. One was, to procure a lancet, take off the handle and place the blade in a book; the other was to put the morphia into one or two capsules. I sometimes think that the reason why he embraced me on the morning of his execution was so that I could slip a capsule, containing poison, from my mouth to his.[24]

Rulloff then said goodbye to his lawyer.

Rulloff and Becker then shook hands cordially. Rulloff said to his counsel: "I hope you will not entertain any hard feelings towards me for anything I may ever have said to you inadvertently. The deplorable situation in which I have always been since I met you has made me irritable and nearly distracted. Please be present to the last."[25]

The sheriff had made sure that persons with an interest in the case would be present as witnesses. Among the crowd were three of Fred Merrick's cousins.

About one hundred and fifty persons assembled in the yard. They were either officials of the Binghamton municipality or else officials of other neighboring cities and counties. They were Sheriffs, ex-Sheriffs, District Attorneys, ex–District Attorneys, Mayors, and ex-Mayors, City Marshals and ex–City Marshals. Besides these were some fifty representatives of the press, mostly of the rural order with huge notebooks, on which they kept continually making notes with a diligence a good deal removed from good taste. The two clergymen, who offered their services, managed to slip out into the yard and, to their shame be it said, had wretched unclerical taste enough to remain witnesses of a scene of strangulation in which, as ministers, they could take no part, and hence should not have gazed upon the agony of a wretched being simply to gratify worse than idle curiosity.[26]

At 11:15, one of the sheriff's deputies struck a bell.

Prompt to the minute, Sheriff Martin passed rapidly up stairs, followed by his deputies, and entering Rulloff's cell announced that the time was come. No muscle moved in the prisoner's stolid face. He got up briskly, and stood forth arrayed in faded and shiny black, greatly the worse for the wear. His linen was spotlessly white, his face calm, and in general he presented the appearance of an honest farmer ready for a "meeting." The Sheriff stepped up and threw the noose over his neck, thrusting the long end in the prisoner's bosom. He sought it, examined it a moment curiously, then replaced it in his breast. Even at this moment, this man of iron smiled grimly, and extended his hand and motioning to the Sheriff, told him to lead on—he was ready.[27]

Now the procession moved toward the stairs leading to the ground-floor corridor, past the coffin draped with army blankets, and out into the sunny yard crammed with nearly 150 people—all of them men. Those who were not present or former officials were made temporary deputies by the accommodating sheriff, even the two Baptist pastors and the reporters from the rural weeklies.

Rulloff's arms were pinioned. As everyone prepared to leave the room, he said,

"Boys, I must shake hands with you all up here, for I'll do nothing of the sort down stairs."

All present shook hands with him, and as they were again about to move Rulloff said:—

"You won't have any clergymen bellowing down there, nor prayers, nor any damned bosh, will you, Mr. Sheriff?"

"No, sir," replied the Sheriff, who appeared much affected.

When the gallows beam was reached, Rulloff was caused to stand on the little square already marked out. The pinioning of the knees and ankles was quickly proceeded with and the halter was fastened to the thick rope above. . . .

The sheriff, still standing before the unrepentant murderer, said:—

"Mr. Rulloff, have you anything to say before the sentence of the law is carried into effect?"

Rulloff answered, after about the pause of five heart beats, "Nothing at all."

The Sheriff moved round to the left side of the dying culprit and said:—

"It now wants twenty-six minutes of the time which I had fixed in my mind for carrying out the sentence of the law upon you and if you have anything to say you shall be given time to utter it."

Rulloff clenched his lips but did not speak. After about a minute he turned to Brown, who was at his side, and said, almost inaudibly, as if apologizing for the pinioning of his limbs,

"I cannot stand still."[28]

The *Sun* reporter was closer to Rulloff than the others, and he enlivened his story with a deadly detail.

The Sheriff was still loath to give the signal, and after a few moments' hesitation entered into a whispered consultation with some of his assistants. While this was going on, the prisoner turned to the keeper on his right and said in a low tone, "I wish they would hurry this thing up." The keeper did not repeat the remark to the Sheriff; but soon afterward the Sheriff advanced again and said:

"Mr. Rulloff, is it your desire that the execution should proceed without further delay?"[29]

Rulloff shook his head.

"You do not desire any delay?"

Another shake of the head.

The Sheriff made a sign to Brown, who took off the cap on Rulloff's head and substituted the white cap, which was pulled down over his face. He then gently pulled the noose, which was run up taut. He then gave a small pull to the signal cord, and the body was raised with a sudden jerk three feet from the ground, apparently dislocating the neck. The force of the upward movement threw his right hand, with a spasmodic movement, out of the pants pocket, but as if the stubborn will of the dying murderer was revived to assert itself in very defiance of the gate of eternity, after a few efforts to find the pocket, the hand slipped in again and remained there. This was the only movement made until life was extinct.[30]

The reporter for the *Sun* looked at his watch. It was precisely forty minutes past eleven.

12
········

A Cabinet of Skulls

The body, dead and despised, of Edward Howard Rulloff was removed from the scaffold on Thursday, May 18, 1871, a little after noon.

Rulloff had been right to worry about the fate of his corpse. Plenty of people, for reasons of curiosity, revenge, or science, would be delighted to dismember it, and Rulloff had already discussed the disposition of his corpse with Sheriff Martin and with George Becker. Yet a third time the gruesome topic arose; with one of the deputies as the hanging party prepared to go down to the execution yard, Rulloff had again asked that his body be kept locked in a vault until his brother could claim it. The deputy, too, made solemn assurances, and George Becker was left with the duty of disposing of the corpse.

One person who wanted access to Rulloff's body was Jefferson Beardsley, who kept an "art gallery" in Ithaca, where interest in Rulloff had been at least as intense as in Binghamton. Beardsley saw money to be made from a death mask and sent two of his men to the jail. After Rulloff's body was removed from the gallows, they shaved his whiskers and applied plaster of Paris to his features. They were pleased that his mold showed, very distinctly, the mark of the noose.[1]

Then the deputies took charge of Rulloff's body. They displayed it in an open coffin in front of the Binghamton jail, flanked by two companies of the New York National Guard. Disgusted, Ham Freeman informed Becker of the "horrid exhibition." Becker asked the sheriff to move the coffin back into the jailhouse, and it was, but not before five thousand people had pressed curiously around for a last glimpse of Rulloff intact.

Rulloff's brother did not claim his body. On Friday morning, Becker made a deal with Dr. George Burr, a professor at the Geneva Medical College and a longtime Binghamton practitioner. In return for the privilege of anatomizing Rulloff, Dr. Burr promised to bury the body in a lot he owned in a cemetery in Binghamton. In return, he wanted to keep the head. His purpose: to determine the nature of evil in human beings by scientific means.

Thirty hours after the execution, Dr. Burr and his son, Dr. Daniel S. Burr, sawed off the head, with a good part of the neck attached. "Rulloff's head was opened in the usual way, by parting the scalp over the top of the head from one ear to the other, and sawing off the top."[2] It was difficult and distasteful work, but the doctors did it with care and accuracy. Extracting the brain and setting it aside, they removed the remaining flesh from the skull by soaking it in a caustic liquid.

Toward evening, the town sexton, Selah P. Rood, brought round his hearse and loaded the coffin into it. A small procession formed, with Dr. Daniel Burr and Ralph Botts, a reporter for the *Binghamton Democrat,* following the hearse in the only buggy. Others followed on foot. At 7:00 P.M. Rulloff's body was buried. But when darkness fell, "medical students from St. Louis, Albany and other places that night invaded the grave and dug up what was left of him, in the vain hope of finding the head."[3]

Four months later, on September 14, George Burr presented his findings to the Medico-Legal Society in New York City. By the end of the year, Dr. Burr's words had been published, enhanced by illustrations of the skull and the brain.[4]

Dr. Burr knew his audience and prefaced his findings with an account of Rulloff's criminal career only slightly less lurid than those that had appeared earlier that summer. Having satisfied his audience with highlights of the well-known story, Burr turned his attention to his findings.

Rulloff had been strangled, an excruciating and lengthy process. The attending physicians at the hanging had been Joseph H. Chittenden, another prominent Binghamton physician, and Dan Burr, who had been present at every stage of the proceedings, from the time the bodies of Jarvis and Dexter had been pulled from the river. Moments after Rulloff's body was hoisted from the ground, both doctors declared that the neck had broken and that death was instantaneous.

But that was not true. First there was the horrifying action of

Rulloff's removing his hand from his pocket and then putting it back. After two minutes, Rulloff had shrugged his shoulders as if gasping for breath. Five minutes passed, and Rulloff again struggled for breath. Eight minutes: "His pulse beats 10 to the quarter. It is going very slow." Nine minutes: "I can't feel any pulse at the wrist." Ten minutes: "A slow motion of the heart." Fifteen minutes. Dan Burr now heard no heart beat. Dr. Chittenden moved him aside and listened. He heard nothing. At twenty-three minutes: "A slight snapping of the heart as if two pieces of tape were snapped together." Rulloff was dead.[5]

When George and Dan Burr began their dissection, they realized at once how long and painful Rulloff's death had been. So slow and steady had been the pressure on his neck that the spinal chord was intact and none of the neck bones broken. Pressure inside the skull had been intense, and the lens of the right eye fractured. Though he did not say so, George Burr must have been surprised, as were the executioners, that, when the white cloth hood was removed from the corpse, the features were hardly contorted and there was no tumefaction of the face.

One thing was immediately obvious as the Burrs examined their specimen: Rulloff's head was unusually large. Interpreting this observation in his lecture, Dr. Burr concluded that the "exterior view [suggests] a dull, heavy, and somewhat coarse organization."[6] As Dan sawed through the head just above the eyes, they also noticed the exceptional thickness of the skull. Above the left eye socket, it was half an inch thick. The thinnest spot was at the right temple where it was a quarter inch. Both dimensions were, the doctors thought, highly distinctive, at least double that of "ordinary skulls."

The physicians present at the lecture did not need Dr. Burr to remind them of the meaning of this heavy skull. Hooper's *Medical Dictionary* had this to say about maniacs: "From Dr. Greding's observations, it appears that the skulls of the greater number of such persons are commonly very thick. Some he found of a most extraordinary thickness."[7]

Dr. Burr and his son set out to determine the capacity of the cranium. Their initial measurement, calculated using the procedure laid down by Dr. J. Aitken Meigs,[8] was 145 cubic inches, an impossibly large number. Inventing a wonderfully American solution, they finally computed its size by filling the skull with cornmeal and adding some extra space for error, at 120 cubic inches.[9] Fiddling the numbers brought Rulloff back from the status of a prodigy into the higher ranges of normal.

The inspection of the interior of the skull and the brain was not much more exacting than their earlier endeavors had been. George Burr did his best to make his observations square with his hypothesis that Rulloff was a criminal type. Further calculations produced the finding that the cerebrum was a smaller share of the total brain mass than usual. The "animal part" of the brain, in short, was more vigorous than the human part of it.

Yet there was no gainsaying that the entire brain was huge—fifty-nine ounces, ten ounces heavier than the average for a man of Rulloff's age. Baron Cuvier, the French naturalist who had died in 1832, had the heaviest brain ever recorded—between sixty-four and sixty-five ounces. Daniel Webster, the titanic orator whose towering brow made him the model for personifying a craggy outcrop in his native New Hampshire, was thought to have had a brain in the same range, though the measurement was a guess since part of it had been destroyed by disease. These two brains had belonged to geniuses, and Rulloff's approached them in weight. But Burr did not draw attention to these comparisons, leaving them to his colleague Dr. Buchanan of Syracuse, who had made the study of the brain a particular specialty. Had Burr provided such a context for Rulloff's weighty brain, he would have been pressed to explain how a man of huge cranial capacity and heavy brain could have become a criminal deserving of the death penalty.

At this point in his lecture, George Burr turned his attention to the parts that had not been of sufficient interest to preserve and anatomize: the remainder of Rulloff's body.

> His entire organization, as has been remarked of the cranium, was coarse. It was not without vigor or powers of endurance, but its material was not of the best quality, and was wanting in that fine finish which is now regarded as the best development of the human structure.[10]

With these scientific deliberations, Dr. Burr put aside his measurements and observations and resumed his narrative of the exciting capture, dramatic trial, and enthralling final weeks of the man whose head he held in his hand.

Yet there was one more medical question to be considered: Was Rulloff of sound mind? This was a matter that had deeply concerned others who followed the trial attentively, especially Ham Freeman. The insanity commissioners had found him sane, and Rulloff himself declared, "I do not pretend to be either insane or an idiot." Prevented by Rulloff, his lawyers had not tried to introduce an insanity plea or to argue for diminished responsibility. Still, the question remained.

> There are, however, many features in Rulloff's case that go to establish the conviction that his mind was not evenly balanced, but that, in many of its operations, it had become disordered and unsound.[11]

Burr was not prepared to say that he was personally convinced of this imbalance, only that "many features" suggested that possibility. But what were these features? How might Rulloff's condition have arisen? Was he destined to murder by the shape of his head, the configuration of his brain, or the lack of "fine finish" expected in persons who did not become criminals? Had he become so obsessed by his mania that he could no longer judge right from wrong? Further evidence distressing to George Burr came from Rulloff's inability to accept responsibility for his conduct, for his persistence in seeing a brutal murder as a "misfortune," or a bungled burglary as a "difficulty."

"This distortion of his mind prevented Rulloff from cultivating the higher moral sentiments, or developing his finer emotional nature,"[12] Dr. Burr declared as he approached the end of this lecture. But in that case, was Rulloff culpable? Had he been "prevented" by the shape of his head from making right moral choices? Was it right that he had been put to death?

These are questions Dr. Burr declined to treat. In the end, he provided both a question and an answer:

> How much the peculiarity of his organization had to do with the mental phenomena he exhibited, or how far it ought to be considered in mitigation of his guilt, it is not yet time to discuss or determine.

When would the time come? He did not say. It was almost as if Dr. Burr were echoing Rulloff's response to Judge Hogeboom's invitation to speak before being sentenced to death: "It is not deemed desirable to say anything at present."

George Burr did recognize that society needed no more of Rulloff's crimes, and the law had judged that the best guarantee that his "depredations should cease" would be to hang him. Such further judgment of his crimes as needed to be made would be made, Dr. Burr declared, by "the tribunal within whose jurisdiction he now is."[13] That is, Rulloff's soundness of mind and fitness of body would have to be judged in heaven.

If the divine appeals court were then sitting, Dr. Burr thought, it might be because some error in the human courts had led to injustice. Not that he was sure, of course. But it might be that the "features" of Rulloff's case suggested insanity, despite the speedy judgment of the lunacy commissioners that his mind was sound. Even while Rulloff had been alive, the question of his sanity was a matter of lively debate. In *The Nation,* in the issue whose publication date was that of the hanging, an editorial writer had savaged the commissioners. Their report, he thought, was "a deal more convincing as testimony to their unfitness for the business they had in hand than as testimony of any value concerning the sanity of the convict."[14]

In his account of Rulloff's life, Ham Freeman gave the same worries prominent attention:

> Rulloff was a ferocious monster, and so far as disposition could relieve him from responsibility, he was not strictly responsible for his acts, though the law held him accountable.[15]

"Disposition" was merely another term for what Dr. Burr had called the "features" of Rulloff's character and the "distortion" of his mind. Ham had liked Rulloff, though he was horrified by his crimes. Neither the experienced doctor nor the young editor of the *Leader* knew quite what to think.

In wrapping up his lecture, Dr. Burr reminded his audience of what they already knew: "The case of Rulloff will rank with the most celebrated criminal trials of our country."[16] Of course there was some self-interest in this exultation. This was his case. He had bartered for the body and dissected the head. There were in it, he said, "peculiar circumstances" and it had aroused "great interest." He had taken the train to New York to enhance that interest before an audience of city doctors, including Dr. R. Ogden Doremus, secretary of the Medico-Legal Society, who had certainly not forgotten his own brush with Rulloff in 1858 and who was keenly interested in forensic medicine. It was a great occasion for a doctor from a small upstate city not yet a century removed from the wilderness.

In his lecture, Dr. Burr had discussed some other celebrated cases. There had been Ephraim K. Avery, acquitted in 1833 for the murder of a young woman whom, most people believed, he had made pregnant. What made Avery interesting? He had been a clergyman.[17] There had been Richard P. Robinson, acquitted in 1836 of murdering a beautiful prostitute, who had been bludgeoned with an ax and her rooms set afire. What made Robinson interesting? He was only nineteen years old and smitten with Ellen Jewett, the dead woman.[18] There was the accused killer Dr. Burr called "Mrs. Cunningham," or Emma Augusta Burdell Cunningham. She had been acquitted in 1857 of murdering Harvey Burdell, a prominent New York dentist. She lived in sumptuous rooms not far from Dr. Burdell's office and declared herself his "secret wife."

Each of these old murder cases, George Burr declared, "attracted a large share of public attention and interest, but none more so than did the trial of Edward H. Rulloff."[19] What they all had in common, his listeners immediately recognized, was lust, illicit sexual connections in a century that prided itself on high morality and spartan denial.

Here the case of Jane Jarvis came in for scrutiny. Speculation about her had begun back in Ithaca in 1858, and her story was revived in the weeks leading up to the Binghamton trial. That they had been lovers in the jail was obvious to everyone, and they kept in close contact in the years that followed: they had corresponded through Rulloff's Pennsylvania brother, and she had come to New York to visit him from Williamstown, Massachusetts, the town in which she had been raised and where she now labored to support herself as a worker in a spinning mill. She had even appeared at the trial, and Rulloff spoke sadly of her in the days before the execution.

Jane Jarvis was a pitiable figure. Her love for Rulloff led to the abrupt collapse of her marriage, public humiliation, and, finally, the death by drowning of her firstborn son. Sentimentalists among those following the trial could easily weep over her fate and wonder that she had been drawn again and again to Rulloff's side. The source of Rulloff's power over others was difficult to pin down, though everyone had an opinion about the "magnetic" and "hypnotic" quality that many very different people experienced when in his company. Such powers were fearful in the hands of evil persons, and therefore dangerous to society.[20]

Ed Crapsey and Ham Freeman wrestled with the relation of the demonic to the psychological, but scientists could not be so easily appeased. They had to find something physical or chemical. George and Dan Burr did not expect a demon to fly out when they sawed off the top of Rulloff's head, but they were in the thrall of ideas about the soul that would soon come to seem absurd. They believed that there was something in that head that would give them the explanation, if they could only reduce it to measurement. The geometry by which they calculated the cubic inches of his cranium, the scales on which they weighed the brain: These would tell the truth.

Race and racial classification were nineteenth-century obsessions. When individuals could be reduced to type and classified, they could be explained. To do so required a taxonomy, and to scientists it seemed natural that this taxonomy be constructed from human heads. The leading thinker in this field was Samuel George Morton, a Philadelphia doctor with medical degrees from both the Universities of Pennsylvania and of Edinburgh. "I commenced the study of Ethnology in 1830," Dr. Morton recalled, and to do so he needed a collection of heads. "When I sought the materials for my proposed lecture, I found to my surprise that they could be neither bought nor borrowed."[21]

To remedy this deficiency, Morton began to collect skulls, both human and animal, and he arranged them in a "cabinet," not a piece of furniture, but what would later be called a "museum." From this collection he wrote learnedly in *Crania Americana,* and he issued, for the benefit of visitors, his *Catalogue of Skulls of Man and the Inferior Animals.* Among his purposes was to create a history of humanity, and so he was especially interested in the images of ancient Egyptians that had aroused so much European and American attention after Napoleon's soldiers had rediscovered the Pyramids and the Sphinx. Morton's focus was to establish "the physical or organic characters which distinguish the several races of men," and he was convinced, along with everyone else, that there were five such races: black, brown, red, white, yellow. By 1849, Morton had collected 867 human skulls (and 601 of "inferior animals"), and his cabinet was a Philadelphia attraction for the scientifically minded. In his *Catalogue,* he invited contributions to his collection. There are as yet no Eskimaux, he wrote, and no skulls of "the long headed people of the Lake of Titicaca in Bolivia."

In an influential work of 1855, *Types of Mankind,* Morton provided the insight of a quarter century of ethnology. "In a word," he concluded,

The whole of Africa, south of 10 N. lat., shows a succession of human beings with intellects as dark as their skins, and with a cephalic conformation that renders all expectance of their future melioration an Utopian dream, philanthropical, but somewhat senile.[22]

Emancipation of American slaves, it followed, was a hopeless ideal held out by wild-eyed Abolitionists and New England ninnies.

Unsurprisingly, given the preoccupation with race, Rulloff's background was deeply interesting to all observers. Ham Freeman reported that Rulloff's father had been a loyalist who left Connecticut for New Brunswick at the end of the American Revolution. Ham thought the family was German. A century later, members of the family regarded themselves as descended from Danes. Crapsey told the world that Rulloff's ancestors were Dutch:

This man came of most reputable and sterling stock, for in his veins flowed the blood which had amazed the world in the last half of the sixteenth century by those sublime exhibitions of heroism and fortitude which shattered the Spanish empire and founded the Dutch Republic.[23]

Rulloff's race, whether Dutch or German, should have bred excellence rather than evil. And "stock" was a term well-known, not only to race theorists like Morton but also to those engaged in the selective breeding of farm animals. Ancestry, in short, would out.[24]

Dr. Morton made no special effort to collect the skulls of criminals, but by 1855 he had a few from "individuals who have been signalized by their crimes." Of course there were only five of them, a number "too small to be of much importance in a generalization like the present," but they were all remarkably small in size, averaging only 96 cubic inches "for the bulk of the brain" (with a range from 91 to 105 cubic inches). Three of these men had died on the gallows for murder, and all five were from "the lowest class of society."[25] Small heads, small minds, small morality.

The correlations were difficult to establish, but what was troubling about murderers like the Reverend Mr. Avery of Massachusetts was that they were not from the lowest class of society but the highest. George Burr was compelled to declare that "Rulloff's intellect was of a superior order." The head refused to disclose its secret.

It was impossible for these doctors to doubt that the head held a secret. In that belief, they were convinced by the most ancient of medical hypotheses, summed up in the word *physiognomy,* which Francis Bacon had defined as the "discovery of the disposition of the mind by the lineaments of the body." A book of anatomy, supposed to be by Aristotle, devoted six chapters to the study of physiognomy, and medieval authors connected the science to astrology and divination of character. In the eighteenth century, however, the science of physiognomy had fallen into disrepute. So pesky had wandering physiognomists become in Britain that in 1743 a law was passed in Parliament declaring them rogues and vagabonds and hence subject to whipping.

The subject was refreshed, however, by the writings of Johan Kaspar Lavater—a religious mystic and eccentric—who, from 1775 to 1778, published a lavishly illustrated work showing the expression of mental states in the human form. He was an inspiration to another German, Franz Josef Gall, who established and popularized the science of phrenology, in which, he asserted, various mental processes that were localized in the brain were, in turn, expressed in the shape of the head. Phrenology consisted of "reading" these external characteristics and translating them into portraits of character. Gall's acolyte in the promotion of this system was Johann Christoph Spurzheim, who, like Lavater and Gall, was a compelling lecturer, and he further popularized phrenology under such names as *craniology, craniometry,* and *zoonomy.* By 1832, there were twenty-nine phrenological societies in Great Britain, and parallel organizations sprouted in North America with lecturers, journals, and almanacs promoting the cause.

Scientific skepticism and even vigorous attacks on phrenology did little to diminish its influence. Robert Southey, the English poet laureate, derided "Spurzheim and the craziologists," but on American shores this new science was greeted with credulous enthusiasm. Its popularity was enhanced by a visit to Boston of Dr. Spurzheim himself and capped by his sudden death there in 1832. Spurzheim's tomb in Mount Auburn cemetery was (and is) a "conspicuous object," commended to the attention of visitors to Boston.[26] Spurzheim's version of phrenology—he had departed in some measure from the theories of Gall—took vigorous hold among the credulous Yankees for whom the wonders of German science were uncritically acclaimed.

In a conduct guide he published in 1850, William Andrus Alcott—a cousin of Louisa May Alcott and centrally located among the gullible Yankees—explained to his young readers the importance of gaining a knowledge of phrenology:

> That Phrenology, in its first or leading principles—that the brain is the material organ of the mind, that different mental faculties have connection with different parts of the brain &c. &c.— is true, I can no more doubt than I could doubt the law of gravitation.[27]

There was no necessity for young people's becoming "adepts in this science," he wrote, but the reading of a few general works would be of inestimable value to a youth entering the wider spheres of adult life.

Alcott was a prominent figure among the intellectual autocracy of Boston. Spurzheim's triumphal visit took place when he was an impressionable young man, recently graduated from Yale Medical School. Alcott was prolific in diagnosing problems and prescribing solutions, and he published his views on many subjects, including the construction of schoolhouses, the physiology of marriage, and the benefits of a vegetable diet. He was genial in directing his readers to the Fowler brothers, who published the *Phrenological Journal,* particularly the elder brother, Orson Squire Fowler.

Like Alcott, O. S. Fowler was a prolific and varied merchant of advice, publishing useful works on the merits of houses built on an octagonal floor plan and a manual on "sexual science." But it was phrenology that made him famous and admired; among the most popular of the works he and his brother published was the *New Illustrated Self-Instructor in Phrenology and Physiology* (1859), with more than a hundred engravings.[28] Following the directions they provided, readers could "chart" characters of friends and family. Lorenzo Niles Fowler, the younger brother, was a hearty combatant when critics expressed skepticism about phrenology. In the *Phrenological Almanac* for 1847, Lorenzo pointed out that the configuration of the critics' heads displayed their character flaws.

> There are many other pop-gun opponents to the science, who sally out occasionally, like a turtle's head, make a witty effort, write a short article, and retreat, and are heard no more.[29]

Popular interest in the science was constantly fed by manuals through which ordinary people could unlock secrets and discern the shape of history from the heads of prominent persons. Writing of her brother, Henry Ward Beecher, the celebrated preacher, Catharine E. Beecher recalled his youthful devotion to "the philosophy of mind." "Beside the standard works on this subject," she reported, "he was deeply interested in the teachings of Gall and Spurzheim, and the science of phrenology."[30] It would help him, he thought, to analyze people in his future congregations. In short, the ideas taught by phrenology were diffused through the intellectual life of midcentury; its principles, as Alcott had declared, as certain as the law of gravitation.

Celebrated public figures were routinely subjected to phrenological analysis, but criminals were even more appealing subjects. In 1850, Milton W. Streeter, of Southbridge, Massachusetts, had murdered his wife in an especially bloody way. The author of a pamphlet describing the crime felt obliged to analyze the causes of the murder:

> A person, having phrenological developments as above, would be destitute of moral principle, reckless and heedless, incapable of analytical reasoning, implacable in his resentments.

This "phrenological character" of Streeter suggested that he was unable to control his "moral conduct," and so it was just that the governor commuted the sentence to life in prison.[31]

George Burr did not lower his scientific mind to the level of the professors of phrenology. Nor did he use the jargon that was so distinctive of its practitioners—*adhesiveness,* for instance, or *philoprogenitiveness* or *vitativeness.* Yet he did address "the peculiarity of [Rulloff's] organization," and "organization" was very much a term of art for the phrenologists.[32] Ham Freeman had no need to avoid the temptations of dubious phrenological science. In summing up Rulloff's character, he noted that "phrenologically the organs of veneration and egotism of his remarkable head were very large."[33] Looking for common ground in interpreting the evidence of the skull, he noted that "in the formation of the brain physicians and phrenologists agree that the animal predominated in him over the intellectual." Rulloff was, in short, "not well balanced."

Still, there was the sheer size of Rulloff's head. Big-headedness, the Fowler brothers asserted, was nearly essential to greatness, and, in addition to Cuvier and Daniel Webster, there were other huge heads to inventory: Washington, Jefferson, Adams, Henry Clay. And of course Spurzheim himself, whose brain had been "among the very heaviest ever weighed."

> The phrenological law is, that size, *other things being equal,* is a measure of power; yet these other conditions, such as activity, power of motive, health, physiological habits, etc., increase or diminish the mentality, even more than size. Quality is more important that quantity, but true greatness requires both cerebral quantity and quality.

It is, the Fowlers said, "a known law of things" that bigger is better, and not only in the size of heads.[34]

The head, of course, was the outward and visible sign of the inward and invisible mind, but the Fowlers were not dissectors given to sawing open skulls to inspect the contents, nor were they anatomists of the brain. Neither were Spurzheim and Gall, but, with only the evidence of this science and their persuasive powers, they shaped nineteenth-century thought about the mind. Of most significance for many was the bump of religious feeling located in Spirituality, a zone above and forward from the ear and adjacent to Hope and Veneration. This domain was seen to be prominent in the magnificent head of Henry Ward Beecher, but what was troubling to thoughtful people was that phrenology suggested that Beecher's great soul was the product of biology rather than of revelation. Gall and Spurzheim "look among the animals" for confirmation of their map of the mind, wrote John Hecker; "the true activity of these faculties as they should be awakened under Christianity, requires names of deeper significance than mere Moral Sentiments."[35] Hecker renamed this portion of the head "Godliness" and located within it the point at which human beings are attached to the Divine. God has "direct, immediate intercourse" with human kind through this spot on the head, Hecker declared.[36]

Naturally, analysts were curious about the size of Spirituality in Rulloff's head, and the ways in which divine intercourse might have activated it. As a youth, wrote Ed Crapsey, Rulloff "had no strong religious convictions of any kind."[37] Ham Freeman did not address the question directly but alleged that Rulloff's mother's convictions had been unusually strong.[38] The lunacy commissioners, too, were interested in this question. "To what church did your father belong?" Drs. Gray and Vanderpool asked. "Episcopalian," Rulloff replied.

> I took no special interest in the church. I went there as a habit and an intellectual pleasure. I never claimed to be pious: never tried to make myself an example.[39]

Over and over again, Rulloff worked to keep his execution free of piety and public prayer; he worried that some member of the clergy might suddenly appear, and said he wanted "no such damn nonsense." As he was led from the cells into the bright sunshine of the jail yard, he spoke to the sheriff again: "You won't have any clergymen bellowing down there, nor prayers, nor any damned bosh, will you, Mr. Sheriff?" Sheriff Martin promised to keep pious exhorters at a distance.[40]

Yet here again there were contradictions in the story Rulloff told of himself. In 1860, he had come upon a Methodist revival in Passaic, New Jersey. Rulloff wandered in and sat down. "It was not a great while," he told Ham, "before the *strange brother* was invited to pray for them." He did and was greeted by affirmations: "Amen—Lord bless the strange brother." Fabricating a life history for himself, he told them he was a member of the Southern Conference, the Methodists having split over the issue of slavery, but he was a "Union man" and had journeyed northward to make the acquaintance of the "Northern brothers." "I remained a week and preached twice." Two collections were taken up for him: "I'll bet these people never heard any better sermons than I delivered them." Yet in telling Ham the story, Rulloff made it plain that these preachings were insincere. Once again, Rulloff had concocted an identity and passed it off for truth. As always, he loved a masquerade.[41]

That was not the last time Rulloff feigned piety and represented himself as a Christian minister. In 1866, Rulloff and accomplices traveled to Nashua and Concord in New Hampshire to case a bank. To gain admission to "good society," Rulloff presented himself as both clergyman and foreigner.

> I played up that I was an Episcopal clergyman, from England. I had letters of introduction in my possession from prominent persons in England, to persons in the United States, and certificates which I exhibited, and which procured me admission into good society in Worcester and Concord and other places. Of course

these papers were all fictitious and forged by me. In this way I was able to procure all the information necessary for the gang.[42]

Rulloff spurned the identity of a repentant Christian, and he politely declined Julius Seelye's efforts to direct him to that condition. He was determined to "die game," and he compared himself to Socrates and Seneca. The spectators crowding the streets of Binghamton hoped that he would fall short of the Stoic ideal and would blubber and squirm. In this hope they were disappointed.

As he readied himself for death, Rulloff had continued to invent new selves. For the lunacy commissioners, it was that of a skeptic about belief and a rationalist about the things of the world. When the commissioners asked if he had ever believed in an everlasting being, Rulloff replied that he had decided against it early. "Before I was twenty; and then I made up my mind that I could believe nothing that I could not demonstrate."

Rulloff said that he had read "German metaphysics," but the speculations, he admitted, "have only tended to perplex my mind." Nonetheless he was ready to allow that there might be a creator of the world who provided the "beautiful adaptation" of a small insect one might inspect under a microscope. But Rulloff was unwilling to accept a morality based on divine rewards and punishments.

> I should do as I intended without regard to the existence of a God or a devil, a heaven or a hell: I have felt this pride during my whole life; I never wished to get anything out of anybody.[43]

With this remark concluding the interview, the commissioners declared him "entirely sane." That opinion put an end to Rulloff's last real chance to escape hanging.

The Nation was skeptical of the connection between the interview and the conclusion.

> Two Albany doctors . . . publish a long farrago of question and answer as containing the basis and justification of their judgment. It is, however, a deal more convincing as testimony to their unfitness for the business they had in hand than as testimony of any value concerning the sanity of the convict. . . . Apparently ignorant of linguistics, and not profound in metaphysics, those

gentlemen stared at Ruloff as a wonder of erudition and ability, and declared him fit for the gallows on evidence which, so far as it makes anything plain, makes it plain that they are incompetent to speak as experts in such a case, and which leaves it as doubtful as ever whether Ruloff is not half a madman.[44]

There had been no need for the anxiety that some people felt about the result of the visit of the lunacy commission.

What might ordinary readers conclude from the long interview that was soon published in the metropolitan dailies as well as the local papers? For Christians, it was obvious that "pride"—the sin of Satan—was Rulloff's ruling passion. He put himself outside the system of sin and repentance conventionally proclaimed by the church. In fact, he would even defy the system, choosing actions that would affront the commandments in order to assert his free will. Yet he also acknowledged the divine mystery and the "revelation" of a creator in the "wondrous relations of things" in the world.

For phrenologists he was, if anything, even more an enigma than he was to the Christians. Surely the expression of Spirituality was fully apparent in this interview, though not readily apparent from inspection of his head. Ham Freeman's amateur analysis led him to conclude that the head was the right shape for the Rulloff he knew: "Phrenologically the organs of veneration and egotism of his remarkable head were very large." The former, Ham thought, was "not of a religious character" but was expressed in Rulloff's devotion to languages, books, and mythology. The latter was "inordinate" and a "weakness," since it was egotism that drove his crimes and made him, sometimes, "a ferocious monster."[45]

Rulloff himself was an adept in the science. When he had pawned his trunk of belongings in Chicago in 1845, it contained, among other things, a manuscript lecture on phrenology of his own composing. Among the papers in his desk in New York was another manuscript on phrenology, written in his own shorthand. George Sawyer, one of Rulloff's more savage attackers in print, said that it "reads, in places, like a medical lecture, and, again, like a funeral sermon." It contained, however, a strong flavor of biological determinism so characteristic of phrenological thinking. "He will do well," Rulloff admonished his audience, "who, in cases of suffering, sets himself rather to inquire wherein the laws of nature have been infringed than impatiently to murmur and fret against our pure humanity." Yet there is a further appeal to "him who ordered all things wisely and well," the deity that shaped the destiny expressed in "organization."[46]

Back in January, Oliver Dyer, the reporter for the *Sun* who had put Rulloff on the national agenda, had asked him about phrenology. Rulloff acknowledged that he had lectured on phrenology and examined the heads of strangers. Dyer asked what he considered the leading phrenological organ in his brain.

> Concentration is what the phrenologists call it; but I do not believe in any such separate organ. . . . It is the natural degree of activity of the faculties according to the constitution of the person. In phrenology concentrations means the drive, the persistent force with which one pursues a thing; and there is no separate organ for that.

Dyer next asked what his next largest phrenological organ was.

> Well, constructiveness, I suppose. I am good at mechanical matters. I am more or less skillful at blacksmithing, carpentering, weaving, cabinet making, designing of patterns for carpets, &c., and various other handicrafts; and also have some knowledge of law and medicine.

Then Dyer asked Rulloff about his temper. "Your destructiveness seems to be formidably developed. When you get angry, your temper is uncontrollable, is it not?"

> No, sir. You are entirely mistaken. I have never had any wrangles, quarrels, or fights. When a person displeases me, I simply want to keep away from him, and I always do that. I never had but one fight in my life, and that was when I was a boy at school, and about 9 or 10 years old. . . . I sometimes play at anger, and pretend to be in a rage, to effect a purpose, and no doubt some people think I have an awful temper.[47]

Even a sketchy knowledge of Rulloff's crimes would make this claim preposterous. Yet Rulloff once again created himself in a new image: the patient, suffering stoic. Only as he began to confess the details of his murders did the disabling rage become apparent.

At the very end, Ham Freeman concluded, as had Ed Crapsey long before, that Rulloff could not be redeemed. "Atheist, infidel, alike to God and man, he was execrated in life, and we fear eternally damned in death."[48]

Yet Ham also saw him as in some ways a giant, a pagan Prometheus come to reveal the secrets of philology.

> *If not insane* he was the incarnation of all that is wicked, and having sown the wind he has reaped the whirlwind. Stoically going into the presence of his Maker, without repentance, without contrition, and leaving a record of all that is evil, and of great intellectual gifts wasted.[49]

He must have been insane; he was too great a man otherwise.

Biological determinism lay at the heart of a judgment passed by the *Binghamton Republican* after the Burrs had reported on the condition of Rulloff's brain:

> In the formation of his brain Rulloff was a ferocious animal, and so far as disposition could relieve him from responsibility, he was not strictly responsible for his acts. There is no doubt that he thought himself not a very bad man on the morning he was led out of his prison, cursing from the cell to the gallows.[50]

This reporter was wrong. Though he might have told bawdy stories and bantered with his guards in the nighttime, in the morning he had shaken hands all around, comforted the sorrowful, and wished well to all who had imprisoned him. He had not gone cursing to the gallows.

At the same time that George Burr was speaking for received medical wisdom before the Medico-Legal Society, the *Phrenological Journal* provided the view of alternative medicine, accompanied by a full-length portrait of Rulloff in which his features were configured to match the findings of the science.

> We can trace in his career, few as the details are, the workings of his lower nature. Secretiveness, Destructiveness, Constructiveness are found working together in close harmony, while in his quiet or studious intervals Self-Esteem, Approbativeness, and the intellectual faculties come in for their share of predominant activ-

ity. Ambition for scholarly reputation stimulates his robust intellect to exertion, but that single aim is not sufficient to repress the large and active organs of Destructiveness, Combativeness, and Acquisitiveness which clamor for indulgence, or to give them a direction which may prove of utility. Conscientiousness small, and weak from long disuse, Veneration apparently wanting, and Benevolence, what there is of it, a mere tool of the intellect, what is there to give an elevated tendency to the physical nature of the man? His selfish qualities governed everything else. The back-head was well developed, but even that was entirely subordinated. Witness the treatment of his wife, child, and friends! His powers of fascination were exercised only to procure certain selfish exacting ends. With his large Human Nature, he knew well how to impose on those who judged only by appearances, or from a superficial examination. There have been and are grave doubts among theologians as to a "personal devil"—a being so low and so bad as to be beyond the hope of regeneration or redemption. Such a personage we may almost venture to pronounce Rulloff. He certainly was but litle [sic] short of a moral idiot, although he had enough intellect to enable him to discriminate between what was right and what was wrong. He knew a thousand times better than he performed. His were not so much the sins of ignorance as of design.

Here was a full-scale phrenological analysis of the man who had held the public imagination in his grasp for many months.

The medical doctors and the phrenologists wanted to reduce Rulloff to a type. But there was something about him that defied easy categorization. And it was this mysterious quality, in the words of the *Phrenological Journal*, that made his case of lasting interest.

Rulloff, however, was unique in his type of villainy. His is a case which is *sui generis*, presenting psychological features never brought to public notice before, and his trial and conviction must take a place among the "celebrated causes" which illustrate the annals of judicial investigation.[51]

Still, the head would not go away. Last seen in the possession of the Drs. Burr, the skull seems to have vanished but not the brain. Preserved in a jar filled with formalin, it went first to Hobart College, where it came to the attention of Bert Green Wilder. Wilder was as persuaded as George Burr had been that something in its appearance, structure, or chemistry would answer the question of evil. Wilder subsequently established a huge collection of brains at Cornell University that was to become as famous as Dr. Morton's cabinet of skulls two generations earlier. Wilder even arranged for his own brain to be added to it.

As for the body, in 1906 it was discovered that George Burr had not kept his promise of contributing a burial plot of his own for Rulloff's remains. In that year, F. B. Hulbert won the contract for moving the bodies from the old and neglected Eldredge Street cemetery to the Glenwood Cemetery at the edge of Binghamton. In lot 265 of the Potters Field Section, he discovered Rulloff's headless corpse among those of others who had died paupers. He was able to identify it from the missing toes on the left foot which were so crucial in linking Rulloff to the murder of Frederick Merrick. The boots in which Rulloff had died were still nearly intact.[52]

The head has one final cameo role in Rulloff's story.

On November 2, 1878, a man fell to his death from a roof in San Francisco. Ambrose Bierce believed he had committed suicide. But the coroner's jury ruled that it was a spectacular accident, the victim having distinctly said as he somersaulted through the air: "My God, I'm killed." The dead man was the youngest of the brothers: William Herman Rulofson.

An elaborate funeral with solemn tributes followed, and many photographic studios closed for the day to memorialize his passing. He was an innovator and a prosperous businessman. The newspapers said nothing about any brothers.[53]

As he fell to his death, legend would later declare, there was in his coat pocket a photograph of his deceased brother Edward's head.

13

I See Him in My Dreams

"What the man was made of is a mystery which the subtlest mental analysis has failed to discover," wrote the editor of the *Weekly Ithacan* on the afternoon when he received the news that Rulloff was, at last, dead. "His character resembles more nearly than any other, the Satan of Milton. He was utterly abandoned. He stood single in his dark crimes."[1] There was something supernatural about him; he seemed to possess an almost magical capacity to put others in his thrall.

Animal magnetism was an expression important to Rulloff and his contemporaries; it described the mysterious psychic power that people might exercise over others and explained the impulses by which mesmerists, hypnotists, and vampires gained their advantage over the weak and innocent. Certainly Rulloff exercised this force in ways that attracted people like Al Jarvis, Billy Dexter, Ham Freeman, Jane Jarvis, and even George Becker. *Magnetism* for them was an apt metaphor.

Rulloff's magnetism was not limited in its effects to the "morbidly curious," so despised by reporters in the crowd on the day of his execution, or to the credulous and superstitious. The lawyer Frances Miles Finch, who had, in the early days of his practice, represented Rulloff at Owego and Albany, composed a long dramatic monologue in which the poetic manner of Robert Browning is very much in evidence. Here speaks, in the poet's imagination, Rulloff himself.

> You wonder why I seem
> So unconcerned.—Pray, do you dream,
> And when you wake the dream despise,
> Scarce worth one look of open eyes?

Well, life is such a dream; and mine
Long nightmare. Think you that I pine
For more? Why not, then, welcome sleep
So sure and sound, so firm and deep,
No dream can break its silence? Why
Should one be so afraid to die?
The pain,—does that some fear awake?
You bear a worse with common ache
Of ulcered tooth, or throbbing head.
'Tis but a pang, and—there—You're dead!
What follows?—Nothing!—only sleep!

Judge Finch was highly regarded for his published poetry, and his verses were well suited to an oratorical age. His lines on Rulloff he did not publish, however. The title, "His Side of the Story," suggests what Finch in fact provides, a sympathetic view of Rulloff the murderer. At the tantalizing end of the poem, Finch's Rulloff promises "tomorrow," before the hanging, to reveal what had become of Harriet and Priscilla. But it is a Rullovian promise: "Tell you then,—perhaps!"[2]

Others favored a different explanation. He was "an infidel without hope," wrote Morris Treadwell in his diary; Treadwell had been outside the jail the day Rulloff was hanged.[3] Seeing Rulloff as an "infidel" was one way to explain, and explain away, his power. That "noble head & face" concealed a mystery, and those who knew him could not get him out of their minds.

In Boston, the literati were in the habit of explaining to the rest of the country what people should think. Writing the day before the execution, the editorial writer in the *Boston Herald* made a judicious argument. John White Webster, the Harvard professor who had murdered and dismembered a colleague in 1849, was different from Rulloff because he had acted in "the heat of passion."[4] Eugene Arum, too, was not to be compared with Rulloff because he had "showed signs of repentance and an acute moral sense." "Rulloff has followed crime *con amore*, and furnished a striking denial of the idea that 'mind is God's best gift to man.' Rulloff's mind was the gift of Satan."[5]

In the wake of the execution were many sermons on the lessons of Rulloff's life and death, and the most prominent preachers addressed them.

First to the pulpit was the Reverend Edward Taylor, one of the savans who had visited Rulloff with the philological delegation. Preaching at the Congregational Church in Binghamton, Taylor selected as his text, "The way of the transgressor is hard" (Prov. 13:15). The *Broome Republican* had a shorthand reporter present in the church, and he recorded Taylor's words.

> The way of the transgressors has a hard end. R. died with a measure of stoicism, but he died wretchedly. No supporting heavenly presence, now frivolous, now blasphemous, without a prayer, he went, and while some shed tears of pity, not one dropped a tear of grief because of loss at his departure. That coffin remaining in the jail for twenty-four hours, and no friend claiming its contents, O, it was a pitiable sight. When his last breath was drawn, society breathed more freely. The grave he found was bought at the price of his brain, to be used for scientific purposes.[6]

The church was crowded, and the reporter praised Taylor's "very earnest, forcible, and eloquent words." "We have rarely," he reported, "seen a congregation give its attention so unreservedly."

In Brooklyn, the most famous clergyman of the day, Henry Ward Beecher, exhorted the congregation of Plymouth Church on the need for "reformation." For Beecher, Rulloff was almost beyond the reach of reform.

> As for RULLOFF, I can scarcely imagine a more repulsive subject. I am glad he is gone. For weeks I have seen nothing in the papers but RULLOFF, RULLOFF. When a man once commits a public crime of this kind, he at once becomes a hero, and every newspaper a picture-gallery. We are shown first how he appeared at the time he committed the act; then we have him on trial, his deportment there; then his behavior after the fact has been ascertained that the Governor won't interfere, and, last of all, a full-length sketch as he appeared at the execution. There is more interest aroused, and more writing done about a poor imbruted murderer than there is over the fate of an Empire, or the destiny of a race, and people are found to gloat over and feed upon these ghastly horrors. For one, when I see a murder in the columns of a paper I

go as far round it as I would round a horse two weeks dead in the month of August. The whole thing argues a low public taste, and a lack of anything approaching refinement of feeling.[7]

Despite his professed aversion to sensation, Beecher was quite well informed about the details of Rulloff's life, even if he did not see that Rulloff's crimes and his execution could be made to illustrate themes of "refinement of feeling."

In so many ways, the story was all about the exercise of feelings, beginning with Rulloff's tears over the novel by Eugène Sue that came to his hand just after he had murdered Harriet. Feelings were just what had brought so many women to Rulloff's trial in Binghamton. As Marshall Champlain had told the jury, the women were there in search of "objects over which their sensibilities [might] expand themselves and their sympathies weep." "Hysterical grief" shook Rulloff's whole frame when he remembered his beloved Al Jarvis slipping from his grasp as the drowning man was swept away by the Chenango River. Feelings nearly overwhelmed Ham Freeman as, an hour before the hanging, Rulloff comforted him with the words: "Stand firm, Ham; do not give way."[8] Here were feelings aplenty being refined by the hot fire of death.

Another minister, Octavius Brooks Frothingham, also addressed himself to the feelings aroused by Rulloff's execution. At Lyric Hall, New York, Frothingham began his sermon by alluding to Rulloff, but then turned his attention to the horrors of capital punishment.

> Were it put to a vote throughout the Union the people who stand most in fear of capital punishment would vote to perpetuate the system. The ignorant, vicious and brutal would retain it, while the thoughtful, the student and the good man would use every exertion to abolish it.

Revealing the skepticism about organized religion that made him at once popular and controversial, Frothingham reminded his listeners that the churches had joined with the "ignorant, vicious and brutal" to keep the system in place.

> The truth—and it is painful for me, a minister, to admit it—is that secular legislation has been struggling for a long time to counteract the evils and the horrors born of ecclesiastical law-making.

To the common sense of the human race, and not to Christianity, do we owe thanks for mercy to men. I must speak the truth, though it is bitter, and by and by the truth will bring peace. I ask now is it well for us to counteract, in our puny way, the will of God? Is it well for us to put a man down in the earth whom God has called from the earth to the sunshine?[9]

Frothingham, a Unitarian turned liberal nonsectarian, reflected progressive ideas about punishment, and he joined Mark Twain in protesting the death penalty.

Another progressive, Robert Bonner, the publisher of the *New York Ledger,* was opposed to carving up corpses in the name of scientific curiosity.

Even Boston, with all its boasted refinement hardly permitted the remains of its greatest man, Daniel Webster, to grow cold before its leading physicians felt constrained to announce, through the public journals, that the great brain which had so often shaken and controlled this continent, had been cut out and put in the scales, and been ascertained to weigh just so many.

Cutting open a skull to weigh the brain was simply barbaric. It bespoke the same "petty ostentation" that led farmers at a county fair to boast of the pigs they had fattened. "We think," Bonner wrote, "that the tendency of this is altogether bad."[10]

Bonner's opinion must have seemed eccentric in an age when science promised to solve all problems. In an editorial, the *Broome Republican* articulated the more common opinion: "The head of the murderer, we are glad to say, is to be submitted to scientific examination."[11]

Rulloff's stoicism at the end, and especially the detail of his removing his hand from his pocket and then putting it back, sent a shudder of horror across the nation.[12] In New Orleans, the *Daily Picayune* editorialized that no one could face so dreadful an execution with complete detachment and indifference: "even as the halter had fixed its death grip to his neck . . . he cared nothing for pain nor for death." At the very end, the insanity doctors were proved wrong, the paper declared, and his death showed that he was "morally incapable" and "diseased and deranged." The headline posed a question: "Was He Insane?" The editorial declared the answer to be yes.[13]

In the immediate aftermath of the hanging, no one could lack an opinion on Rulloff's meaning. Convinced that if he had been spared, he would have murdered again, the editor of the *Weekly Ithacan* saw him as a "mystery," but his end as deeply satisfying.

> Criminal records do not, we venture to say, present a case more absolutely abandoned by all thoughts of compassion. Rulloff died a horrible death. Even the scaffold has its claims to the offices of humanity in the hearts of the people as well as in the hands of the executioner. But in the case of this man it stands as barren of sympathy as it is rude in construction. The hanged man ascended utterly alone, utterly forsaken, utterly unworthy of any slight office or mercy, either expressed or silently entertained by the world. He died like a dog, only with less claims to compassion.
>
> The shadow of the hangman's hand hangs gloomily over a community always, but now that the awful event is over in this case, we seem to be lifted into a higher plain of morality and to breathe a purer social atmosphere. The name of Rulloff will no more startle us as the coming of some frightful object. Those who were stricken by him in the long years past will sleep more soundly now that he is beyond fear of approach.[14]

Such a view was certainly satisfying to the Schutt family and the many other Ithacans who had been howling for Rulloff's blood for a quarter century and more. It was impossible for them to believe that anyone could shed a tear at his death.

Rulloff had not been quite as alone and forsaken as the *Ithacan* supposed. Ham Freeman was almost confessional in the final pages of his biography.

> I see him in my dreams, and I contemplate him in my daily walk. I sometimes think of him as a poor unfortunate; a child of genius, whose whole life was embittered by an unlucky blow struck in the heat of ungovernable passion, the consequences of which he immediately deplored; that this one terrible deed rendered his pathway in life forever dark and obscure; turned every man's hand against him and made him an outlaw, but that he realized all and regretted it more keenly than any one, and that the way down in the deep recesses of his heart there was a great soul, and a foun-

tain of human kindness frozen up in the most terrible ordeal of adversity and woe, that it was ever the lot of man to suffer. But for this one irremediable event in his early life this man might have been an ornament to society, and his great talents joined to a perseverance that nothing could daunt, and an industry that never tired would have placed him in the front rank of any of the learned professions, or have shed luster upon any science by which he might have devoted the energies of his powerful intellect. I again sometimes see him as a cool, cold blooded designing villain and murderer, going about seeking where he might rob and filch from his fellow man, the associate of hardened criminals, not hesitating to kill or destroy whoever might come in his way when prosecuting his nefarious designs.[15]

Rulloff had undergone a metamorphosis, and Ham had been taken in by his argument that he had been merely "unlucky" and ever thereafter had suffered from continual remorse. It was not the "event" of his early life that sent him to the gallows but a work of his maturity: the murder of Frederick Merrick.

One of Rulloff's victims could not so easily be explained away by the "ungovernable passion" of his youth (as when he killed Harriet) or by an act of impetuous loyalty (as when he shot Frederick Merrick in an effort to save his beloved Albert Jarvis). That victim was his infant daughter, the pitiful baby whose cries must soon have broken the silence of that shabby little house in Lansing where her mother lay dying.

Ham Freeman found an explanation.

Rulloff was a very proud man, and his pride, his personal self-respect, would never allow him to acknowledge that he murdered, in cold blood, a sweet little infant. He would have been cut into pieces first.[16]

Here hope far outstrips plausibility, but Ham had an explanation: the infant survived and was raised as Priscilla Jane Rulofson in his brother's household in Pennsylvania. In support of that theory, Ham quoted a letter Scilla sent to her "Uncle Ed" on January 10, 1870. Full of endearments, "it seems to us," wrote Ham, "more like the expressions of a *daughter* writing under the disguise of a *niece* to a man she has been taught to believe is *her father*, but who, for prudential reasons, she does not recognize before the world as her father." In it, Scilla tells how her husband, Samuel Ridgeway Stratton, hearing read a letter Rulloff had written, had declared: "Bless his old heart, that letter sounds just like him—that is the way the dear old boy talks."[17]

Priscilla Jane Rulofson Stratton was born in the same year as the vanished infant. She grew up in a capacious mansion in Pennsylvania in a family of wealth and the utmost respectability. If she really was Harriet's daughter, hers was a Cinderella story.

People wanted to believe the fanciful tale, and Rulloff had led Ham again and again to the edge of disclosure: "She is living and well enough," he had told him.[18] A letter arrived at the office of the *Binghamton Republican* shortly after the end of the trial from "one of our well-known citizens of Clarion, Penn." It implied that Priscilla Rulofson was the long-lost daughter, and the *New York Times* duly reprinted the story.[19]

What was missing were facts. How could Rulloff have spirited away the nursing baby even to Pennsylvania and yet be in Lansing the following morning when Tom Robertson and his boy Newton helped him load the ominous chest into their wagon? At the time, Rulof Rulofson and Amanda Jane Emerson lived in Maine, and there they were when Scilla was born. Struggling to give substance to the idea that Rulloff had spirited his baby away to his brother, Ham wondered if he had employed those Indian women who had appeared in Lansing to transport the baby. He made much of the fact that Scilla is named for her paternal grandmother. But what Ham wanted to believe could not be true.

Rulloff persisted as a representative figure of the age. In July 1871, a prosecutor in Chicago had fulminated that a person he was trying for murder was "cleverer than Rulloff." In an editorial rebuke, the *New York Times* was unwilling to concede that a midwestern murderer could be smarter than one from New York.[20]

An Iowa suffragist took up the cry. Elizabeth Cady Stanton and Susan B. Anthony had been criticized for visiting a woman convicted of murder, and Annie Savory wrote to the paper in Des Moines that she saw nothing wrong with a "condoling visit." Acidly she exclaimed that women and men had equal rights to be visitors and visited.

You must have lost sight, too, of Ruloff, the cold-blooded murderer, whom the Professors of Harvard and Yale—to say nothing of numberless Doctors of Divinity, and the scores of *lovely pure women*—did not scorn to visit.[21]

Almost universally despised in life, Rulloff gained prominent (if fictional) friends in death.

Even in distant Japan, Rulloff's philology was a topic of discussion. William Elliot Griffis later reported a remarkable conversation.

> The undersigned remembers vividly a prolonged discussion at a dinner of the professors of the Imperial University of Japan, in Tokio in 1872, in which German, French, American, British, Russian, Korean and Chinese scholars, directly or indirectly took part. Most of those had heard of Rulloff as a great philologist, or at least of a very industrious person who pretended to be such. The common judgment arrived at was that Rulloff was untrained, had but little insight, and that his conclusions were unscientific.[22]

For a man whose main intellectual contributions had been written in jail and published in the pages of a small-town newspaper, his reputation was astonishingly widespread.

Loose ends needed to be tied up. In June 1872, a dispute over the reward offered for Rulloff's capture came into the press. Posse members thought they had earned it. Chauncey Livingston wanted a share since it was his outhouse where Rulloff had been found. Henry Hedden and Phillip Reilley, the two New York police officers who had assisted in locating Rulloff's haunts, thought they had earned a share even though Rulloff was in jail by the time they heard of the case. Somewhat resignedly, the *Binghamton Republican* concluded: "Law suits over the rewards cannot be averted and the dispute may just as well be settled in three law suits as by thirty."[23]

Objects associated with his imprisonment and death were preserved as relics: the padlock on his cell door in Binghamton, the silk noose, the leg irons that held him at short range in the final months of his life. In the way of folklore, imagination began to unravel circumstance and knit up legend. Governor Hoffman, in later accounts, became Rulloff's special friend, Tolstoy an advocate of his philology. His story became another Knickerbocker tale and, like Washington Irving's horseman, Rulloff rides through the dark nights in search of his head.[24] Macabre fascination with his brain still draws visitors to

Ithaca to inspect it, a huge gray organ floating in turbid fluid in a large glass cylinder.[25]

The contradictions of his life so fascinating to his contemporaries are now less apparent. Measuring skulls and weighing brains no longer constitute respectable scientific practice; the shape of the skull is not now viewed as a sign of character, so his huge head is no longer seen as a fact at odds with his moral depravity. Philology is now far from the center of educational practice, and claims about the miraculous formation of language no longer lure the widespread attention of the public. An improved ratchet drill or a vivid new carpet pattern would hardly attract interest. Intimate knowledge of New Testament Greek is not now seen as a guarantor of good behavior.

Rulloff's legend has remained alive by being transformed to suit successive generations. His collateral descendents in California in the 1950s had so far forgiven him as to describe his life as "fabulous but erratic."

His linguistic genius had made him an object of wide public sympathy which nearly saved his neck. Horace Greeley set out to visit him in prison but turned back, afraid that he would break down completely if confronted by the prisoner; Tolstoi, impressed with Rulloff's theory of universal language, tried to intervene from abroad. Rulloff was as free in quoting character references— W. T. Sherman, S. F. B. Morse, Governor Hoffman—as he was in adopting aliases. He died believing himself misunderstood, feeling that no man had ever had higher or nobler ambitions than he; and he astounded the spectators by putting his hands into his pockets after the death trap had fallen.[26]

All these endorsers of Rulloff's genius are figments of airy imagination. He died persuaded of his own genius. But not even Ham could quite believe it. In Ham's opinion, Rulloff had died, not, as he might have, in the arms of Jane Jarvis or even in those of her son Al but "affectionately embracing the cold statue of Philology."[27]

If the twenty-first century is mostly indifferent to philology and universally scornful of phrenology, we remain deeply curious about Rulloff's affectionate embrace. Rulloff's open-mouthed kiss as he parted from Ham Freeman on the way to the gallows strikes us as an act more cordial than merely searching for a capsule of poison. Yet it may have been no more than a last effort to cheat the gallows. Sharing a bed with his young disciple seems to us to imply a physical intimacy between Rulloff and Al Jarvis; these sleeping arrangements did not carry the same import in the nineteenth century, yet they also, then as now, could enable homoerotic love. One of the few conclusions that Ed Crapsey and Ham Freeman reached together was that Rulloff loved Al Jarvis more than any other person; he risked his own life to save him—and lost them both.

In the southern tier of counties in New York, where Rulloff's story is best preserved, it continues to fascinate. The picture history of Broome County devotes a two-page spread to his trial and execution;[28] in Ithaca a restaurant bears his name and its menu a lively, if fantastic, account of his life. Present-day versions are written in successive layers over those of the recent and more distant past. Modern storytellers can approach Rulloff, but never quite reach him.

Murder remains a mystery.

Notes

1. Typical of this press coverage is the headline from the *Elmira Advertiser:* "Rulloff! The Great Criminal of the Century," April 8, 1871, 3.1.

2. Crapsey had already written a two-part ruminative essay whose headline inquired: "Will Murder Out?"; he concluded, on review of lurid cases, that it would. *Galaxy* 7 (1869): 383–94; 10 (1870): 536–45. In 1872 he would publish *The Nether Side of New York; or, The Vice, Crime and Poverty of the Great Metropolis* (New York: Sheldon and Co.).

3. Rulloff tried to seduce Ham into giving him the means to kill himself: "One was to procure a lancet, take off the handle and place the blade in a book; the other was to put the morphine into one or two capsules. I sometimes think that the reason why he embraced me on the morning of his execution was so that I could slip a capsule, containing poison, from my mouth into his" (E. H. Freeman, *The Veil of Secrecy Removed* [Binghamton, N.Y.: Carl and Freeman, 1871], 99).

4. See "Edward H. Rulloff," *Phrenological Journal* 53 (1871): 159–65.

5. Even the raw materials snatched from daily journalism and trial transcripts could be slapped together into a quickie book for rapid consumption. Barclay and Company of Philadelphia specialized in such works: *Runaway Girls and their Startling Adventures* (1878); *The Life of Anson Bunker* (1875), a serial killer; *The Great "Trunk" Mystery of New York City* (1871), the tale of the corpse of Alice Bowlsby, *The Thrilling Adventures of Alice Dunbar* (1869), a horse thief; *The Terrible Hay-Stack Murder* (1869), and other lurid titles. Barclay's contribution to this case was rather plainly titled: *Life, Trial and Execution of Edward H. Rulloff* (1871).

6. Andie Tucher argues persuasively that the "penny press" (especially in the ingenious papers of James Gordon Bennett) established a national narrative for sensationalism in the 1830s. See her *Froth and Scum: Truth, Beauty, Goodness, and the Ax Murder in America's First Mass Medium* (Chapel Hill: University of North Carolina Press, 1994).

PROLOGUE

1. *The Papers of Ulysses S. Grant: November 1, 1870–May 31, 1871*, ed. John Y. Simon (Carbondale: Southern Illinois University Press, 1998), 37.

2. Lonnie Athens, *Violent Criminal Acts and Actors Revisited* (Urbana: University of Illinois Press, 1997), 145.

3. Ibid., 157. Athens quotes with approval the idea of C. Wright Mills that scholarly work should not be "split" from one's life (121). In the winter of 2002, on a dark, cold day, my friend Bernard Van't Hul and I drove across Michigan to witness the final day of testimony in a trial of a man accused (and soon after convicted) of a savagely violent murder. Rulloff seemed revived in this killer. Both of us reflected on a similarly cold and dark day in December 1980 when we had been caught up in the events surrounding the murder of my daughter, Eleanor Bowman Bailey. Both murderers were repeaters.

4. See John C. Honeyman, "Zion, St. Paul, and Other Early Lutheran Churches in Central New Jersey," *Proceedings of the New Jersey Historical Society*, n.s. 14 (1929): 467.

5. The battalion was commanded by Lieutenant Colonel Isaac Allen, whose name was incorporated into that of one of Rulofson's famous grandsons.

6. See Lorenzo Sabine, *Biographical Sketches of Loyalists of the American Revolution* (Boston: Little, Brown, 1864), 246.

7. *Clarion Democrat*, November 2, 1899, 5.3.

8. *Clarion Republican*, November 2, 1899, 1.3.

9. According to the records preserved in the Prothonotary's Office, Henniger became a U.S. citizen on September 6, 1876, in Clarion County, Pennsylvania. Of Priscilla Howard's sons, he is the most mysterious because the least notorious.

10. Freeman, *Veil of Secrecy Removed*, 7.

11. Here the allusion in the fireworks is to a famous painting, *Westward the Star of Empire Makes Its Way, Near Council Bluffs, Iowa* (1867) by Andrew Melrose. The scene shows the headlamp of an onrushing locomotive looming through the vast landscape toward the viewer. The painting is now in the Autry Museum of Western Heritage, Los Angeles. Melrose's picture itself alludes to *Westward the Course of Empire Takes Its Way* (1861) by Emanuel Gottlieb Leutze, another allegorical picture that hangs in the U.S. Capitol. Such cultural references were expected to be entirely plain to a mass audience of the day.

12. These particulars are from the *Daily Alta California*, July 5, 1870, and the *San Francisco Chronicle*, July 5, 1870.

13. See Peter E. Palmquist, "William Herman Rulofson: 'The P. T. Barnum of American Photography,'" *Daguerreian Annual 1993* (Green Bay: Daguerreian Society, 1993), 136–54, 259–71.

14. *San Francisco Chronicle*, November 3, 1878, 8.6; *San Francisco Morning Call*, November 5, 1878, supplement 1.7.

15. Robert Bartlett Haas, "William Herman Rulofson," *California Historical Society Quarterly* 35 (1956): 47.

16. Palmquist, "William Herman Rulofson," 267.

17. William Herman [Rulofson], *The Dance of Death*, 3d ed. (San Francisco: Henry Keller and Co., 1877), 20.

18. Ibid., 24.

19. Ambrose Bierce, *A Sole Survivor: Bits of Autobiography,* ed. S. T. Joshi and David E. Schultz (Knoxville: University of Tennessee Press, 1998), 138. Other authorities describe it as a "literary hoax" and assign its authorship to Bierce and Thomas Arundel Harcourt, Rulofson's son-in-law. See Robert L. Gale, *An Ambrose Bierce Companion* (Westport, Conn.: Greenwood Press, 2001), 66.

20. Quoted by Peter E. Palmquist, "*The Dance of Death* Revisited," *American Bookman,* February 8, 1993, 480.

21. See Helen Hughes, *Lumbering in Early Elk County* (Ridgway, Pa.: Elk County Historical Society, 1998), 15. I am grateful to Ms. Hughes for correspondence on these matters.

22. "Rulof Ruloffson and John Cobb" (1898), *Elk Horn,* second issue, 1998, 7.

23. John Reck, "My First Trip on a Raft," in *True Tales of the Clarion River,* ed. George P. Sheffer (Clarion: Northwestern Pennsylvania Raftmens Association, 1933), 112. See also Alice L. Wessman and Harried Faust, *Ridgway, Lily of the Valley: 1824–1974* (Ridgway, Pa.: Ridgway Sesquicentennial Celebration, 1974).

24. Aaron J. Davis, *History of Clarion County, Pennsylvania* (Syracuse: D. Mason and Co., 1887), 641.

25. Freeman, *Veil of Secrecy Removed,* 9.

26. The *New York Times* for July 4 and 5, 1870, provided these details.

27. In his address to the jury in 1871, the attorney-general of New York played upon the homoerotic aspects of this relationship, calling the two men "boon companions" and reminding jurors that they slept side by side in the same bed. See Marshal B. Champlain, *The People vs. Edward H. Rulloff: Argument of Marshal B. Champlain* (Albany: Argus Co., 1871), 15.

28. *The Diary of George Templeton Strong: Post-war Years, 1865–1875,* ed. Allan Nevins and Milton Halsey Thomas (New York: Macmillan, 1952), 294.

29. *Life, Trial and Execution,* 76.

30. Ibid., 77.

31. Ibid., 78.

CHAPTER 1

1. Quoted dialogue here and following from Freeman, *Veil of Secrecy Removed,* 35–38. See also Edward Crapsey, *The Man of Two Lives* (New York: American News Co., 1871), 32–34. Richmond's account of Rulloff was widely reprinted in newspapers across the country; it appeared in the *Binghamton Republican* on January 21, 1871.

2. See Walter Jack, "Greater Than Darrow, and Far More Saintly," *Times-News* (Erie, Pa.), May 4, 1958, 14e.

3. The interpretation of Nelson as a fiend and a carnivore was an embellishment of hindsight; it certainly expressed the taste for rhetorical flourish that was at the heart of A. B.'s courtroom eloquence.

4. Crapsey, *Man of Two Lives,* 34.

5. Ibid., 35.

6. Freeman, *Veil of Secrecy Removed,* 38–39.

7. Ibid., 4. Ham had trouble keeping his spelling up to the level of his psy-chologizing.

8. Crapsey, *Man of Two Lives,* 6.

9. Ibid.

10. "He was very suspicious and cautions, and generally had but little confidence in men" (Freeman, *Veil of Secrecy Removed,* 4).

11. Ibid., 11.

12. Names in the region reflect a yearning for literary elegance: *Dryden, Ithaca, Ulysses, Jackson* and *Franklinville* celebrated national heroes. *Hard-scrabble* and *Sodom* had connotations that led to their rapid obsolescence. See W. Glenn Norris, *The Origin of Place Names in Tompkins County* (1951; Ithaca: DeWitt Historical Society of Tompkins County, 1984).

13. After Rulloff's death in 1871, a writer in the *Phrenological Journal* would declare: "He had magnetized her." See "Edward H. Rulloff," *Phrenological Journal* 53 (1871):159–65.

14. I appreciate the help of a descendant of the Schutt family, Ann Louns-bury Owens, in supplementing census and cemetery records.

15. This is the first recorded instance of Rulloff's declaration of an intention to murder. It was probably not the first time he had uttered such words.

16. These details and those that follow were inserted in both Crapsey's and Freeman's biographies. They relied upon testimony from Rulloff's 1856 trial. See Amasa J. Parker, ed., *Reports of Decisions in Criminal Cases,* vol. 3 (Albany, N.Y.: W. C. Little, 1858), 401–64. The minister's conduct is described by Will Schutt, 411–12, and Jane Schutt, 417.

17. Robert J. Hooper, *Lexicon Medicum; or, Medical Dictionary,* 4th American ed. (New York: J. and J. Harper, 1829).

18. This Dr. Bull is one of the figures in Rulloff's story who comes into sharp focus only at a few crucial junctures. Rulloff told Ham Freeman that he was an "old-school doctor," while Rulloff himself had been "an advocate of the new botanical method" (Freeman, *Veil of Secrecy Removed,* 13). Ed Crapsey gave his name as "W. H. Bull," and Rulloff's subsequent biographers repeated that name. In fact, he was Henry W. Bull, an 1839 graduate of the College of Physicians and Surgeons in New York, and very much a modern physician. In 1881 he was still practicing in Slaterville, a town just south of Dryden, and so had been present all during Rulloff's notorious career. Bull seems to have been adept at keeping himself outside the glare of publicity surrounding Rulloff, though testimony at the 1856 trial dragged his reputation to the edge of it. See John H. Selkreg, *Landmarks of Tompkins County, New York* (Syracuse: D. Mason and Co., 1894). In May 1858, Phoebe Wood, a sister of Ezra Cornell's, wrote to her brother that she believed Rulloff "guiltless" of the murder of his wife. Priscilla, she thought, had run off with Dr. Bull, and they were living under the assumed name of Young. "I did not get up this rumor or any of our friends here and the first who noticed it was a man who heard it talked of in a bar room not among women. Even if R killed his wife you make too light of this. It would do Young no harm to prove his woman was not Mrs R. and certainly the Law aught to give R any chance. . . . Schutts family could easily have

trumped up all. . . ." (Phoebe Wood to Ezra Cornell Papers, Kroch Library, Cornell University, Box 19, folder 8).

19. Finch Papers, Kroch Library, Cornell University, Archives 2594, Box 1, S-13–F-4.

20. Finch's notes add here words alleged to be Rulloff's: "I will knock you to hell."

21. Ibid., 416–18.

22. Guy C. Clark had murdered his wife with an ax on December 11, 1831; she had had him arrested for domestic violence and he had been in jail for ten days as a consequence. At trial, he said: "I swore I would kill her, I have killed her, and I am glad of it." Clark was hanged in Ithaca in 1832.

Rulloff often mentioned Clark but without, apparently, arousing suspicion that he was capable of such a murder. His calling Clark a "gentleman" reflects yet another of Rulloff's lifelong obsessions. In remarkable ways, Clark was a model for Rulloff. He had a "mind rather above mediocrity, which had been cultivated by various reading." Among his readings were works by Paine, Volney, and Voltaire, and these, it was thought, had made him a "free thinker" and hence indifferent to damnation. Before his execution, Clark turned to composing poetry: "How silly would it be to think / That on the scaffold he should shrink; / Firm and undaunted he will go / From a life to him a scene of wo." See *A Sketch of the Life of Guy C. Clark* (Ithaca: n.p., 1832).

Ben Jonson had once said that John Donne, "for not keeping of accent, deserved hanging."

So too did Clark.

23. Freeman, *Veil of Secrecy Removed*, 92–93.

CHAPTER 2

1. Whitney R. Cross, *The Burned-Over District: The Social and Intellectual History of Enthusiastic Religion in Western New York, 1800–1850* (1950; New York: Harper Torchbooks, 1965), 307. Whitney's pioneering cultural study does much to illuminate the beliefs that shaped the Rulloff story.

2. Freeman, *Veil of Secrecy Removed*, 94.

3. Cross, *Burned-Over District*, 308.

4. When Vosbury visited him in the Binghamton jail, Rulloff first denied knowing him. Vosbury persisted. "You recited to me in Latin and Greek, in the village of Ithaca." "I cannot distinctly remember that fact, but I recognize your voice as one which I have heard before. There is something so peculiar about it." *New York Herald*, April 30, 1871, 10.1.

5. Describing her impressions of a visit to the United States in 1834–35, Harriet Martineau reported the enthusiasm by which "the great mass of society became phrenologists in a day" (180). Americans, she declared, were given to such fads: animal magnetism, spiritualism, homoeopathy, for instance. See Harriet Martineau, *Retrospect of Western Travel* (1838), ed. Daniel Feller (Armonk, N.Y.: M. E. Sharpe, 2000).

6. Parker, *Reports of Decisions*, 415.

7. Ibid.

8. Freeman, *Veil of Secrecy Removed*, 93–94.

9. See Crapsey, *Man of Two Lives*, 11.

10. Parker, *Reports of Decisions*, 420–21.

11. Freeman, *Veil of Secrecy Removed*, 94.

12. Ibid., 95.

13. Ibid., 19, 94–95.

14. Ibid., 95.

15. Ibid., 99–101. Ham was not alone in believing that the baby had been spirited away to be raised by her paternal relations. As evidence, he quoted a letter from Priscilla Rulofson, dated January 10, 1870. "It seems to us more like the expressions of a daughter writing under the disguise of a niece to a man she has been taught to believe is her father but who, for prudential reasons, she does not recognize before the world is her father" (100). This hypothesis was popular because people wanted it to be true.

16. Crapsey wrote of the "ghastly wagon" and its "frightful burden" (13). The children singing "gay songs" as Rulloff whistled were described in *Life, Trial and Execution*, 20. The corpses delivered to the Geneva Medical College were mentioned by Freeman, *Veil of Secrecy Removed*, 18.

17. Parker, *Reports of Decisions*, 424.

18. Samuel D. Halliday, *Rulloff: The Great Criminal and Philologist* (Ithaca, N.Y.: Ithaca Democrat Press, 1905), 39.

19. Bayard Taylor, trans., *Faust: A Tragedy* (Boston: Houghton Mifflin, 1871), 291.

20. Freeman, *Veil of Secrecy Removed*, 96.

21. Ibid., 97.

22. Ibid.

23. Ibid.

24. Halliday, *Rulloff*, 31. The desire to plumb the depths continues to this day. See Lauren Bishop, "Believe It or Not: Cayuga Lake's Legends," *Ithaca Journal*, June 23, 1999, D8.

25. Freeman, *Veil of Secrecy Removed*, 96.

26. Ibid., 98.

27. Parker, *Reports of Decisions*, 425.

28. Ibid., 420.

29. Ibid., 424–25.

30. Ibid., 425.

31. Crapsey, *Man of Two Lives*, 14–15.

32. Parker, *Reports of Decisions*, 421.

33. Ibid., 427.

34. Ibid., 426.

35. Eugène Sue, *The Mysteries of Paris*, trans. Charles H. Town (New York: Harper and Brothers, 1844).

36. Ostrander would come to know Rulloff far better a decade afterward when he had become a police officer and Rulloff was a prisoner in the Ithaca jail.

37. Parker, *Reports of Decisions*, 429.

38. "Dyn" was a stenographic or typographic mistake for Dr. Charles V.

Dyer, one of two dozen physicians practicing in Chicago when the chest was opened.

39. Ibid., 430–31.

40. *The Poetical Works of Beattie, Blair, and Falconer,* ed. George Gilfillan (Edinburgh: James Nichol, 1854), 105.

CHAPTER 3

1. Parker, *Reports of Decisions,* 421.

2. Freeman, *Veil of Secrecy Removed,* 22.

3. Parker, *Reports of Decisions,* 427–28.

4. Ibid., 432.

5. In 1871, Ham would declare that Hayes had been as famous in his day as Allan Pinkerton was in the 1870s. Freeman, *Veil of Secrecy Removed,* 25. Diligent investigation at the Rutherford B. Hayes Presidential Library, Fremont, Ohio, has failed to yield further information about the detective.

6. See the *Ithaca Chronicle,* September 10, 1845, 3.1.

7. See the *Ithaca Journal,* November 19, 1845, 3.

8. Freeman, *Veil of Secrecy Removed,* 28.

9. Minute particulars of the system are described by Philip Klein, "Prison Methods in New York State," Ph.D. diss., Columbia University, 1920.

10. Francis Bonnivard had been imprisoned in a dungeon on Lake Geneva from 1530 to 1536, and his cell was a regular stop for Protestant tourists. Byron, visiting the Castle of Chillon that contains the dank room where Bonnivard had been chained to the wall, had added to the fame of the place by carving his own name in the cell and by writing the poem.

11. Freeman, *Veil of Secrecy Removed,* 28.

12. Crapsey, *Man of Two Lives,* 22.

13. George C. Sawyer, "Edward H. Rulloff," *American Journal of Insanity* 28 (1872): 471.

14. Crapsey, *Men of Two Lives,* 23.

15. John Perdue Gray, "Thoughts on the Causation of Insanity," *American Journal of Insanity* 29 (1872): 277.

16. See Sawyer, "Edward H. Rulloff."

17. Freeman, *Veil of Secrecy Removed,* 33–34. The handwritten indictment with the names of the grand jurors survives in the Clerk's Office, Tompkins County, New York. For the duration of Rulloff's sentence for abduction, this indictment seems to have remained a secret.

18. Ibid., 405.

19. Notes on the jury selection are found in the Finch Papers at Cornell, Box 1, S-13–F-4.

20. Parker, *Reports of Decisions,* 431.

21. Freeman, *Veil of Secrecy Removed,* 34.

22. Parker, *Reports of Decisions,* 444.

23. Ibid., 445. The judge cited "lamentable mistakes" in which persons had been wrongly convicted by "direct evidence" and others in which "circum-

stances" led to justice. In illustrating the latter, he cited the murderer Eugene Aram, a parallel case later used in discussing Rulloff (448).

24. Ibid., 464.

25. Jane Jarvis had borne seven children before Rulloff entered her life, and she and her husband had grieved over those who had died. The first daughter to be called Frances had died in 1846 at age ten and just twelve days later the first to be called Helen Louise died just before her third birthday. Another daughter, Jane Josephine, had died in infancy in 1842, and the second Frances died in 1853 at age six. See George A. Jarvis et al., *The Jarvis Family* (Hartford, Conn.: Case, Lockwood, and Brainerd, 1879), 171. This genealogy records that Jane M. Curtis was born on Christmas Day in 1814, but other sources report her birth in January 1820. See *Vital Records of Williamstown, Massachusetts, to the Year 1850* (Boston: New England Historic Genealogical Society, 1907), 49.

26. Freeman, *Veil of Secrecy Removed*, 102–3.

27. Stenography, or shorthand writing, was an essential skill for clerks and an accomplishment that led to better employment.

28. Crapsey, *Man of Two Lives*, 30.

29. I am grateful to Elizabeth Smith, Senior Recording Clerk, Office of the Tompkins County Clerk, Ithaca, for supplying copies of these records.

CHAPTER 4

1. A copy of this notice is preserved at the DeWitt Historical Society of Tompkins County, Ithaca.

2. "Escape of Rulloff," *Ithaca Journal*, May 13, 1857, 3.

3. "The Escape! Stop The Murderer! $500 Reward!" *American Citizen*, May 13, 1857, 2.

4. A voluminous condensation of the testimony appeared in the *Ithaca Journal*, May 20, 1857, 3; it provides the details given in the following paragraphs.

5. Freeman, *Veil of Secrecy Removed*, 35.

6. Salacious tales of this imprisonment continued to blossom and flourish. The anonymous author of *Life, Trial and Execution* wrote: "Scandal has it that the mother of this same boy gave the learned reprobate many unusual favors" (68).

7. *Ithaca Journal*, May 20, 1857, 2.

8. Ibid., May 14, 1857, 1.

9. Ibid., May 27, 1857, 3.

10. Ibid., May 29, 1857, 2.

11. The *Ithaca Journal* would shortly declare: "We learn in some quarters our article in regard to the escape of Rulloff is construed to imply censure on Sheriff Ives. Nothing was farther from our intention" (May 20, 1857, 2).

12. *American Citizen*, May 20, 1857, 2; May 27, 1857, 3.

13. *Tompkins County Democrat*, June 12, 1857, 2.

14. *Ithaca Journal*, June 3, 1857, 3.

15. A *weasel-skin* was, in the vernacular of western New York, a purse. *Tompkins County Democrat*, May 29, 1857, 2.

16. John King was the first of the New York governors to increase his political fortunes by attaching his reputation to the outrage against Rulloff.

17. The newspapers provided copious details: *Tompkins County Democrat,* May 29, 1857, 3; *American Citizen,* June 3, 1857, 2.

18. *Tompkins County Democrat,* June 5, 1857, 3.

19. *Ithaca Journal,* June 10, 1857, 3.

20. *Ithaca Journal,* June 12, 1857, 3.

21. *Tompkins County Democrat,* June 5, 1857, 3; *Ithaca Journal,* June 10, 1857, 3. A report that a man jailed in Pittsburgh was Rulloff proved false. *Ithaca Journal,* June 17, 1857, 3.

22. Ibid.

23. Perhaps he became a citizen as a precaution should something go wrong with the escape plans he, Edward, and James Henniger were formulating. It would be more difficult to convict a citizen than to deport an alien, so becoming a citizen was attractive. Additional biographical details are found in Davis, *History of Clarion County,* 641–42; Irene Furman Rogers, *Souvenir History of Strattanville, Pennsylvania* (Strattanville Centennial Committee, 1928), 16–17. I am grateful to Sandra G. Assalone, Deputy Prothonotary, Elk County, for providing a copy of R. Rulofson's naturalization certificate.

24. Wessman and Faust, *Ridgeway,* 107.

25. Ibid., 10.

26. Freeman, *Veil of Secrecy Removed,* 38–39.

27. Crapsey, *Man of Two Lives,* 36. Like most of the personal names in these reports, Merrick was variously spelled.

28. Ibid., 36. If Crapsey's account is true, this was the first time that Rulloff had ever furthered his career by force of arms.

29. Freeman, *Veil of Secrecy Removed,* 40.

30. *Ithaca Journal,* March 24, 1858, 3.3.

31. *Ithaca Journal,* March 31, 1858, 2.3–4.

32. *New York Times,* October 26, 1857, 5.2.

33. The transcript of Dr. Doremus's deposition is preserved at the DeWitt Historical Society of Tompkins County, Ithaca.

34. Hooper, *Lexicon Medicum.* Richard K. Swift recalled this work had been among the items left as security for Rulloff's loan in 1845 (Parker, *Reports of Decisions,* 431).

35. Seelye had spent one year at Halle and then, in 1853, was ordained and appointed pastor of the First Dutch Reformed Church in Schenectady. He was an effective Christian apologist and, after Rulloff's death in 1871, lectured in India and on his return published *Lectures to Educated Hindus* (1873).

36. Rulloff to Seelye, October 7, 1858, p. 2, Amherst College Library, Archives and Special Collections.

37. In his letter of December 28, 1858, he quotes Thomas Reid, *An Inquiry into the Human Mind* (1764). A modern edition of this work has been edited by Derek R. Brook (University Park: Pennsylvania State University Press, 1997).

38. Halliday, *Rulloff,* 15. Spencer's argument can be found in Parker, *Reports of Decisions,* 439–44.

39. *Ithaca Journal,* June 23, 1858, 3.2.

40. The *Ithaca Journal* explained the selection of the place of execution:

NOTES TO PAGES 71–84

"The law prescribes that the condemned shall be executed in the county where the trial is had and the prisoner found guilty."

41. *Ithaca Journal,* July 14, 1858, 3.2, provides the details of the proceeding.

42. Direct popular election of U.S. senators did not take place until the ratification of the Seventeenth Amendment in 1913.

43. *Speeches, Correspondence, Etc. of the Late Daniel S. Dickinson of New York* (New York: G. P. Putnam and Sons, 1867), 1:28.

44. See Halliday, *Rulloff,* 16–18.

45. When, following Dickinson's death in 1866, his brother published two hefty volumes of his speeches and legal briefs, the senator's effort in the case of *Ruloff v. The People* was not included.

46. See E. Penshine Smith, ed., *Cases Argued and Determined in the Court of Appeals of the State of New York* (New York: Bobbs and Brothers, 1863), vol. 4.

47. Finch's letter appeared as an appendix to Halliday, *Rulloff,* 51–53.

48. Halliday, *Rulloff,* 20.

49. Ibid., 15.

50. *Tompkins County Democrat,* March 11, 1859, 3.

51. *Ithaca Journal,* March 9, 1859, 3.

52. Halliday, *Rulloff,* 20.

53. Ibid., 48–50, published Robertson's letter.

54. Halliday, *Rulloff,* 21–22. Defending Rulloff did no harm to Douglass Boardman's career, and he was soon elected to serve as district attorney of Tompkins County. See Selkreg, *Landmarks of Tompkins County.*

55. *Ithaca Journal,* March 16, 1859, 3.4.

56. *Ithaca Journal,* March 3, 1859, 3.4.

57. *Tompkins County Democrat,* March 18, 1859, 2–3.

58. Ibid., March 18, 1859, 3. The *Ithaca Journal* repeated the news reported in the *Democrat,* March 23, 1859, 3.

59. These letters are preserved among the Finch Papers, Kroch Library, 2594, Box 1, Folders 20–26.

60. Freeman, *Veil of Secrecy Removed,* 105. Rulloff told Ham that he had had the offer of positions at Chapel Hill College in North Carolina and at Oglethorpe University in Georgia. No trace of him is to be found in the records of these institutions, lacunae owing perhaps to the Civil War and perhaps to a lack of interest in correspondence with this unknown scholar.

61. Crapsey, *Man of Two Lives,* 39.

CHAPTER 5

1. Freeman, *Veil of Secrecy Removed,* 91. "Every man is the architect of his own fortune" first appeared in English in 1533 in Nicholas Udall's translation of Terence's *Flowers for Latin Speaking.* See Wolfgang Mieder, Stewart A. Kingsbury, and Kelsey B Harder, *A Dictionary of American Proverbs* (New York: Oxford University Press, 1992), 25.

2. This is the first time in his career that Rulloff is known to have impersonated an Englishman and apparently nothing in his manner of speaking contradicted that claim.

3. Freeman, *Veil of Secrecy Removed*, 104.

4. Ibid., 103.

5. Ibid.

6. Ibid., 105–6.

7. I. Richmond Barbour, *The Silk Culture in the United States* (New York: Greeley and McElrath, 1844), 55.

8. Freeman, *Veil of Secrecy Removed*, 106.

9. Crapsey, *Man of Two Lives*, 43. Dutchess County should be the repository of records of Rulloff's imprisonment; nothing survives for either Rulloff or "James Kerron."

10. Ibid., 44.

11. Freeman, *Veil of Secrecy Removed*, 107–8.

12. Oliver Dyer, "The Modern Eugene Aram," *New York Sun*, January 25, 1871, 1.1–5.

13. *New York Sun*, May 19, 1871, 2.4.

14. When the war was over in the spring of 1865, John Dexter went back to his trade as a lathe operator and became respectable. Billy, however, was content to be a thief, but he was also proud of his military service, however brief and inconsequential it had been. In 1870, he contemplated joining the veterans organization founded in 1866, the Grand Army of the Republic.

15. Crapsey, *Man of Two Lives*, 47–49.

16. Freeman, *Veil of Secrecy Removed*, 108–9.

17. Ibid., 109.

18. Crapsey, *Man of Two Lives*, 49–50.

19. See Jarvis et al., *The Jarvis Family*.

20. This time, Rulloff represented himself as an Episcopal minister born in England. He had forged various letters of introduction from prominent people and used them to ingratiate himself with the bankers of Nashua and Concord.

21. Freeman, *Veil of Secrecy Removed*, 110. The New Hampshire State Library was unable to provide me with corroborating details of this crime, and thus we have only Rulloff's extremely unreliable testimony for it.

22. Ibid., 110–11.

23. Crapsey, *Man of Two Lives*, 51.

24. Freeman, *Veil of Secrecy Removed*, 112.

25. Ibid., 112–13.

26. Sarah Bradford Landau, the historian of New York, tells me that Jews were establishing themselves in the retail trades in this neighborhood in the 1860s. The family name is variously spelled in the records of Rulloff's life: Jacob, Jacobs, and Jakob.

27. The story was included in *Life, Trial and Execution*, 75–77.

28. This interview was subsequently published in ibid., 77.

29. Ibid., 120–21.

CHAPTER 6

1. *Democratic Leader,* August 19, 1870, 6.
2. Ibid.
3. *Broome Republican,* August 24, 1870, 6.5.
4. Ibid.
5. *New York Evening Post,* as republished in the *Broome Republican,* August 31, 1870, 1.5.
6. *New York Times,* August 18, 1870, 1.3–4.
7. Freeman, *Veil of Secrecy Removed,* 126.
8. On Friday, Merrick's funeral was held in the Baptist Church in Walton. Like most of the men in Rulloff's story, he was a member of a secret order, and his friends in the Good Templars—an association devoted to the cause of temperance—organized the service. To recognize their dead townsman, all the proprietors in Walton closed their stores, and school was suspended so everyone could attend and join the procession to the cemetery. Between four hundred and five hundred people turned out for the occasion. (*Broome Republican,* August 24, 1870, 6.6.)
9. She was eighteen years old. Among her papers were letters from her mother, Ann Jones, posted from Chittenango, a village just east of Syracuse. Her life seemed to fit a familiar pattern: a fall from virtue, despair, despondency, and death.
10. *Democratic Leader,* August 19, 1870, 6.
11. Crapsey, *Man of Two Lives,* 63.
12. *Broome Republican,* August 24, 1870, 6.6.
13. *Life, Trial and Execution,* 23.
14. Ibid., 24.
15. Crapsey, *Man of Two Lives,* 66.
16. Ibid., 66–67.
17. Although the newspapers provided detailed accounts of much of this story, this part of the investigation was not described precisely. The reporter for the *New-York Herald* wrote:

> It is not proper to state exactly how the information received was obtained by Hedden and Reilley, and the reader must be content with knowing that by the aid of these officers Mr. Hopkins was enabled to present an almost impregnable case to the jury.

Perhaps the third degree was administered as they pursued the chain of evidence.
18. Crapsey, *Man of Two Lives,* 68.
19. Ibid., 68–69.
20. This piece of fortune-telling ephemera has often been reprinted. Below I quote from the facsimile distributed by the Lucky Mojo Curio Company, Forestville, California. The *Oraculum* appears as a chapter of *Aunt Sally's Policy Players Dream Book* (Chicago: Lama Temple, 1994).

CHAPTER 7

1. Freeman, *Veil of Secrecy Removed*, 61.

2. Ibid., 63.

3. Ibid., 65. Freeman here supposed that the brothers provided some help, however meager. There is no surviving testimony to what this help might have been.

4. For biographical details, see ibid., 58–60.

5. The "veiled murderess" had been a mysterious woman who called herself Henrietta Robinson and was sentenced to be hanged on August 3, 1855. Subject to various kinds of odd and threatening behavior, Robinson was declared insane and her sentence commuted to life. Mitigation for her crime was found in the fact that she had been seduced and abandoned by a powerful New York politician, a canal commissioner whose opportunities for graft and extortion were nearly unbounded. She explained why she kept her face concealed during her trial: "On my trial, *I felt I could not be looked at*. It seemed to me *I should make other women ashamed.*" Many jurors and even the judge signed her plea for clemency, but Henry Hogeboom did not. As a prosecutor, he had not been sympathetic to an insanity plea. After her conviction, one interviewer provided a characterization of her brain: "She has two projections in the region of what is called constructiveness, extending backward, which of themselves would be sufficient to throw the whole character out of balance" (quoted by Karen Halttunen, *Murder Most Foul* [Cambridge, MA: Harvard University Press, 1998], 221). You could tell by looking at her that she was a criminal; her unbalanced character doomed her; Henry Hogeboom never doubted that she deserved to hang. See D[avid] Wilson, *Henrietta Robinson* (New York and Auburn: Orton and Mulligan, 1855).

6. *New York Times*, January 7, 1871, 1.6.

7. January 7, 1871, 1.6.

8. Freeman, *Veil of Secrecy Removed*, 56–57.

9. Ibid., 69–70.

10. Summoning "talesmen" was a time-honored practice, the term itself appearing in legal papers from as early as the thirteenth century. The "tales"— pronounced as two syllables—were persons taken from among those in court or standing by, to serve on a jury in a case where the original panel had become deficient in number by challenge or other cause, these being persons such as those originally summoned.

11. In February, Judge Platt Potter reviewed this issue (Freeman, *Veil of Secrecy Removed*, 69–70). In 1861, the legislature instituted a requirement that, when the original panel was exhausted, the sheriff should "draw names from a box" containing a list of jurors residing in the town who could be conveniently brought to court. However, this requirement proved "impracticable," and the act of 1861 was repealed. The prior law was thus brought back into force, but amendments enacted in 1870 contained another inconvenient provision, namely that additional jurors called from the talesmen could not be required to appear in court for two days. Judge Potter could see no reason that

the "public interest" could not be as easily served by drawing from the bystanders some possible jurors who would be ready to be sworn without a two-day delay.

Since the 1870 amendment did not forbid the practice of selecting jurors prepared to take seats in the box immediately, Judge Potter found that Judge Hogeboom had made no mistake in declaring eligible the three bystanders from whom the last, John W. Travis, had been chosen.

12. *Life, Trial and Execution,* 31.

13. Ibid.; Crapsey, *Man of Two Lives,* 73.

14. The siege and fall of Paris was taking place as the trial proceeded. On July 18, 1870, a front-page story had been a translation of an essay explaining "the reasons of France's hostility to Prussia." It was a particularly turgid piece, hardly likely to have been read even once, let alone cut out and preserved. But Rulloff had found it of sufficient interest to keep by him, and the telltale tear between the *e* and the *s* of *Times* on the masthead was a damning clue linking the carpetbag to his New York apartment.

15. Crapsey, *Man of Two Lives,* 73.

16. Ibid., 73–74.

17. *Ithaca Journal,* January 10, 1871, 1.3–5.

18. Transcript, 169–80. The printed transcript of the proceedings is preserved by the Broome County Historical Society, Binghamton. The cost of producing it had been borne by the public, the tax-conscious *Binghamton Daily Republican* noted (January 12, 1871, 2.7).

19. Freeman, *Veil of Secrecy Removed,* 123.

20. Ibid., 123–25.

21. Ibid., 124.

22. Ibid., 125–26.

23. Ibid., 126.

24. *Life, Trial and Execution,* 33.

25. Transcript, 35.

26. Ibid., 34.

27. *Ithaca Journal,* January 10, 1871, 1.4.

28. Freeman, *Veil of Secrecy Removed,* 55–56.

29. *Ithaca Journal,* January 10, 1871, 1.6–7.

30. *Ithaca Journal,* January 10, 1871, 1.7.

31. Crapsey, *Man of Two Lives,* 78.

32. *Ithaca Journal,* January 10, 1871, 1.7.

CHAPTER 8

1. *New York Sun,* January 25, 1871, 1.1.

2. *Ithaca Journal,* January 10, 1871, 1.6.

3. A reporter overheard these words (see *Life, Trial and Execution,* 37); they were not recorded in the transcript.

4. Transcript, 186.

5. *Life, Trial and Execution,* 38.

6. Ibid., 38.

7. Transcript, 104.

8. Ibid., 217.

9. *Ithaca Journal,* January 17, 1871, 1.3.

10. *Life, Trial and Execution,* 39.

11. Transcript, 230–31.

12. That robbery had also been effected by removing a panel from the back door of the store.

13. In the ensuing appeal, Judge Platt Potter upheld the use of photographic evidence.

> No authority was cited to show this to be error, or upon the other side, to sustain the rulings; nor, in my opinion, does it require any. It is the every day practice to use the discoveries in science to aid in the investigation of truth.
>
> As well might we deny the use of the compass to the surveyor or mariner; the mirror to the truthful reflection of images; or spectacles to aid the failing sight, as to deny, in this day of advanced science, the correctness, in greater or less degree depending upon the perfection of the machine and the skillful admission of light, to the photographic instrument, in its power to produce likenesses; and upon the principle, also, that a sworn copy can be proved when the original is lost or cannot be produced, this evidence was admissible. (Austin Abbott, *Reports of Practice Cases, Determined in the Courts of the State of New York,* n.s., vol. 11 [New York: Diossy and Co., 1872], 290–91.)

For a discussion of the legal status of photographs in Rulloff's era, see Thomas Thurston, "Hearsay of the Sun: Photography, Identity, and the Law of Evidence in Nineteenth-Century American Courts," *American Quarterly: Hypertext Scholarship in American Studies.* This fascinating essay was available online in 1998. Thurston discusses the uncertain fate of online scholarship in "New Questions for New Media: Scholarly Writing and Online Publishing," *American Quarterly* 51 (1999): 250–53. In the essay no longer available, he drew attention to contemporary discussion of photography in jurisprudence: "The Legal Relations of Photographs," *American Law Register* 17 (January 1869): 1–8; "The Legal Relations of Photography," *Albany Law Journal* 50 (January 25, 1873): 50–51; "The Use of Photographs of Proof of Identity in Criminal Cases," *Central Law Journal* 2 (July 16, 1875): 462. In the second of these essays, Rulloff's case is cited; in the third, the state of the question in Britain is reported.

14. *Life, Trial and Execution,* 40.

15. Ibid, 41.

16. Ibid.

17. *Ithaca Journal,* January 17, 1871, 1.4.

18. *Life, Trial and Execution,* 41.

19. Ibid.

20. Ibid., 42.

21. Transcript, 270.

22. Ibid., 271.

23. *Democratic Leader,* January 13, 1871, 8.1.

24. *Life, Trial and Execution,* 43.

25. Champlain, *People vs. Ruloff,* 7.

26. Ibid., 11.

27. Ibid., 22.

28. Ibid., 31.

29. Ibid., 33.

30. Ibid., 38. Names in the transcript were given variously phonetic spellings.

31. Ibid., 39–40.

32. Ibid., 42–43.

CHAPTER 9

1. Transcript, 278.

2. Ibid., 282.

3. Ibid., 283.

4. Ibid., 284.

5. Ibid., 285–86.

6. Ibid., 286.

7. Ibid., 287.

8. Ibid., 287–88.

9. Ibid., 288.

10. Ibid., 291.

11. Ibid., 292.

12. Later George Becker would tell Rulloff that he had presented a line of argument that seemed to him very unlikely to succeed. Almost certainly this attempt to turn Frederick Merrick from victim to murderer is that argument. Once again, Rulloff was attempting to shift the burden of his guilt to someone else.

13. Transcript, 293. "Truth is mighty and will prevail" has a long history as a proverb. See Mieder, Kingsbury, and Harder, *Dictionary of American Proverbs,* 617. Mark Twain would later write: "'Truth is mighty and will prevail.' There is nothing the matter with this except that it ain't so." See Albert Bigelow Paine, ed., *Mark Twain's Notebook* (New York: Harper and Brothers, 1935), 345.

14. Transcript, 253–54.

15. Ibid., 294.

16. *Ithaca Journal,* January 17, 1871, 1.6.

17. Transcript, 295.

18. Ibid., 295–96.

19. Ibid., 302.

20. *Democratic Leader,* January 13, 1871, 1.4.

21. An undated newspaper clipping at the Broome County Historical Society gives the history of the jury's ballots. Since it declares the documents to be seventy-nine years old, the story was apparently published in 1943.

22. *Ithaca Journal,* January 17, 1871, 1.6.

23. Crapsey, *Man of Two Lives*, 91.
24. *Ithaca Journal*, January 17, 1871, 1.6.
25. *New York Times*, January 12, 1871, 8.2.
26. *Ithaca Journal*, January 17, 1871, 1.7. Rumors of Rulloff's escape were also publicized in the *Binghamton Daily Republican*, January 12, 1871, 2.7.
27. Ibid., 1.8.
28. *Life, Trial and Execution*, 45.
29. Transcript, 304–6.
30. Crapsey, *Man of Two Lives*, 49.
31. This issue of the *Police Gazette* does not, apparently, survive. Ham Freeman drew attention to it in his newspaper (*Democratic Leader*, January 20, 1871, 4.3). The American Antiquarian Society preserves a copy of a similar account in the *Gazette*'s competitor *The Day's Doings* (New York), February 4, 1871, 14.3–5.
32. *New York Sun*, February 16, 1871, 1.1. See also *New York Sun*, January 15, 1871, 1.1–6.
33. Ibid., 300.
34. Reprinted from the *New York Express*, February 15, in the *New York Sun*, February 17, 1871, 3.3.
35. *Ithaca Journal*, February 28, 1871, 1.4.
36. Freeman, *Veil of Secrecy Removed*, 71–72.
37. *New York Times*, March 1, 1871, 2.6.
38. *Ithaca Journal*, March 7, 1871, 1.3.
39. Abbott, *Reports of Practice Cases*, 310.
40. Freeman, *Veil of Secrecy Removed*, 73.
41. *New York Times*, March 29, 1871, 4.6.
42. *New York Daily Tribune*, April 25, 1871, 4.2–3.
43. *Ithaca Journal*, May 2, 1871, 1.2.
44. *Mark Twain's Letters: 1870–1871*, ed. Victor Fischer and Michael B. Frank (Berkeley and Los Angeles: University of California Press, 1995), 382–84. Mark Van Doren discussed this letter as an example of Twain's rhetorical practice in "A Century of Mark Twain," *The Nation*, October 23, 1935, 472–74.
45. *Appleton's Journal*, July 1, 1871, 22. *Appleton's* had already expressed revulsion at Rulloffs' "unspeakable corruption of heart" (March 25, 1871, 358).

CHAPTER 10

1. *The Poetical Works of Henry Alford* (London: Strahan and Co., 1868), sonnet 55. A novel by Bulwer-Lytton had also dramatized this story for those who, like the women in Judge Hogeboom's court, wished to find some "objects over which their sensibilities may expand themselves and their sympathies weep."
2. *New York Sun*, January 25, 1871, 1.1.
3. "Dim, religious light" is a quotation from John Milton, and Dyer would expect his readers to immediately recognize and to connect Rulloff with the studious subject of Milton's poem "Il Penseroso," from which the words come.
4. *New York Sun*, January 25, 1871, 1.2–4.

5. Newspaper readers were minutely informed about Rulloff's library. See the *New York Sun,* February 16, 1871, 1.2. Books kept in his desk in the Jacobs' parlor were also noted for posterity; see *Life, Trial and Execution,* 78.

6. *Galaxy* 11, March 1871, 475–76. The "learned editor" was Ham Freeman. White was identified as the author of these anonymous essays by Frank Luther Mott, *A History of American Magazines, 1865–1885* (Cambridge, MA: Harvard University Press, 1933), 368–69. *Supremest* was commonly used in poetry in the English tradition. In a striking parallel to Rulloff's case, William Dodd, a learned man, had been hanged in 1777 for forgery. In his *Thoughts in Prison,* Dodd had written: "Grim death itself, in all its horrors clad, / Is man's supremest privilege! It frees / The soul" ([London: Charles Dilly, 1793], 137).

7. Rulloff to Seelye, March 27, 1871, Amherst College Library, Archives and Special Collections.

8. Macbeth's famous soliloquy was in Rulloff's mind: "If it were done, when 'tis done, then 'twer well, / It were done quickly." The bloody occasion of Macbeth's speech—he contemplates killing the king—was a subtext of Rulloff's reflections and yet another evidence of the literary culture so ready to hand. Mather's report first appeared in the *Springfield* (Massachusetts) *Republican.* It was reprinted in the *New York Times,* April 23, 1871, 1.3; and the *New York Herald,* April 24, 1871, 8.1.

9. Freeman, *Veil of Secrecy Removed,* 132. Such allusions were common in conversations in those days. "The last quotation from the poets he ever made," Ham Freeman later recalled, was from James Russell Lowell: "Truth forever on the scaffold, / Wrong forever on the throne." As in the lines from *Macbeth* quoted here, this quotation is not quite accurate. In Lowell's poem, *truth* was on the scaffold; Rulloff, the philologist, put *wisdom* in that place of execution. Thus he transformed himself from a murderer to a philological martyr. In a letter of Seelye (May 1, 1871), he quotes from Young's *Night Thoughts:* "Voracious learning, often overfed, rarely to sense / Digests its motley meal." This quotation is similarly transformed. Young had written: "Voracious learning, often over fed, / Digests not into sense her motley meal." In his studious labors, in other words, Rulloff had found inward nourishment, though "rarely."

10. Mather was not a clergyman. This brief notice was torn (not cut) from a local Binghamton paper and pasted to the end of a letter Rulloff wrote to Seelye on April 20, 1871. Rulloff was not allowed scissors for fear he would kill himself with them. Amherst College Library, Archives and Special Collections.

11. Rulloff to Seelye, April 20, 1871, Amherst College Library, Archives and Special Collections.

12. Freeman, *Veil of Secrecy Removed,* 78.

13. Ibid.

14. *New York Herald,* April 30, 1871, 10.1–2.

15. Sawyer, "Edward H. Rulloff," 482.

16. These stamps remain stuck to the top of the letter Rulloff wrote to Seelye, April 26, 1871, Amherst College Library, Archives and Special Collections.

17. This extract is from the manuscript diary of the Rev. Edward Taylor held by the Broome County Historical Society. On May 21, the Sunday after the execution, Taylor preached his afternoon sermon "on the lessons of Ruloff."

18. Monboddo's ideas were ponderously displayed in a book that occupied much of his life: *On the Origin and Progress of Language* (London: T. Cadell, 1773–92). In the pre-Darwinian age, Monboddo was ridiculed for making this comparison, and even more for believing stories of "men with tails" who constituted the missing link between apes and humans. See E. L. Cloyd, *James Burnett, Lord Monboddo* (Oxford: Clarendon Press, 1972).

19. *New-York Tribune*, April 25, 1871, 4.2–3.

20. *New York Herald*, May 18, 1871, 3.6.

21. Sawyer, "Edward H. Rulloff," 465–66.

22. Ibid., 495.

23. William A. Hammond, "Medical Jurisprudence: Report of the Commission Appointed to Determine the Mental Condition of Edward H. Rulloff," *Journal of Psychological Medicine* 5 (1871): 612–20.

24. Sawyer, "Edward H. Rulloff," 513.

25. Charles Kraitsir, *Significance of the Alphabet* (Boston: E. P. Peabody, 1846), 4.

26. Stephen Pearl Andrews, *Discoveries in Chinese; or, The Symbolism of the Primitive Characters of the Chinese System of Writing* (New York: Charles B. Norton, 1854), 5.

27. William Dwight Whitney, *Language and the Study of Language* (New York: Charles Scribner and Co., 1867).

28. Ibid., 14.

29. J. P. Lesley, *Man's Origin and Destiny Sketched from the Platform of the Sciences* (Philadelphia: J. B. Lippincott and Co., 1868), 159.

30. Ibid., 177.

31. Ibid., 178.

32. Ibid., 230–31.

33. Waite's letter first appeared in *The Nation*, March 30, 1871, 217, and it was immediately summarized in the *New York Times*, March 31, 1871, 6.5, and in the *New York Herald*, March 31, 1871, 4.6.

34. Waite, letter in *The Nation*, 217.

35. The sarcasm so memorable to Waite is also apparent in the commentary kept by Seelye. Pointing to a particular footnote in Lewis's edition, Rulloff wrote: "The failures of our worthy Professor are in some places quite amusing, and not a little in the note before us." Rulloff, "Remarks on Excursus 69th," March 21, 1853, Amherst College Library, Archives and Special Collections.

36. See the entry in *The National Cyclopedia of American Biography*.

37. *New York Times*, May 4, 1871, 5.1–2. Lewis did not oppose the death penalty in general; see George B. Cheever, *A Defence of Capital Punishment and an Essay on the . . . Penalty of Death by Tayler Lewis* (New York: Wiley and Putnam, 1846).

38. Crapsey, *Man of Two Lives*, 54–55.

39. *New York Times*, May 23, 1871, 4.7.

40. In addition to being a founder of the American Philological Association in 1869, Comfort was in the same year an organizer and subsequently a trustee of the Metropolitan Museum of Art in New York.

41. Comfort, *New York Times*, May 23, 1871, 4.7.

42. This circular appeared in full or in part in many newspapers. Its publi-

cation, in an anonymous letter, at the end of January 1871 led to the sudden flowering of interest in Rulloff's theories. See *Life, Trial and Execution,* 79.

43. *The Nation,* February 23, 1871, 127.

44. The committee appointed to examine Rulloff's manuscript was hardly unqualified to form an opinion of his work. The "young man" was Porter C. Bliss, just thirty years old then, a specialist in the native languages of the Americas, and eventually president of the Philological Association. The two others were Albert Harkness, an accomplished professor of Latin, and John Howard Raymond, a classicist, president of Vassar College, and the moving force behind the organization of the association. Freeman, *Veil of Secrecy Removed,* 116–17.

45. Comfort, *New York Times,* May 23, 1871, 4.7.

46. *Democratic Leader,* January 20, 1871, 5.1.

47. *American Educational Monthly* 8 (April 1871): 169.

48. Ibid., 173.

49. *New York Times,* May 13, 1871, 8.2.

50. *New York Times,* April 29, 1871, 8.2.

51. *New York Times,* May 13, 1871, 5.4.

52. *New York Herald,* May 17, 1871, 2.6.

53. Lesley, *Man's Origin and Destiny,* 239.

54. Sawyer, "Edward H. Rulloff," 497.

55. Ibid., 498–99.

56. Ibid., 505–6.

57. Freeman, *Veil of Secrecy Removed,* 79–80.

58. Ibid., 80.

59. Rulloff to Seelye, May 14, 1871, Amherst College Library, Archives and Special Collections.

60. *New York Herald,* 3.2; see also *Life, Trial and Execution,* 60.

CHAPTER 11

1. *Mark Twain's Letters,* 391–92.

2. *New York Herald,* May 17, 1871, 2.5.

3. Ibid.

4. *New York Sun,* May 18, 1871, 1.1.

5. On March 21, he had written to Ham Freeman and told him that, if worse came to worse, Ham could publish his life:

> You have my full consent to make use, at the proper time, of the facts in my history confided by me *to you alone.* This, if *I must die,* is the only way I can reward *your* fidelity. My brother will recompense Mr. Becker and Mr. Beale. (*New York Herald,* May 18, 1871, 3.5)

Since then Ham had been writing feverishly, recording Rulloff's story as soon as he possibly could after each visit. Now Ham felt obliged to print in the *Leader* Rulloff's denunciation of biographers.

Binghamton, May 17, 1871

This is to certify that I have never in any way contributed to the preparation of a work to be sold as my life, and such work purporting to be written from information furnished by me, will be fraudulent and untrue.

EDWARD RULLOFF

When, in early June, Ham's book was published, he printed a facsimile of the March letter opposite the title page and appended to it declarations by George Becker and Peter Hopkins that the handwriting was Rulloff's.

6. The Wallace Sisters were English comediennes: Jennie, Agnes, and Nellie. In the Harvard Theatre Collection is a large volume bound in red morocco: J. S. G. Hagen's *Records of the New York Stage* grangerized by Augustus Daly. In vol. 9, facing p. 72, is a portrait of two of the sisters taken from the *New York Clipper* (1870).

7. *Po-ca-hon-tas* (New York: Samuel French, n.d.).

8. *New York Herald,* May 19, 1871, 3.2.

9. *New York Sun,* May 18, 1871, 1.2. The manuscript has since disappeared.

10. *New York Tribune,* May 19, 1871, 1.6.

11. *New York Times,* May 18, 1871, 5.5.

12. *New York Tribune,* May 19, 1871, 1.6.

13. *New York Herald,* May 19, 1871, 3.1. The French tag is yet another example of literary allusion newspaper readers were expected to recognize. Loosely rendered in English, it means "a few anxious moments." More literally, it means the time when one is expected to "pay up" for a round of drinks in a tavern.

14. Ibid., 3.2.

15. *Life, Trial and Execution,* 52–53.

16. *Ithaca Journal,* May 23, 1871, 1.3.

17. *Weekly Ithacan,* May 19, 1871, 5.2.

18. Eph Schutt would later deny that he had been driven by morbid curiosity. "I was present at the execution, not with any taste or wish of my own. But the people hereabouts would have me see the man dead. I can assure you it was a sorry sight to see a man die so wicked and depraved, defying both God and man." Sawyer, "Edward H. Rulloff," 484.

19. Ham elsewhere described this letter as "singular" but did not describe it further. Freeman, *Veil of Secrecy Removed,* 64.

20. *New York Tribune,* May 19, 1871, 8.1.

21. Ibid.

22. Ibid.

23. Freeman, *Veil of Secrecy Removed,* 80–81.

24. Ibid., 99.

25. *New York Sun,* May 19, 1871, 3.3.

26. *New York Herald,* May 19, 1871, 3.2.

27. *New York Tribune,* May 19, 1871, 8.1.

28. *Life, Trial and Execution,* 58–59.

29. *New York Sun,* May 19, 1871, 3.1–2.

30. *Life, Trial and Execution,* 59.

CHAPTER 12

1. *Ithaca Journal,* May 23, 1871, 1.6. According to the *Broome Republican,* a second death mask was made by Daniel Burr (May 24, 1871, 4.1).

2. Freeman, *Veil of Secrecy Removed,* 128.

3. Ibid., 83. See also the *Binghamton Daily Democrat,* May 20, 1871, 2.1. More soberly, the *New York Times* reported, "Three different parties opened the grave at Binghamton on Friday night, with a view to disinter the part of the body which had never been buried." What this odd circumlocution meant was the head.

4. George Burr, "Medico-Legal Notes on the Case of Edward H. Rulloff," *Journal of Psychological Medicine* 5 (January 1872): 67.

5. *Ithaca Journal,* May 23, 1871, 1.6.

6. Burr, "Medico-Legal Notes," 79.

7. Hooper, *Lexicon Medicum,* s.v. "mania."

8. J. Aitken Meigs, *The Mensuration of the Human Skull* (Philadelphia: J. B. Lippincott, 1861).

9. Burr, "Medico-Legal Notes," 81.

10. Ibid., 83.

11. Ibid., 91.

12. Ibid., 93.

13. Ibid., 94.

14. *The Nation,* May 18, 1871, 3306.

15. Freeman, *Veil of Secrecy Removed,* 129.

16. Burr, "Medico-Legal Notes," 94.

17. See David Richard Kasserman, *Fall River Outrage: Life, Murder, and Justice in Early Industrial New England* (Philadelphia: University of Pennsylvania Press, 1986).

18. See Patricia Cline Cohen, *The Murder of Helen Jewett* (New York: Alfred A. Knopf, 1998).

19. Burr, "Medico-Legal Notes," 94.

20. See J. P. F. Deleuze, *Practical Instruction in Animal Magnetism,* trans. Thomas C. Hartshorn (New York: D. Appleton and Co., 1843).

21. Samuel George Morton, *Catalogue of Skulls of Men and Inferior Animals,* 3d ed. (Philadelphia: Merrilew and Morgan, 1849), iii.

22. Josiah Clark Nott gathered papers by Morton and other race theorists in *Types of Mankind* (Philadelphia: Lippincott, Grambo and Co., 1855). For this quotation see p. 185.

23. Crapsey, *Man of Two Lives,* 5. John Lothrop Motley's *Rise of the Dutch Republic* (1855) had given Americans an especial reverence for this nation, not only because it was a parallel example of throwing off a foreign monarchy but also because it was Protestant.

24. See especially Henry Flagler Rulison, *Genealogy of the Rulison, Rulifson, Ruliffson, and Allied Families in America, 1689–1918* (Chicago: Privately printed, 1919). I am grateful to the Newberry Library for access to this volume.

25. Nott, *Types of Mankind,* 309.

26. Frederika Bremer, *The Homes of the New World: Impressions of America,* trans. Mary Howitt (New York: Harper and Brothers, 1853), 1:150.

27. William Andrus Alcott, *Familiar Letters to Young Men on Various Subjects* (Buffalo: Geo. H. Herby and Co., 1850), 133.

28. O. S. Fowler and L. N. Fowler, *New Illustrated Self-Instructor in Phrenology and Physiology* (New York: Fowler and Wells, 1859).

29. L. N. Fowler, *Phrenological and Physiological Almanac for 1848* (New York: Fowler and Wells, 1847), 45.

30. Catharine E. Beecher, *Educational Reminiscences and Suggestions* (New York: J. B. Ford and Co., 1874), 59.

31. Hosea Tingley, *Incidents in the Life of Milton Streeter* (Providence, R.I.: A. W. Pearce, 1850), 191–92.

32. Burr, "Medico-Legal Notes," 83, 84.

33. Freeman, *Veil of Secrecy Removed*, 129.

34. Fowler and Fowler, *New Illustrated Self-Instructor*, 39. In the *Encyclopedia Britannica* of 1910–11, the professor of physiology at the University of Liverpool declared that research on brain weight was "not altogether conclusive," and that "brains over 60 oz. in weight are frequently found in quite undistinguished people." A generation later this "measurement" would be described as a "heavy-headed anthropological fraud." Earnest Albert Hooton, *The American Criminal: An Anthropological Study* (1939; New York: Greenwood, 1969), 212.

35. John Hecker, *The Scientific Basis of Education* (New York: A. S. Barnes and Co., 1868), 197.

36. Ibid., 107–8.

37. Crapsey, *Man of Two Lives*, 6.

38. Freeman, *Veil of Secrecy Removed*, 7.

39. *New York Times*, May 13, 1871, 8.2.

40. *New York Herald*, May 19, 1871, 3.2.

41. Freeman, *Veil of Secrecy Removed*, 115.

42. Ibid., 110.

43. *New York Times*, May 13, 1871, 8.1–2.

44. *The Nation*, May 18, 1871, 3306.

45. Freeman, *Veil of Secrecy Removed*, 129.

46. Sawyer, "Edward H. Rulloff," 507–8.

47. *New York Times*, January 25, 1871, 1.4–5.

48. Freeman, *Veil of Secrecy Removed*, 132.

49. Ibid.

50. *Broome Republican*, May 24, 1871, 4.1.

51. "Edward H. Rulloff," *Phrenological Journal* 53 (1871): 165.

52. See "Skeleton in Binghamton's Closet," *Binghamton Press*, January 29, 1950.

53. See Robert Bartlett Haas, "William Herman Rulofson," *California Historical Society Quarterly* 34 (1955): 188–300; 35 (1956): 47–58.

CHAPTER 13

1. *Weekly Ithacan*, May 19, 1871, 4.1.

2. Finch's poem in manuscript is preserved at the DeWitt Historical Society, Ithaca.

3. Treadwell's manuscript diary is preserved at the Broome County Historical Society, Binghamton.

4. The definitive account of this murder to date is Simon Schama's *Dead Certainties: Unwarranted Speculations* (New York: Knopf, 1991).

5. *Boston Herald,* May 18, 1871, 4.1. The phrase "God's best gift to man" was applied to several different things in the language of the day: the Bible, Abraham Lincoln, music, and suicide.

6. *Broome Republican,* May 24, 1871, 1.2.

7. *New York Times,* May 20, 1871, 5.3. Richard Grant White applauded Beecher's protest "against the absurd fuss made about Rulloff." Echoing his own denunciation of Rulloff's philology back in March, White wrote: "Society is merely acting in self-defense when it exterminates such wild beasts, and it ought to exterminate them swiftly and silently, with no more delay or publicity than is necessary to secure strict justice." *Galaxy* 12 (July 1871): 145–46.

8. Freeman, *Veil of Secrecy Removed,* 80.

9. *New York Herald,* May 23, 1871, 4.5.

10. *Life, Trial and Execution,* 65.

11. *Broome Republican,* May 24, 1871, 4.1.

12. Rulloff's "firmness" was noted in newspapers very distant from the scene of the execution. See, for instance, *The Intelligencer* (Seattle), May 22, 1871, 2.3.

13. *Daily Picayune,* May 21, 1871, 1.7.

14. *Weekly Ithacan,* May 19, 1871, 4.1.

15. Freeman, *Veil of Secrecy Removed,* 130.

16. Ibid., 100.

17. Ibid. Written almost exactly a year before Rulloff's conviction for Merrick's murder, the letter was filled with lighthearted banter. Priscilla reported that her husband, Ridgeway Stratton, "thinks there never was such a man in the world as uncle E. He has made me almost believe you are something more than human" (101).

18. Ibid., 99.

19. *New York Times,* January 23, 1871, 1.8.

20. *New York Times,* July 18, 1871, 4.3.

21. *Iowa State Register,* July 23, 1871. I am grateful to the historian of suffrage, Louise R. Noun, for bringing this letter to my attention.

22. Preface to Halliday, *Rulloff,* 9–10.

23. Reprinted in the *New York Times,* June 18, 1871, 6.4.

24. This idea is expressed on the menu at a campus tavern near Cornell University: Rulloff's.

25. The rope, the noose, and other relics were photographed in the *Binghamton Press* (February 12, 1950) and the same paper later published a picture of a comely young woman with Rulloff's brain (in a jar) on the table in front of her (December 11, 1955). Various summaries of Rulloff's life appear from time to time, some with mythical elements, for instance, Carl Carmer's *Listen for a Lonesome Drum* (New York: Farrar and Rinehart, 1936), 337–44, and Herbert A. Wisbey Jr., "The Trial and Hanging of Edward H. Rulloff," *New York Folklore Quarterly* 16 (1960): 126–31. A stoneware gallon jug with Rulloff's name

and a crude picture of a gallows has recently come to light; see Steven B. Leder, "The Rulloff 'Gallows' Jug," *Maine Antique Digest*, March 1996, 40–41D.

26. Haas, "William Herman Rulofson," 35:53.

27. Freeman, *Veil of Secrecy Removed*, 131.

28. Gerald R. Smith, *The Valley of Opportunity: A Pictorial History of the Greater Binghamton Area* (Norfolk, Va.: Conning, 1988).

Bibliography

"A. B. Richmond." *Tribune-Republican* (Meadville, Pa.), May 12, 1938, D9.3–4.

Andrews, Stephen Pearl. *Discoveries in Chinese; or, The Symbolism of the Primitive Characters of the Chinese System of Writing.* New York: Charles B. Norton, 1854.

Athens, Lonnie. *Violent Criminal Acts and Actors Revisited.* Urbana: University of Illinois Press, 1997.

Aunt Sally's Policy Players Dream Book. Chicago: Lama Temple. 1994. Reprint of a much earlier imprint; contains *The Oraculum; or, Napoleon Buonoparte's Book of Fate*, 52–61.

Burr, George. *Historical Address Relating to the County of Broome in the State of New York.* Binghamton: Carl, Stoppard and Co., 1876.

———. *Medico-Legal Notes on the Case of Edward H. Ruloff.* New York: Appleton, 1871. Also published in the *Journal of Psychological Medicine* 5 (January 1872), 67–94.

Carmer, Carl. *Listen for a Lonesome Drum: A York State Chronicle.* New York: Farrar and Rinehart, 1936.

Cassidy, Michael John. *Warden Cassidy on Prisons and Convicts.* Philadelphia: Patterson and White, 1894.

Champlain, Marshall B. *The People vs. Edward H. Ruloff: Argument of Marshal B. Champlain.* Albany: Argus Co., 1871.

Cohen, Patricia Cline. *The Murder of Helen Jewett: The Life and Death of a Prostitute in Nineteenth Century New York.* New York: Alfred A. Knopf, 1998.

Costello, Augustine E. *Our Police Protectors: History of the New York Police.* New York: Published by the Author, 1885.

Crapsey, Edward. *The Man of Two Lives.* New York: American News Co., 1871.

———. "Will Murder Out?" *Galaxy* 7 (1869): 383–94; 10 (1970): 536–45.

Cross, Whitney R. *The Burned-Over District: The Social and Intellectual History of Enthusiastic Religion in Western New York, 1800–1850.* 1950; New York: Harper and Row, 1965.

Davis, A. J., ed. *History of Clarion County, Pennsylvania.* Syracuse: D. Mason and Co., 1887.

Deleuze, J. P. F. *Practical Instruction in Animal Magnetism.* Trans. Thomas C. Hartshorn. 1843; New York: Da Capo Press, 1982.

Dieckmann, Jane Marsh. *A Short History of Tompkins County.* Ithaca: DeWitt Historical Society of Tompkins County, 1984.

Doremus, Charles A. "A Retrospect in Biochemistry." *Biochemical Bulletin* 1 (1911): 245–55.

Doremus, Charles A., and B. A. Witthaus. "Chemistry of the Cobb-Bishop Poisoning." *Bulletin of the Medico-Legal Society* 12 (1879): 71–96.

"Edward H. Rulloff." *Phrenological Journal* 53 (1871): 159–65.

Ellis, Havelock. *The Criminal.* London: Walter Scott, 1890.

Fink, Arthur E. *Causes of Crime: Biological Theories in the United States.* Philadelphia: University of Pennsylvania Press, 1938.

Fox, Richard Wightman. *Trials of Intimacy: Love and Loss in the Beecher-Tilton Scandal.* Chicago: University of Chicago Press, 1999.

Freeman, E[dward] H. *The Veil of Secrecy Removed.* Binghamton, N.Y.: Carl and Freeman, 1871.

Haas, Robert Bartlett. *A Biographical Sketch of William Herman Rulofson (1826–1878).* Los Angeles, author's typescript (12 pp.). Bancroft Library, University of California at Berkeley.

———. "William Herman Rulofson: Pioneer Daguerreotypist and Photographic Educator." *California Historical Society Quarterly* 34 (1955): 188–300; 35 (1956): 47–58.

Halliday, Samuel D. *Rulloff: The Great Criminal and Philologist.* Ithaca, N.Y.: Ithaca Democrat Press, 1905.

Halttunen, Karen. *Murder Most Foul: The Killer and the American Gothic Imagination.* Cambridge: Harvard University Press, 1998.

Hammond, William A. "Medical Jurisprudence: Report of the Commission Appointed to Determine the Mental Condition of Edward H. Ruloff, under Sentence of Death *(since hanged)* for Murder." *Journal of Psychological Medicine* 5 (1871): 612–20.

Harder, J. Russell. "Daguerrotypists and Portrait Takers in Saint John." *Dalhousie Review* 35 (1955): 259–70.

Hearn, Daniel Allen. *Legal Executions in New York State: A Comprehensive Reference, 1639–1963.* Jefferson, N.C.: McFarland, 1997.

Hinman, Marjory Barnum. *Court House Square: A Social History.* Endicott, N.Y.: Published by the Author, 1984.

Holbrook, Stewart H. *Murder Out Yonder: An Informal Study of Certain Classic Crimes in Back-Country America.* New York: Macmillan, 1941.

Hooper, Robert. *Lexicon Medicum; or Medical Dictionary.* 4th American ed. New York: J and J Harper, 1829.

Jack, Walter. "Believer in Return of Dead: A. B. Richmond, Famed Lawyer, Looked to Life in Hereafter." *Erie* (Pa.) *Sunday Times,* April 24, 1949, E11.1–5.

———. "Greater Than Darrow, and Far More Saintly: Noted Criminal Lawyer Practiced in Meadville." *Erie* (Pa.) *Times-News,* May 4, 1958.

Jarvis, George A., et al. *The Jarvis Family.* Hartford: Case, Lockwood, and Brainerd, 1879.

Kasserman, David Richard. *Fall River Outrage: Life, Murder, and Justice in Early Industrial New England.* Philadelphia: University of Pennsylvania Press, 1986.

Klein, Philip. "Prison Methods in New York State." Ph.D. diss., Columbia University, 1920.

Kraitsir, Charles. *Significance of the Alphabet.* Boston: E. P. Peabody, 1846.

Lawyer, William S. *Binghamton: Its Settlement, Growth, and Development.* New York: Century Memorial Publishing Co., 1900.

Lesley, John Peter. *Man's Origin and Destiny.* Philadelphia: J. B. Lippincott and Co., 1868.

Lewis, W. David. *From Newgate to Dannemora: The Rise of the Penitentiary in New York, 1796–1848.* Ithaca: Cornell University Press, 1965.

Life, Trial and Execution of Edward H. Ruloff. Philadelphia: Barclay and Co., 1871.

MacDonald, Arthur. *Abnormal Man, Being Essays on Education and Crime and Related Subjects.* Washington: Bureau of Education, 1893.

McDade, Thomas M., comp. *The Annals of Murder: A Bibliography of Books and Pamphlets on American Murders from Colonial Times to 1900.* Norman: University of Oklahoma Press, 1961.

Meigs, J. Aitken. *The Mensuration of the Human Skull.* Philadelphia: J. B. Lippincott, 1861.

Morrison, William Douglas. *Crime and Its Causes.* London: Swan Sonnenschein and Co., 1891.

Morton, Samuel George. *Catalog of Skulls of Man and the Inferior Animals.* 3d ed. Philadelphia: Merrihew and Thompson, 1849.

———. *Types of Mankind; or, Ethnological Researches Based upon the Ancient Monuments, Paintings, Sculptures, and Crania of Races.* Philadelphia: Lippincott, Grambo and Co., 1855.

Norris, W. Glenn. *The Origin of Place Names in Tompkins County.* 1951; Ithaca: DeWitt Historical Society of Tompkins County, 1984.

O'Hara, Ward. *Ten Murders in the Finger Lakes.* Auburn, N.Y.: Ward O'Hara, 1994.

Packard, Frederick Adolphus. *Memorandum of a Late Visit to the Auburn Prison.* Philadelphia: J. Harding, 1841.

Palmquist, Peter E. "Bradley and Rulofson's Funny Money." *History of Photography* 4 (1980): 72.

———. "*The Dance of Death* Revisited." *Bookman's Weekly* 91 (1993): 476–88.

———. "William Herman Rulofson: 'The P. T. Barnum of American Photography.'" In *The Daguerreian Annual 1993,* ed. Peter E. Palmquist. Eureka, Calif.: Daguerreian Society, 1993.

Peabody, Andrew P., trans. *Cicero's Tusculan Disputations.* Boston: Little, Brown, and Co., 1886.

Pearson, Edmund. *Instigation of the Devil.* New York: Charles Scribner's Sons, 1930.

Reynolds, Davis S. *Beneath the American Renaissance: The Subversive Imagination in the Age of Emerson and Melville.* Cambridge: Harvard University Press, 1988.

Rhodes, Richard. *Why They Kill: The Discoveries of a Maverick Criminologist.* New York: Alfred A. Knopf, 1999.

Richmond, A. B. *Leaves from the Diary of an Old Lawyer: Intemperance, the Great Source of Crime.* New York: American Book Exchange, 1880.

Rulison, Henry Flagler. *Genealogy of the Rulison, Rulifson, Ruliffson, and Allied Families in America, 1689–1918*. Chicago: Privately printed, 1919.

[Rulofson], William Herman. *The Dance of Death*. 3d ed. San Francisco: Henry Keller and Co., 1877.

Savage, Minto Judson. *The Religion of Evolution*. Boston: Lockwood, Brooks, Y Co., 1876.

[Sawyer, George C.] "Edward H. Rulloff." *American Journal of Insanity* 28 (1872): 463–514.

Selkreg, John H. *Landmarks of Tompkins County, New York*. Syracuse: D. Mason and Co., 1894.

Seward, William Foote. *Binghamton and Broome County, New York: A History*. New York: Lewis Publishing Co., 1924.

Schama, Simon. *Dead Certainties*. New York: Alfred A. Knopf, 1991.

Sheffer, George P. *True Tales of the Clarion River*. [Clarion:] Northwestern Pennsylvania Raftmens Association, 1933.

Smith, Gerald R. *The Valley of Opportunity: A Pictorial History of the Greater Binghamton Area*. Norfolk, Va.: Conning, 1988.

Smith, Goldwin. *Reminiscences*. Ed. Arnold Haultain. New York: Macmillan, 1910.

Smith, H. P. *History of Broome County*. Syracuse: D. Mason and Co., 1885.

Souvenir History of Strattanville, Pennsylvania. Clarion, Pa.: Centennial Committee, 1928.

Srebnick, Amy Gilman. *The Mysterious Death of Mary Rogers: Sex and Culture in Nineteenth-Century New York*. Oxford: Oxford University Press, 1995.

Sue, Eugène. *The Mysteries of Paris*. New York: Harper and Brothers, 1844.

Thurston, Thomas. "Hearsay of the Sun: Photography, Identity, and the Law of Evidence in Nineteenth-Century American Courts." <http://chnm.gmu.edu/aq/photos/index.htm>. 1999. Acquired June 28, 2002.

Tingley, Hosea F. *Incidents in the Life of Milton W. Streeter*. Pawtucket, R.I.: A. W. Pearce, 1850.

Townsend, George Alfred. *The Life, Crime, and Capture of John Wilkes Booth*. New York: Dick and Fitzgerald, [1865].

Triplett, Frank. *History, Romance and Philosophy of Great American Crimes and Criminals*. New York: N. D. Thompson and Co., 1884.

Tucher, Andie. *Froth and Scum: Truth, Beauty, Goodness, and the Ax Murder in America's First Mass Medium*. Chapel Hill: University of North Carolina Press, 1994.

Vital Records of Williamstown, Massachusetts, to the Year 1850. Boston: New England Historic Genealogical Society, 1907.

Wells, Samuel Roberts. *How to Read Character*. New York: Samuel R. Wells, 1874.

Wessman, Alice L., and Harriet Faust. *Ridgway, Lily of the Valley, 1824–1974*. Ridgway, Pa.: Ridgway Sesquicentennial Celebrations, 1974.

"W. H. Rulofson." In *Sketches of Leading and Representative Men of San Francisco*. San Francisco: n.p., 1875.

Wilder, Bert G. "The Head of a Murderer" (abstract). *Journal of Nervous and Mental Diseases* 13 (1886): 633.

Wilson, D[avid]. *Henrietta Robinson.* New York: Miller, Orton and Mulligan, 1855.

Wisbey, Herbert A., Jr. "The Trial and Hanging of Edward H. Rulloff." *New York Folklore Quarterly* 16 (1960): 225–31.

Young, Andrew. *History of Chautauqua County, New York.* Buffalo: Matthews and Warren, 1875.

LEGAL REPORTS

The People agt. Edward H. Rulloff. Ithaca: Ithaca Journal Steam Press, 1856.

The People v. Edward H. Rulloff (Supreme Court, Tioga General Term, May 1857). In *Reports of Decisions in Criminal Cases Made at Term, at Chambers, and in the Courts of Oyer and Terminer of the State of New-York,* ed. Amasa J. Parker, 3:401–64.

Ruloff v. The People (December term, 1858). In *Reports of Cases Argued and Determined in the Court of Appeals of the State of New-York,* ed. E. Peshine Smith, 4:179–99. (18 New York 179.)

Ruloff's Case. (Oyer and Terminer, Broome County; January 1871; Again, Supreme Court, Third District, February; and Court of Appeals, March 1871). In *Reports of Practice Cases, Determined in the Courts of the State of New-York,* ed. Austin Abbott, vol. 11, n. s., pp. 245–310. New York: Diossy and Co., 1872.

Edward H. Ruloff, Plaintiff in Error, v. The People, Defendants in Error. Argued March 15, 1871; decided March 28, 1871. *Reports of Cases Argued and Determined in the Court of Appeals of the State of New York,* ed. Samuel Hand, 6: 213–25. New York: Banks and Brothers, 1871. Reprinted in *Reports of Criminal Cases Decided in the Appellate Courts of the State of New York and of Other States,* ed. Patrick H. Cowen, 1:359–69 (Albany: Weare C. Little and Co., 1884).

Acknowledgments

Without the splendid resources of the University of Michigan Library, this book could never have been written. The Clements Library at the university, thanks to the shrewd decision of its Director, John C. Dann, to purchase the James V. Medlar Crime Collection, put the basic resources for this book at my disposal.

Making of America, a digital library created at Michigan with support from the Mellon Foundation, gave me instant access to books and periodicals containing the name *Rulloff*. The World Wide Web also brought me to a commercial site, the Lucky Mojo Curio Company of (where else?) California, where I purchased a copy of Billy Dexter's fortune-telling book.

For access to collections, I am happy to acknowledge the help of the following institutions: the American Antiquarian Society; Amherst College Library, Archives and Special Collections (especially Peter A. Nelson); the Bancroft Library at the University of California, Berkeley (especially Corliss Lee); the Boston Public Library; Broome County Library and Broome County Historical Society (thanks especially to Marjory B. Hinman) in Binghamton, New York; the California Historical Society (especially Ellen Harding and Emily Woolf); Chicago Public Library; Clarion Free Public Library, Clarion, Pennsylvania (especially Kerry A. Kline and Marianne Battista), Clarion County Historical Society (Lindsley A. Dunn, Director-Curator), Clarion County Prothonotary Office, Clarion Pennsylvania; Cornell University Library (especially the late Tom Turner); Dartmouth College Library (especially Ridie W. Ghezzi); DeWitt Historical Society of Tompkins County, New York (especially the former Director, Lorraine S. Johnson, and Donna Eschenbrenner, Archivist); the Elk County Historical Society of Ridgway, Pennsylvania (especially Helen Hughes); the Harvard Theatre Collection (for information on the Wallace Sisters); the Historical Society of Pennsylvania; the Library of Michigan, Lansing; James Prendergast Library Association, Jamestown, New York; the Library of the Rutherford B. Hayes Presidential Center, Fremont, Ohio; Liberty Public

Library, Liberty, New York; Los Angeles Public Library; the National Library of Medicine (especially Elizabeth Tunis); the New York Historical Society; the New York Public Library; the New Orleans Public Library; the Newberry Library (especially Rachel Bohlmann), Oglethorpe University Library (especially George Stewart); the Pennsylvania State University Library; Seymour Public Library, Auburn, New York; Sandusky Public Library; Toledo-Lucas Public Library, Toledo, Ohio; Tompkins County Clerk, Ithaca (especially Liz Smith); University Archives and Records Service, the University of North Carolina, Chapel Hill (especially Mike Martin); the University of Washington Library, Seattle.

Individuals who helped especially include Allan Metcalf and Patricia Stock (who firmly declared that a short anecdote I told them should turn into a book), Sandra G. Assalone (Deputy Prothonotary, Elk County, Pennsylvania), Adam D. Blistein (Executive Director, American Philological Association), Sarah Bradford Landau (for investigating Rulloff's haunts in lower Manhattan), Ann Lounsbury Owens of Seattle (a genealogist of the Schutt family), the late Peter E. Palmquist (photographic historian with a special interest in the studio of Bradley and Rullofson, San Francisco), William H. Rulofson of Holmsted, Pennsylvania (a descendant), Gerald R. Smith (historian of Broome County, New York).

Historians of the era have also encouraged me—especially Patricia Cline Cohen (University of California, Santa Barbara) and Karen Hulttanen (University of California, Davis). Readers engaged by the Press provided valuable critiques of an earlier version of this book: Daniel A. Cohen of Florida International University and Randolph A. Roth of the Ohio State University. Two graduate students provided invaluable help: Martin Heggestad (in Ithaca) and John T. McGuire (in Binghamton).

A Michigan Humanities Fellowship, awarded on the basis of a proposal that had nothing whatsoever to do with Rulloff, gave me time to write this book. For this and other support from the University of Michigan, I am very grateful.

Of course it is to one's closest friends and family that one's greatest thanks are owed: Judith C. Avery, C. A. S. Bailey, Barbara Beaton, Anne Curzan, Marsha L. Dutton, Julia Huttar Bailey, John Price-Wilkin, Carol Shannon, Bernard Van't Hul, Donna L. Wessel Walker, Mary White. They suffered through endless anecdotes, all the while repaying me with gifts of wisdom, insight, and love.

Index

Brown, Robert, 107, 126, 206–7
Browning, Robert, 229
Buffalo, New York, 44
Bull, Henry W., 21–23, 27–28, 32, 244n. 18
Bullock, Seneca, 102, 128–29, 156
Bulwer-Lytton, Edward, 257n. 1
Burdell, Harvey, 215
Burdick, John F., 29, 41–42
Burnett, James, 174, 259n. 18
Burr, Daniel S., 102, 126, 134, 210, 226
Burr, George, 210, 226
Burritt, George, 56–59
Burrows, Gilbert S., 103, 104, 116, 118–19, 125, 127–28, 130, 131–32, 134–35, 139, 141–42, 145, 155, 156, 166
Bush, Timothy F., 95
Byron, Lord, George Gordon, ix, 46, 60

Calais, Maine, 18
California Pioneers, Society of, 5
Campbell, Thomas, 137
Capital punishment, 162–63, 233
Cayuga, Lake, 34, 39, 45, 81
Chamberlain, Jack, 102–3
Champlain, Marshall B., 109, 135–40, 147, 159
Chapel Hill College, 250n. 60
Chenango River, 101–3, 115, 144
Chittenden, Joseph H., 210–11
Christianity, 222–23
Church, Sanford E., 157
Circus, 99
Clark, Guy C., 23, 245n. 22
Clark, Lyman, 130
Clay, Henry, 72, 221
Clemens, Samuel Langhorne. See Twain, Mark
Cleveland, Ohio, 44, 67
Cobb, John, 8
Comfort, George Fisk, 183–85, 259n. 40
Cornell, Ezra, 244n. 18

Cornell, Phoebe. See Wood, Phoebe Cornell
Cornell University, 228
Crapsey, Edward, vii–viii, 15–16, 17, 47, 52–53, 59, 67, 83, 92, 105, 121, 149, 153, 160, 182, 199–200, 221, 226
Crosby, Stafford, 131, 135
Cunningham, Emma Augusta Burdell, 215
Curran, Benajah S., 125
Curran, O. B., 81
Curtis, Charles, 68
Curtis, Charles G. See Jarvis, Albert F.
Cushing, Stephen B., 31, 45
Cuvier, Georges, 212

Darrow, Clarence, 14–15
Darwin, Charles, 186
Denio, Hiram, 73
Dennin, James, 67–68
Dexter, John, 90, 250n. 14
Dexter, William T. (aka William Davenport, William D. Thornton), 88–99, 107–18, 120–21, 124–25, 127–30, 132–37, 142–44, 155–56, 182, 210, 250n. 14
Dickens, Charles, 16
Dickinson, Daniel S., 50–51, 72–75, 250n. 45
Dodd, William, 258n. 6
Donne, John, 245n. 22
Doremus, R. Ogden, 69, 214
Dostoyevsky, Fyodor, viii
Drake, C. B., 55, 63
Drew Theological Seminary, 183
Dryden, New York, 19
Dyer, Oliver, viii–ix, 90, 123, 154–55, 156, 165, 174, 187, 225

Elmira, New York, 199
Emerson, Ralph Waldo, 177
Episcopal church, 222
Etymology, 189–92

Farnham, Francis L., 130